THE BEST SCHOLARSHIPS FOR THE BEST STUDENTS

Donald Asher
Jason Morris
Nichole Fazio-Veigel

PETERSON'S
Publishing

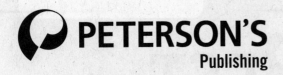

About Peterson's Publishing

To succeed on your lifelong educational journey, you will need accurate, dependable, and practical tools and resources. That is why Peterson's is everywhere education happens. Because whenever and however you need education content delivered, you can rely on Peterson's to provide the information, know-how, and guidance to help you reach your goals. Tools to match the right students with the right school. It's here. Personalized resources and expert guidance. It's here. Comprehensive and dependable education content—delivered whenever and however you need it. It's all here.

For more information, contact Peterson's, 2000 Lenox Drive, Lawrenceville, NJ 08648; 800-338-3282 Ext. 54229; or find us online at www.petersonspublishing.com.

Stephen Clemente, Managing Director, Publishing and Institutional Research; Bernadette Webster, Director of Publishing; Mark D. Snider, Editor; Ray Golaszewski, Publishing Operations Manager; Linda M. Williams, Composition Manager

ISBN-13: 978-0-7689-3260-7
ISBN-10: 0-7689-3260-2

Printed in the United States of America

10 9 8 7 6 5 4 3 2 1   12 11 10

First Edition

By printing this book on recycled paper (40% post-consumer waste) 92 trees were saved.

Certified Chain of Custody

60% Certified Fiber Sourcing and
40% Post-Consumer Recycled

www.sfiprogram.org

*This label applies to the text stock.

Sustainability—Its Importance to Peterson's, a Nelnet company

What does sustainability mean to Peterson's? As a leading publisher, we are aware that our business has a direct impact on vital resources—most especially the trees that are used to make our books. Peterson's is proud that its products are certified by the Sustainable Forestry Initiative (SFI) and that all of its books are printed on paper that is 40 percent post-consumer waste.

Being a part of the Sustainable Forestry Initiative (SFI) means that all of our vendors—from paper suppliers to printers—have undergone rigorous audits to demonstrate that they are maintaining a sustainable environment.

Peterson's continually strives to find new ways to incorporate sustainability throughout all aspects of its business.

OTHER RECOMMENDED TITLE

Scholarships, Grants & Prizes

Contents

About the Authors

Donald Asher is an internationally acclaimed author and speaker specializing in careers and higher education. He is the author of 11 books, including the best-selling guide to the graduate admissions process in America *Graduate Admissions Essays: Write Your Way into the Graduate School of Your Choice*. He has been a columnist or contributing writer for *The Wall Street Journal*'s online editions, CareerJournal.com and CollegeJournal.com, the MSN home page, *USAirways Magazine, The San Francisco Chronicle,* CareerBuilder.com, and College.Monster.com.

Dr. Jason Morris is a two-time Fulbright grantee. He is an assistant professor of higher education and program director at Abilene Christian University, where he trains master's-level students to be administrative leaders in higher education settings. He also currently serves as the director of the McNair Scholars Program, a federal program designed to prepare undergraduates for graduate research opportunities. Dr. Morris' areas of academic interest include college student retention, multicultural and international education, and educational access and equity issues. His articles have appeared in several national academic journals. He is a member of the National Association of Fellowship Advisors.

Nichole Fazio-Veigel currently provides scholarship and fellowship advising to students attending SCIO's Scholars' Semester in Oxford and Oxford Summer Programme (since 2007). Previously, she helped to develop the University of Washington's Office of Merit Scholarships, Fellowships, and Awards and undergraduate research program, serving as an adviser and assistant director for both programs. She is an active member of the National Association for Fellowship Advisors and the Council on Undergraduate Research. Ms. Fazio-Veigel is also completing her Ph.D. at the University of Oxford. She is a postgraduate fellow at Trinity College, and her studies are supported by scholarship funding from the Overseas Research Scheme (Clarendon Bursaries).

Acknowledgments

The authors would like to thank the many, many people who helped make this book a reality. We would especially like to thank Stephen Clemente and Bernadette Webster at Peterson's. We are delighted with the content, and it would not have been possible without the assistance of

Jennifer Vega La Serna
Kornélia Litkei
Lisabeth Bertschi
Heidi W. Morris
Nada M. Zohdy
Julie Kern Smith
Lesa Breeding
Chris Myers Asch
Jeff Haseltine
Kyle Beaulieu
Brent Eaton
Deirdre Baskin
Dwayne Keiffer
Adam Farrar
Huba Brückner
Alison Cohen
Bethany Smith-Polderman
Jessica Dyer
Alison Ensminger
Rhonda Collier
Aimee Friberg
Kelley Greenman
Chris Munn
Samuel Harrold
Michele Haynes
Mona Pitre-Collins
Carissa Hipsher
Donald J. Bungum
Lee Clemon
Kelly Sargent

Kristina Poznan
Karen Ho
Michael J. Adelman
Terry Schenold
Agata Clevenger
Calla Hummel
Sanja Jagesic
Michael Ji
Todd Ream
Vivian Jiang
Nora Cook
Joy Kiefer
Laura Michelle Jiles
Natalie Bowlus
Jessica Lee
Orlando Taylor
Alex Merkovic-Orenstein
Jentery Sayers
D. Wesley Miller
Jacob Barr
John Gibney
Jane Morris
Janice DeCosmo
Jacob Nickels
Paul Anderson
Maria Fernandez
Lucas E. Nikkel
Thomas Heineman
Bryan Rolfe
Hannah Salim

Pamela Tang
Aarti Sharma
Wally Englert
Ian Simon
Amanda Burrows
Stephanie Smith
Jamie Davies
Ben Towne
Julie Villegas
Ryan K. Walter
Mary Gonzalez
Karen Morris
Chris Willerton
Joaquin Baldwin
Brian Wilson
Matthew Worthington
Danaelle Bell
Margaret Moran
Janet Goebel
Josh Willis
Ruby Ausbrooks
Judy Jones
Christopher Brooks
Thao Do
David Fitts

and talented and diligent scholars everywhere. Thank you all!

Don wants to thank his mother, Dr. Ruby Faye Asher Ausbrooks, who taught him to read, the greatest gift one human can give to another.

Jason wishes to dedicate this work to the memory of Dr. Kelly Hamby; a great friend, mentor, and educator.

Nichole wishes to thank her husband who has supported her efforts with this book as well as her extensive educational journey. Her family has also inspired her as have the many wonderful mentors, colleagues, friends, and students who have encouraged her to "build castles in the sky."

A Note from the Authors

We designed *The Best Scholarships for the Best Students* to assist the highly ambitious, high-performing student in planning to get the most out of his or her educational process. This guide will help you find honors, awards, and opportunities that can be *life-changing*. It is designed to bridge the curriculum of college or university with critical summer experiences and critical cocurricular experiences (such as undergraduate research) that are proven to lead to both academic and career success. And, we kept high school students in mind as we compiled and wrote because early planning can lead you in new directions and open opportunities that you never dreamed of.

The Best Scholarships for the Best Students is designed to be an *idea book*. The profiles are not designed to provide exhaustive program information. They are here to pique your curiosity, to send you in directions you had never considered or even knew about. A listing for a Wall Street internship should make you think about all the *other* Wall Street possibilities: banks, hedge funds, investment advisory groups, and so on. The listing for the Peace Corps should make you think about the Peace Corps, but it is also designed to make you aware of other, similar options such as City Year and Americorps in the United States, and Save the Children, Bridge Span Group, which are active globally, and so on. You may know a bit about the Rhodes, but we want you to consider the Marshall, the Watson, and the Fulbright as well.

Our goal is to help you think about a variety of options and then guide you through the application and interview process. Happy hunting and good luck!

Donald Asher
Jason Morris
Nichole Fazio-Veigel

Foreword

During the 2009–10 academic year, more than 3,000 applications were submitted for thirty-two Rhodes Scholarships, forty Marshall Scholarships, and sixty Harry S Truman Scholarships. While the odds of winning one of these highly competitive awards are low, thousands of highly qualified U.S. college students each year undertake the daunting task of completing the application process for the chance to study at prestigious British universities and to secure a network of opportunities to make important changes in the world. The benefits of winning are high. The benefits of the application process, although not quite as obvious, are equally high.

As a scholarship adviser, my task is to provide guidance to students through the application process and, more important, to help them recognize that while they are applying for a scholarship, they are also articulating a plan for their lives. Writing compelling personal statements and project statements for nationally competitive scholarships requires each applicant to assess his or her academic programs, extracurricular commitments, and future goals. Such a process of active self-reflection in order to develop intentional, mindful, postgraduation plans has a value to our students well beyond that of winning scholarships. All students, whether or not they are scholarship candidates, can benefit from this process that will lead them to seek opportunities in line with their interests and make authentic choices that will fuel their achievement. Mary Tolar, a Truman/Rhodes Scholar and former Deputy Executive Secretary of the Harry S Truman Scholarship Foundation, once commented that all of us would benefit from writing a personal statement every five years. That is the value of "the process."

The qualities that comprise a successful scholarship candidate are qualities that are found in all well-educated people. Academic excellence is certainly an important component of a scholarship recipient, but it is most definitely not sufficient. A review of the criteria for the Rhodes Scholar, as stated in the will of Cecil Rhodes, reveals that "literary and scholastic attainments" are listed along with requirements for physical vigor, courage, leadership, and devotion to duty. These are characteristics that are not necessarily developed in the classroom; rather, they are acquired through participation in such activities as undergraduate research, community service, international study, and internships. While many of our colleges and universities provide access to such extracurricular pursuits, it can be challenging to navigate the systems that lead to these opportunities. *The Best Scholarships for the Best Students* provides a wonderful tool for motivated students to use as they map their path for successful undergraduate and graduate experiences.

So, what happens when you work hard in the classroom and get good grades, when you serve as a leader in your school and broader civic community, when you engage in undergraduate research and publish in peer-reviewed journals, when you successfully complete an internship in your field? Well, sometimes you win a scholarship. More often than not, you discover your vocation—your life's calling. I have had the honor of working with hundreds of students over the last ten years, some of whom have won prestigious scholarships, most of whom did not. They have all been successful in gaining acceptance to and funding for highly competitive graduate programs, law schools, medical schools, and public service positions around the world. Learning to see themselves as potential

Marshall Scholars or Gates Cambridge Scholars or Fulbright Scholars has provided them not only the insight to see where their lives are going but also the capacity to develop a confidence in their abilities to achieve those goals. Many of these students have gone on to postgraduate studies at Cambridge, Harvard, Stanford, MIT, and Oxford. Many are now using their undergraduate learning experiences and postgraduate preparation to improve the lives of people around the world. The process works. The process is transformative.

The Best Scholarships for the Best Students is unique. While there may be other resources and Web sites that supply advice for writing personal statements or that list internship and scholarship opportunities, there is no other book that has gathered all of this information in one place. Furthermore, the authors have culled their collective experiences in higher education, career counseling, and scholarship advising to provide assistance to readers about the best ways to develop an academic plan that will position them to become strong candidates for nationally competitive scholarships as well as well-educated leaders prepared to change the world. This book will be a valuable resource to highly motivated students, especially when used in conjunction with the sound guidance provided by a fellowships adviser. Members of the National Association of Fellowships Advisors (NAFA, http://www.nafadvisors.org/index.php) will welcome this guide as an important tool in the work they do with scholarship candidates.

NAFA is an organization whose members share best practices in scholarship advising. NAFA was founded in May 2000, and its mission is "to guide advisors in promoting the full potential of fellowship candidates through the application process, and to foster the continued growth and professionalization of fellowship advising in higher education." Members of NAFA include not only the individuals engaged in scholarship advising and the institutions of higher education that support them, but also the foundations and organizations that administer competitive scholarship and fellowship programs. In July 2009, NAFA adopted a Code of Ethics that specifies the responsibilities and ethical obligations for each of these constituents and that emphasizes the importance of the value of the process above the outcome. As a result, NAFA has made significant contributions to the competitiveness of individual scholarship competitions. In the past couple of years, the number of applications for the Fulbright U.S. Student Grant has increased dramatically, as noted in the October 30, 2009, issue of *Inside Higher Education*. While factors such as the economy may have contributed to the rise in application numbers, the efforts of NAFA members—both advisers and foundations—have certainly played a role in the success of the program. As NAFA has contributed to the transformation of scholarship programs, *The Best Scholarships for the Best Students* will further contribute to the competitive nature of these programs by making the information more accessible to a wider audience.

Access and opportunity serve as foundational guideposts for the work that NAFA does in supporting faculty and staff who assist students through the complex process of applying for nationally competitive scholarships. We look forward to working with this new book as we continue to reach out to all the students on our campuses. This type of guide might serve as an excellent component of first-year programs that help incoming freshmen with the transition to university life. The sooner new students can learn about all of the opportunities afforded to them through their undergraduate educational experiences, the more they will benefit from their programs overall and hopefully come to discover helpful ways to achieve their academic goals. Students who may never have otherwise considered themselves qualified to apply for nationally competitive scholarships may come to see themselves as potential scholarship candidates and will perhaps challenge themselves to engage in learning experiences that will allow them to realize their full potential as scholars, citizens, and leaders. Some may even become Rhodes Scholars.

During his address to the NAFA membership at the July 2009, NAFA Conference in Seattle, Bill Gates, Sr., provided the following words of encouragement:

> When it comes to the hard work of democratizing, you are both a scout and a coach. You find the young people with the most talent, and then you nurture that talent. Perhaps most important of all, you encourage students to believe in themselves. And you also encourage professors to believe in their students.

> It is true at all levels there are young people whose potential is much greater than they think it is. Many don't think about fellowship opportunities at all because they simply aren't encouraged to see their futures in that way. Others assume they're not cut out for the top fellowships. Part of your task is to give them the confidence to be bold when thinking about what's in store for them.

As NAFAns, we eagerly accept this challenge. We look at a guide such as *The Best Scholarships for the Best Students* to help us unlock the potential in all of our students so that we can give them the tools they need to achieve their goals and "the confidence to be bold."

Jane Morris
Director of the Center for Undergraduate Research and Fellowships, Villanova University
President of the National Association of Fellowships Advisors

CHAPTER 1

For the Ambitious: Competitive Scholarships and Experiential Opportunities

We wrote *The Best Scholarships for the Best Students* for ambitious, hard-working students who want to compete on the global stage. If this describes you, our book can help you create a track record of excellence and leverage that track record into prestigious, life-changing opportunities for your future. We designed *The Best Scholarships for the Best Students* to be of maximum benefit for students—forward-thinking high school students as well as college and graduate students—who wish to prepare and position themselves to be candidates for the most elite and exclusive scholarships, honors, internships, and other experiential programs. The requirements for programs vary widely, and we have included programs with very stringent requirements as well as those with less demanding qualifications, but that also provide valuable and exciting opportunities for personal and academic growth.

You will find the following five types of information in *The Best Scholarships for the Best Students:*

1. **Scholarships and Fellowships.** We have assembled a list of the most prestigious scholarships and fellowships in the world. Some are available to undergraduates, some are for those enrolling at the graduate level, and some are open to current graduate students. Some are available only to students wishing to study abroad, whereas others are available only to students with certain majors. These scholarship and fellowship opportunities differ greatly and have widely differing requirements as well.

2. **Undergraduate Research Programs.** The programs we have chosen under this heading are designed to prepare students for graduate research opportunities and are strong preparation for many of the other honors and awards explained in this book. Some research programs are summer programs drawing students from all over the world, whereas others are activities a student may pursue during a semester or quarter.

3. **Access and Equity Programs.** These are elite scholarship, research, and experiential opportunity programs designed for underrepresented populations, including students of color, first-generation college students, students from low-income families, and women in science, technology, engineering, and mathematics degree programs.

1

4. **Internships.** We have built a list of the most competitive and sought-after internships, ranging from Wall Street to the jungles of Central America, with information on when and how to apply. Internships like these often serve as the gateway to some of the most highly sought-after jobs in the United States.

5. **Service Programs.** Increasingly, service programs are considered as important as the types of opportunities described above in gaining a foothold to future achievement. As a result, service programs have become very competitive. Included in this book is a list of some of the most interesting and competitive ones, with guidance as to what wins an appointment.

The scholarships, fellowships, and experiential learning programs that are the focus of this book offer you life-changing experiences, provide you with huge career advantages later, and aid you financially along the way. In picking up this book, you may be considering applying soon for some of these opportunities. We suggest that you back up and take another approach. Zoom out to 30,000 feet and see your educational process from another perspective—the big picture view. What is your plan to maximize your educational experience and to become one of the top performers in our society? That's what we want for you and what *The Best Scholarships for the Best Students* can help you prepare for—whether you are a high school junior, a college freshman, or a graduate student.

IF YOU ARE A HIGH SCHOOL STUDENT

The Best Scholarships for the Best Students was written to be read by anyone—from a forward-looking high school student to a graduate student considering a post-doc. If you are a high school student reading this book, you may feel that graduate fellowships and Wall Street internships are a bit over your head. It is true that to apply for many of the opportunities described in this book, a student would have to be a college junior or senior or even a graduate student. However, this book has the greatest potential to change your trajectory of success if you read it at the earliest possible moment, as a high school student or a freshman beginning his or her college career.

TEN PRESTIGIOUS SCHOLARSHIPS FOR HIGH SCHOOL STUDENTS

Check out the following ten prestigious awards available to high school students:

1. **AXA Achievement Scholarships for High School Seniors**

   The AXA Foundation offers the AXA Achievement Scholarship for High School Seniors preparing for postsecondary education. Each year, 52 students are recipients of $10,000 scholarships (one recipient is selected from each U.S. state, the District of Columbia, and Puerto Rico). Ten of the 52 winners are selected for national awards and receive an additional $15,000.

   See: http://www.axa-equitable.com/axa-foundation/AXA-achievement-scholarship.html

2. **Bank of America Student Leaders**

   Bank of America offers a Student Leadership Program that provides recipients a paid eight-week internship at a nonprofit or charitable organization as well as a weeklong Leadership Summit held in Washington, DC.

   See: http://www.bankofamerica.com/foundation/index.cfm?template=fd_studentleaders

3. **Coca-Cola Scholars Program**

   The Coca-Cola Foundation annually selects 250 finalists for the Coca-Cola Scholars Program. Of those, 200 are identified as "Regional Scholars" and receive a $10,000 scholarship; 50 students are identified as "National Scholars" and receive a $20,000 scholarship.

   See: https://www.coca-colascholars.org/cokeWeb/page.jsp?navigation=15

4. **Dell Scholars Program**

   The Michael and Susan Dell Foundation offers the Dell Scholars Program. This scholarship program evaluates students on individuality, unique experiences inside and outside the classroom, financial need, work ethic, and future dreams. Each year, the program awards approximately 300 scholarships. Each recipient receives $20,000 toward his or her education expenses.

   See: http://www.dellscholars.org/public/

5. **Gates Millennium Scholars Program**

   The Bill and Melinda Gates Foundation offers the Gates Millennium Scholars (GMS) Scholarship. This award is designed to assist qualified students with financial and academic support throughout their undergraduate education and possibly into graduate school. The Foundation selects approximately 1,000 students annually to receive awards.

   See: http://www.gmsp.org/publicweb/AboutUs.aspx

6. **Intel Science Talent Search**

The Intel Science Talent Search invites high school seniors to participate in a science research competition. Students submit independent research projects in the areas of science, math, engineering, and medicine to be judged by a panel of experts. Each of 300 semifinalists receives $1,000. Forty finalists receive at least $7,500. Ten top winners receive between $20,000 and $100,000.

See: http://www.societyforscience.org/sts

7. **Jack Kent Cooke Foundation's Young Scholars Program**

The Jack Kent Cooke Foundation's Young Scholars Program is designed to provide financial and academic support to talented students with financial need who apply during their 7th grade year for support through grades 8 through 12 and into college. Approximately 50 students are named as Jack Kent Cooke Young Scholars annually.

See: http://www.jkcf.org/scholarships

8. **John F. Kennedy Profile in Courage Essay Contest**

The John F. Kennedy Profile in Courage Essay Contest is held annually by the Kennedy Library Foundation. The contest invites U.S. high school students to construct an essay considering the topic of political courage. The winning essayist receives $10,000.

See: http://www.jfklibrary.org/Education+and+Public+Programs/Profile+in+Courage+Award/Essay+Contest+for+High+School+Students/

9. **National Merit Scholarship Program**

The National Merit Scholarship Program is administered annually by the National Merit Scholarship Corporation (NMSC). High school students are eligible for scholarships for college by taking the PSAT/NMSQT. This test serves as an initial screening mechanism. About 50,000 students annually receive recognition; 15,000 are named "finalists."

See: http://www.nationalmerit.org/nmsp.php

10. **Siemens Competition in Math, Science & Technology (in partnership with the College Board)**

The Siemens Competition in Math, Science & Technology is funded by the Siemens Foundation and administered by the College Board. According to The College Board Web site, "The Siemens Competition seeks to promote excellence by encouraging students to undertake *individual or team research projects*. It fosters intensive research that improves students' understanding of the value of scientific study and informs their consideration of future careers in these disciplines." Scholarships for winning projects range from $1,000 to $100,000.

See: http://www.collegeboard.com/siemens/

Sitting down and carving out some time to strategize about your future will pay big dividends later. We encourage you to think seriously about the opportunities listed in this book that you would like to purse in the future. Once you have identified a handful, begin to ask questions and do a little research of your own. Take a careful look at the timeline driving academic and career-readiness success in Chapter 2. Knowing when to do what can really change your educational outcome! Please realize that it takes years to prepare for, say, a Rhodes or a Marshall application, so you're approaching these topics in a timely manner and well ahead of your peers.

Consider applying for an internship for the summer *before* you enter college, a summer that many students use for naught. Freshmen absolutely should apply for creative or science-, research-, or business-preparatory internships. No one will hold it against you if you don't get one, but (1) the practice will get you ready to apply for highly competitive internships for the following summer, with applications due in December and January, and (2) you may get one, thus catapulting yourself ahead of the masses of other students who don't even realize they need to build this part of their resumes.

There are many opportunities described in this book that are available for ambitious high school students and freshmen (which you will soon be!). Check out the

- The Posse Foundation in Chapter 4, perhaps one of the coolest college-entry programs in the country.

- Xerox Technical Minority Scholarship Program in Chapter 4, and the Xerox College Experiential Learning Programs (XCEL) in Chapter 5, both of which will allow you to get industrial experience at an early age as will the INROADS program, described in Chapter 4.

- Boren Undergraduate Scholarships: National Security Education Program (NSEP) that will allow you to *start* your college experience with a year abroad, Chapter 3.

- Hispanic Scholarship Fund Programs for Graduating High School Seniors mentioned in Chapter 4.

- National Institutes of Health Summer Internship Program (SIP) available to high school students and students in the summer between high school and college, Chapter 5.

- U.S. International Trade Commission—Student Temporary Employment Program (STEP), a paid internship available to high school students, Chapter 5.

- CIA Undergraduate Scholarship Program open to applications from high school seniors, described in Chapter 5.

- Americorps and City Year, open to high school graduates and GED holders (and making a great gap-year experience), both described in Chapter 5.

- elite White House Internship Program available to military veterans who hold a high school diploma, Chapter 5.

- NASA Programs for High School Students covered in Chapter 5.

- Jack Kent Cooke Undergraduate Transfer Scholarship Program, designed to assist students in the transition from a community college to a four-year-degree program, is covered in Chapter 3.

FROM COLLEGE FRESHMAN TO ALUMNUS

Right about now, some of you may be thinking, *Wait a minute! This is more than I bargained for. I just wanted some free money or an awesome summer experience. I don't want to plan out every minute of my life and study 24/7!* But you have what it takes to compete and excel, or you wouldn't have picked up this book. There is a wide range of opportunities described within these pages. Some of them are, quite frankly, statistically daunting. At one end of the spectrum, to be realistic, you would have to have proper guidance from a scholarship office as well as your own personal qualities to be successful. But other opportunities will go to thoughtful students who have prepared a well-constructed application working entirely on their own—and that may as well be you!

Success is mostly about planning and work. You don't have to be the most brilliant student who ever studied for an exam to win prestigious honors and awards. In fact, intelligence by itself is overrated. Bestselling author Malcolm Gladwell, in *Outliers: The Story of Success,* posits that truly successful people need only above-average intelligence; an astronomic IQ is not required.

Psychologist Carol Dweck of Stanford has discovered that students who attribute their success or failure on a task to intelligence are *less* likely to persevere and learn than students who attribute their success or failure to the effort they put into the endeavor. Focusing on intelligence leads to weak performance, and focusing on effort leads to continuing improvement and excellence. Decide to put *planning* and *effort* into your prework and your applications and many of these opportunities will be available to you, no matter where you grew up, which college you attend, or what your major is. These awards are not intelligence tests. They are more a test of your preparation, research skills, diligence, and ability to attract good advising.

The Matter of Grades

We will say right up front, however, that grades do matter. Personality and unique life experiences will *in some cases* offset lower grades. Among the three of us, we do know of a student with a 3.2 GPA who won one of the most prestigious national scholarships, a student with a 2.87 GPA admitted to a good medical school, and another with *less than a 2.0 GPA* admitted to a doctoral program! But in each of these cases there were extraordinary circumstances that came into play.

For example, the student with a 1.85 undergraduate GPA was, by her own admission, lackadaisical in her undergraduate career. She partied and goofed off. After graduation, she got a job on campus and at some point she became serious about her life. She talked her way into a master's program at the university where she worked and achieved a 4.0 GPA. She wanted to be admitted to the doctoral program, but the department chair said her undergraduate grades were far too low, in spite of her 4.0 graduate GPA. So she took, one by one, all the core classes for the doctoral program, earned an A in every single one of them, and appealed the decision. She was admitted to the doctoral program, and now has a doctorate—along with her 1.85 undergraduate GPA.

This is an interesting example, but, as Malcolm Gladwell would say, this student is an "outlier." For some of the competitive opportunities in this book, most of the successful applicants are going to have stellar grades. For some opportunities, this is going to be the norm. One of our goals in writing this book is to help you gain an understanding of the level of competition for some of these awards and of what a typical selectee brings to the process. So even though everyone should look for an award that's appropriate to his or her interests, do know that students who win some of these awards will indeed be nearly perfect.

WHY SHOULD YOU APPLY FOR HIGHLY COMPETITIVE OPPORTUNITIES?

This is a more complex question than it might at first appear. Why apply for competitive opportunities, especially those which have a 1 or 2 or 5 percent success rate? Why get involved in such an endeavor? We believe that there are at least six good reasons.

1. **We think the application process itself has great value.** You learn things about yourself as part of preparing a strong application. You will think deeply and introspectively about yourself; most students simply do not. One fellowship adviser we interviewed said,

    > The process of applying for a fellowship changes students. It forces them to think hard about goals and future direction. It helps them dream big about the possibilities that lie before them. After going through the application process it is true that you see students transform. Students gain great satisfaction and benefit from a well prepared, well thought-out application.

    All of the fellowship advisers that we interviewed for this book made similar comments. So if you choose to apply for one of these fellowships or programs, realize that you are embarking on a journey of self-discovery—and that the journey is just as important as the destination.

2. **Learning how to compete gracefully is an advantageous skill to learn if you intend to maximize your life experience.** You live in a very competitive world, and if you don't learn how to stretch yourself toward goals that are uncertain, you will skip the majority of what's possible. If you win every goal you attempt, you're not attempting large enough goals.

   Although he was not the first to say something like this, Dr. Benjamin Elijah Mays, former president of Morehouse College, said it well:

   > It must be borne in mind that the tragedy of life doesn't lie in not reaching your goal. The tragedy lies in having no goal to reach. It isn't a calamity to die with dreams unfulfilled, but it is a calamity not to dream. It is not a disaster to be unable to capture your ideal, but it is a disaster to have no ideal to capture. It is not a disgrace not to reach the stars, but it is a disgrace to have no stars to reach for. Not failure, but low aim is a sin.

   As part of this point—and we know it's hard to accept—we believe there is value in losing, in not being selected, in being passed over, and seeing your prize awarded to another. This is part of the richness of a full life. Pity those unfortunates who are afraid to attempt great things because they fear they will not be able to handle a failure. Dealing with failure builds toughness of character. There is a Japanese proverb that sums up the situation well: Fall down seven times; get up eight. Dealing with failure is all about learning to get up again.

   Jack London collected his rejection slips on a wire in the backyard shed he was using for an office. The wire had 6 feet of rejections on it before he earned enough money to get a better writing space. He went on to become the highest-paid writer in history up to his time. Dealing with failure is part of pursuing and achieving success. Fall down seven times; get up eight.

3. **Planning for these highly competitive opportunities will encourage you to maximize your college experience.** Once you realize it takes *years* of preparation to make a solid Rhodes application, you may set out to get the most out of those years. Whether you win a Rhodes scholarship or not, your life may be enhanced by the decisions you make to prepare for it.

   By the way, we sincerely hope you won't simply make a check-off list of items that march you one step closer to some application requirement or other. We hope you'll take joy and interest in your service experiences, your athletic endeavors, and your academic pursuits.

4. **A prudent student applies for several opportunities.** Efficiencies are in your favor. You will be able to recycle your essays and your interview preparation, and your recommenders will be happy to tweak a letter used for one program to the slightly differing requirements of another. By viewing the project of planning your future as a *series* of applications, you will see that a rejection here and there is just a normal part of the process. If you mix into your project some opportunities with a higher acceptance rate, you can absorb the nasty probabilities of rejection from those with very small success rates.

5. **Even if you don't win a single opportunity, you will be more prepared than your colleagues for the job search or for graduate school applications.** The types of document preparation, research, networking, reference priming, and interview preparation that you do for these scholarships and awards are perfect preparation for getting a great job out of college or for making a sophisticated application to competitive graduate schools. You will learn to write well, interview well, and represent yourself well.

6. **You may win.** In an article in the *Chronicle of Higher Education,* author Michael Kiparsky described the process this way: "Trying to win a graduate fellowship can sometimes feel like playing the lottery—long odds for a big payoff." After years of research and fact-checking, we have come to an astonishing finding: The students who win these highly competitive opportunities are among the ones who apply. There's an old saying in sports: You have to play the game to win the game.

We think these six points are valid reasons to decide to go for these opportunities, even if some of them are quite competitive. But there is yet another reason, which has less to do with you and the benefits that you will gain.

Simply stated, the world needs you; the world needs your contribution to make it a better place. From teaching in inner-city schools in the United States, to advocating for the education of Roma children in Central Europe, to helping Africans develop sustainable crops—at the heart of the scholarships and programs listed in this book is the ideal of improving society. These improvements begin on the individual level with an investment in one person's human capital. They end with universal benefits, a leveraged gain for the world.

LIFE-CHANGING OPPORTUNITIES

If you are ready to make a difference, this book will provide you with the tools to prepare a stellar application that, if accepted, will give you the funding, training, and experience you need to make significant contributions to our broader global community. Through our own experiences and through witnessing the effects of these opportunities on others, we can attest that these opportunities are often transformational. The person one becomes upon completing these programs is not the same person who sat down to apply.

Here's what some awardees say:

> Receiving a Harry S Truman Scholarship is something I had never dreamed would happen to me. However, after taking great interest in public service work with non-profits in high school and college, one of my professors encouraged me to apply. I always considered myself as a 'change agent' for the public good. By now having the experience of being a Truman Scholar, I have the credibility to go with it. This honor has opened new doors of opportunity for me.
>
> —Rachel W., Harry S Truman Scholar

> When I graduated from college, I was looking for a way to have a direct impact on society and grow as a leader. I couldn't imagine a better way to accomplish both of those goals than by joining Teach For America. I taught fifth graders in a low-income community, and the experience changed the way I view the world. I saw the huge challenges facing children growing up in poverty, but I also saw incredible potential in every student I taught. I learned that through setting big goals, partnering with my students and their families, working relentlessly, and constantly reflecting to improve our approach that my students could make tremendous academic improvements. These are leadership lessons that apply to any sector, and they have become the way I approach any professional endeavor. And most importantly, through my Teach For America experience, I have become a lifelong advocate for children in low-income communities.
>
> —Mary R., Teach For America Participant

> My time in Hungary on a Fulbright grant was a highlight in my academic career. My worldview was expanded dramatically.
>
> —Steve G., Fulbright Grantee

> Not only did winning a Goldwater Scholarship provide needed funding for college, but it also drew my attention to these nationally competitive scholarships, so that when graduate school came around, it was natural to me to seek them out. I suspect also that it helped to have a nationally competitive award on my resume when applying both to graduate school and for graduate fellowships; those considering my applications had

at least one other instance when a national board had looked at my qualifications and approved them.

—Josh W., Goldwater Scholar

Just before my senior year I decided to become a Peace Corps Volunteer. I did this because I wanted experiences that would broaden me as a person, and I wanted to spend some time doing something practical so as to confirm whether or not I wanted to pursue a career in medicine. I was selected to go to Kenya and work in the public health sector. I am now conversant in Swahili and also know a little of the local dialect. The major skills that I feel I have acquired while in Kenya are leadership, how to assess specific target areas in a community, and finally how to begin to make efforts which meet the community's goals. Working in this rural community showed me that in order to alleviate long-existing health problems, there must first be an understanding of one another. Now that I am in medical school I see that that principle of understanding becomes all the more true. Oftentimes the doctor and patient are a team, especially when working in areas where even basic healthcare is lacking. Most cases are not one-sided scenarios where the doctor hears the symptoms and then gives an immediate drug to fix the problem. My experiences in Kenya showed me that much of medicine and public health is listening to and discussing with people ways to promote health together. I was fortunate to see and meet individuals while in the Peace Corps (both medical and nonmedical) who invested in me so I could invest in others through medicine.

—Brent E., Peace Corps Volunteer

Hot Tip

For more inspiration, skip ahead and read Chapter 12, "Advice from Student Winners: What's the Secret?"

Applying for the Truman Scholarship was a life-changing experience in itself. The rigorous scope of the application requires you to declare and define your priorities, lay out your ideal graduate program, and describe where you see yourself five to seven years after graduation. These are all things that the average college student rarely thinks about! It helped me structure my thinking about my life. Since winning the scholarship, I have recognized another great benefit—the Truman community. The program selects people highly focused on service and the public good, and I have developed a large number of close friends with whom I share common values. With people I met through the Truman community, I went on a diplomatic trip to the Middle East and co-founded a political participation project in conjunction with the recent election—opportunities I never would have had!

—John S., Harry S Truman Scholar

TWO NOTES OF CAUTION

First, you should not attempt an application if you cannot deal with a rejection. The brutal fact is that students who are *not* selected can be indistinguishable from those who are. Those who are passed over can be just as charming in an interview, just as accomplished, just as well prepared, and have just as good grades and preparatory experiences. So keep this in mind at all times.

Second and of paramount importance, your application needs to reflect who you really are. This resource is not designed to help you create a "packaged" application filled with the ideas of others, however successful those ideas may have been *for them*. Rather, this resource was created to help you find your true voice and express it in your application. These award processes can be protracted, with many interviews and ancillary essays, and multiple stages of selection. If you manufacture a persona, it may unravel somewhere along the way, which would be unbearably uncomfortable and embarrassing for you and your school. Your goal is to put your best foot forward, but it must be *your* foot.

THE ROLE OF ADVISERS

Many college campuses have an office of scholarships advising, or a scholarships adviser or committee. You should reach out to this person, office, or committee as early in your process as you possibly can. Some of these scholarships *require* sponsorship by your committee; you cannot initiate or process an application for one of these on your own. Other opportunities are well known to be so complicated and peculiar that successful applicants will always have had the benefit of strong advising at every stage of the application and selection process.

Should you do another summer of research, or round out with a field experience to best prepare for _____ scholarship? Should you take Latin or Spanish as a foreign language? How should you dress for an interview? What questions should you expect? What answers have in past years killed otherwise promising applicants? What political views should be avoided or embraced? Only a scholarship adviser who has been intimately involved in these processes year after year can answer questions like these. This book is designed to augment and support the advice and counsel of your scholarships office, not to replace it. In fact, the deeper into the process you go, the more important your advising office will become.

Scholarship advisers usually belong to the National Association of Fellowship Advisors (NAFA, www.nafadvisors.org). They know which colleagues to call to get answers to your unique questions. They get regular bulletins on changes in procedures and criteria and attend annual conventions and meetings where these elite programs present information on their processes. Scholarship advisers can call officers of these programs and speak directly with them, which is simply impossible for the student/candidate to do. In the case of an apparent conflict between the advice in this book and your scholarships adviser, you can bet that your scholarships adviser is right in your particular case.

The same will be true of your internships coordinator and your service learning officer. They can best tell you the changing details of Teach For America, the Peace Corps, and internship programs. If you're not sure where on your campus to get advice, stop by the president's office and ask. The secretary to the president would be happy to tell you who handles all these functions. *Do it early!* You cannot put together a great background overnight.

If your campus has no one handling these types of functions, approach a faculty member who has had experience with students gaining scholarships, grants, and internships and ask him or her to mentor you through the process. It is our opinion that every student should have advice and counsel through these applications and that this book (or any other) is insufficient in and of itself. Our book should serve as a catalyst for you to aim high, but you need coaching along the way.

WARNING! THE CLOCK IS TICKING!

It takes years to prepare the kind of resume that some of these programs are seeking, and the deadlines for application can be shockingly early. The deadline for the Rhodes, for example, is early September. Several very large graduate scholarships have *early* September deadlines. A student's semester may not even have begun before she or he has to be ready to submit a complete application. Likewise, the most elite summer internships tend to collect resumes in November and December of the previous year and may not consider any applicants who begin the process after January. Deadlines really matter, and it can take a considerable amount of time to prepare your materials. *Early action is recommended for all applicants.*

HOW TO USE THIS BOOK

In writing *The Best Scholarships for the Best Students*, we have purposely focused on some of the most widely sought-after scholarships and experiential opportunities available to under graduate and graduate students. As you can see by now, winning one of these opportunities requires hard work, creativity, vision, and preparation. *The Best Scholarships for the Best Students* is designed to give you a competitive edge by blending information and requirements about these competitive programs with winning strategies and advice from previous winners and fellowship advisers.

As you read, you will note that the profiles are not all identical. We made the conscious decision to let the material dictate the form and structure of each profile. It would have been artificial and less useful to force each opportunity into an exact template. Each profile provides basic information about the opportunity and its requirements and tells you where to go to find out quickly the rest of the story.

> **A Word to High School Students**
>
> Please be sure to check out the chapters that will be helpful to you as you apply for college scholarships! These include Chapter 7 on developing personal statements, Chapter 9 on obtaining letters of recommendation, and Chapter 10 on interviewing.

The best way to use this book is to read it in its entirety. The chapters are carefully crafted to help you move through the application process and produce your highest quality applications for competitive scholarships, honors, internships, and other experiential programs.

- Chapter 1, as you have already read, talks about laying a foundation of accomplishment, which you can leverage into continuing opportunities.

- Chapter 2 walks you through the nuts and bolts of application preparation, providing general strategies designed to help you succeed.

- In Chapters 3, 4, and 5, we review the most prestigious scholarships, fellowships, and programs available to U.S. undergraduate and graduate students. You will find specific tips and strategies that have helped past applicants produce successful applications.

- Chapter 6 provides resources for international students.

- Chapter 7 provides solid tactics and proven strategies for clearly articulating who you are as an applicant. Many times this "personal statement" is the only item in the packet that lets a selection committee really get to know you. It is critical that this document clearly illustrate who you are and where you want to go.

- Chapter 8 will help you develop a strong curriculum vitae or resume, depending on which one you need to submit with your application.

- In Chapter 9, we thoroughly examine a critical aspect of the application process—obtaining strong letters of recommendation. This chapter will coach you on how to approach faculty and ensure the best recommendations possible.

- In Chapter 10, we cover winning interview strategies designed to help you prepare for tough questions and assist you as you articulate your unique qualities, attributes, and strengths.

- Chapter 11 is for parents and mentors, who may be wondering how they can best support you in these processes.

- In Chapter 12, we let the winners speak. We asked numerous winners from a variety of awards to talk about their approach to applying for major awards.

- The Appendix provides additional resources to help you with your planning.

There is a lost art of engagement with a text; it's called "browsing." If you are in a section of this book that doesn't appear to apply to you, flip through a few pages and suddenly you may find a spot-on opportunity that you had never dreamed of! We invite you to take on the whole book, even if your original interest was just how to prepare to apply for a Marshall or how to get an internship on Wall Street.

Let your process of self-discovery begin!

CHAPTER 2
Strategies and a Timeline for Success

This chapter provides an overview of the strategies that you can use and the steps that you should take to plan and apply for scholarships, honors, awards, and experiential opportunities described in this book. In writing this chapter, we not only relied on our own experiences in applying for prestigious awards and advising students, but also reviewed fellowship program Web sites, interviewed fellowship advisors, and consulted fellowship winners. The strategies that we call "preplanning" are those you need to consider well in advance of application— ordinarily, one or two years ahead. "In-process" strategies are useful as you and your recommenders work on applications. The timeline, or calendar, takes you through the steps from freshmen year through graduation.

PREPLANNING STRATEGIES

Plan Ahead

Remember: Those who win competitive awards don't do it by sheer luck. They follow solid strategies that encompass preplanning, intentionality, and persistence.

Preparation is a key ingredient to success in almost any endeavor. Winning competitive awards is no different. The following preplanning strategies are designed to put you in the best position to apply for scholarships, honors, awards, and experiential opportunities. These strategies will help you set a solid foundation that you can build on as you begin to prepare your applications. Many of the suggestions discussed in this section are used by top student who are looking to get the most out of their academic experience. Regardless of whether you actually apply for an award, many of these tips will help you maximize your educational experience.

Preplanning Strategy 1

Determine if applying for a competitive program is right for you. Applying for prestigious awards attracts many students, which is good for the funding bodies because the awards are geared toward a variety of students with differing backgrounds, interests, and abilities. However, there are thousands more applicants than there are awards. Before you start down this path, ask yourself if applying for a competitive scholarship—or fellowship or service program—is right for you. For the most prestigious awards, an applicant will invest 50 to100 hours in applying. Those hours will be wasted if the student is not a "fit" for the award in the first place. Do a careful self-assessment before you do anything else.

Your self-assessment should help you better understand yourself in relation to the competitive process. It's a given that successful applicants are ambitious, methodical, persistent, good at networking (to cultivate recommendation letter-writers), and poised in interviews. Beyond that, various qualities in this inventory will be important to one program or another. Expect to engage in this self-examination throughout the entire application process.

Be honest. If you realize that your personal characteristics and future ambitions do not align with competitive award application processes, then consider whether you really want to invest months of effort. If you realize that your professors or parents are more eager than you are about a big-name fellowship, then chances are you will not invest enough time and energy into the process. Your time might be better spent in a job or volunteer work that builds your skill set and enhances your resumé or *Curriculum Vitae*. Competitive award application processes are not for everyone, so don't worry if you decide this is not the route for you.

Caution: No one will check off every item on this self-assessment inventory (at least not without multiple personalities). Some items are contradictory, because we're describing a varied group. We're just showing you a range of personality traits and priorities that can determine an applicant's fit for various scholarships and opportunities.

- ❑ I like to read for fun.

- ❑ I am passionate about justice issues.

- ❑ I am more passionate about my career than about social justice.

- ❑ I am goal-oriented and hate to be distracted from achieving what I've set my sights on.

- ❑ I am adaptable and optimistic. I can seize unexpected opportunities, and I can roll with punches.

- ❑ My strongest motivations are intrinsic. Some things are worth doing for their own sake.

- ❑ My strongest motivations are extrinsic. I will work hard if I am sure of a reward.

- ❑ Sometimes I enjoy being alone with my thoughts.

- ❑ Being alone with my thoughts is a bore. I'm more of a doer than a thinker.

- ❑ Discussing ideas with other people is exciting.

- ❑ I find myself thinking differently from those around me.

- ❑ I have been gathering information about postgraduate education (law schools, med schools, graduate school, etc.).

❑ I solve problems more quickly than most people.

❑ I enjoy being with friends who are as smart as I am.

❑ I can tolerate living with "loose ends"—unanswered questions, unsolved problems.

❑ I expect to meet interesting people and be exposed to new ideas in my postgraduate work.

❑ I would like to go abroad for study or travel.

❑ I have the language competency to study in another country.

❑ I enjoy doing projects or research on my own.

❑ I am a good team-player. I enjoy doing projects with others.

❑ I have a track record as a leader. I can bring out the best in people.

❑ A good college course is one that is an adventure in thinking and that tackles big issues. I have taken some with no guarantee of an A because they fit my curiosity or career aims.

❑ I'm pretty sure of who I am, even if I haven't locked into a career.

❑ I pay attention to current events.

Preplanning Strategy 2

Do your research. If you have caught the bug to apply for a major fellowship one of the first things we recommend is that you thoroughly research the program or programs for which you plan to apply. Obviously, start with the program Web site. These sites are thorough and often provide information on the make-up of a strong application. If you're fortunate, a site will be candid about what the selection committee is looking for in applicants. Such tips are very important. Selection committees look at so many applications that it is almost formulaic, that is, they are looking for a certain set of key ingredients in each application. When the Web site describes what the committee is looking for, it's always wise to follow those instructions.

Your initial research should also focus on your "fit" for various programs. Your personal background, experiences, and interests will more naturally fit with certain opportunities than with others. It takes some honest assessment of yourself to determine what type of opportunity is best for you. Someone who desires a teaching and research career in higher education should pursue a different scholarship than one whose goal is to develop a career in law or be a social entrepreneur. If you're considering graduate school, you will need to research the fit of the graduate programs in your discipline and faculties as well. Someone with proven financial need is better suited for a Jacob K. Javits Fellowship than someone who may have had an easier time paying for college. Sifting through the application processes will be less painful and more likely successful if you know why you are a good fit for certain opportunities than others.

Another valuable technique as you are researching various scholarships is to study the web biographies of winners. The operative question is, "Do I look like that?" If not, now is the time to craft a plan. In building your plan, ask yourself, "How can I use my summers, my elective courses, my student-government service, my parents' political connections, and my part-time job to build a record of achievement like that?"

Finally, as you research programs and narrow your choices, if at all possible, try to find alumni or someone in your campus community who has won the award you are interested in. Take them out for coffee and informally interview them; ask them to reflect on their application process. This will provide invaluable information and insight that you can apply to your own application process.

Preplanning Strategy 3

Keep your GPA as high as possible. We said this in Chapter 1 and we'll say it again: The one thing that all major awards have in common is close inspection of your collegiate academic record, and in rare cases your high school record. We can't stress strongly enough that you need to set your academic goals high and work toward top marks in every class, not only your major classes, but also electives.

For one thing, scholarship boards find the GPA an easy way to weed out the mediocre. A near-perfect grade point is a given. It's not that committees have a special affection for "grinds" or bookworms, it's that grades are one measure, however faulty, of a student's self-discipline and versatility. If you're smart enough to make A's in everything but don't, the scholarship committee wants to know why.

But there are exceptions to every rule, and there are some important exceptions to the sky-high-grades rule. A scholarship board looking for entrepreneurs, problem solvers, and innovators is consequently looking for risk-takers. If you have perfect grades, but a transcript full of safe or easy courses, you're not the person they're looking for. Depending on the aims of the scholarship, the board could be happier with the physics major who took electives in social work or philosophy, the accounting major who took electives in history, or the English major who learned computer programming—and sometimes students get B's in those adventuresome courses. Sometimes they collect a few B's for taking an honors program. Prestigious scholarship review committees are looking for more than good-grade-getters, and they may forgive some B's that were earned by an ambitious and questing student. Your transcript supports every other part of your application. It is a record of your efforts to create an academic path that is rigorous and intentional. So, while it is good to explore courses outside of your major, it is equally important that your transcript testifies to the way you have crafted your undergraduate experience with your ultimate ambitions in mind.

Various books with detailed strategies have been written about getting good grades. Find a strategy that works best for you and use it through the duration of your undergraduate career. Good grades will pay off not only as you begin to apply for fellowships, but they are a key factor in graduate school admissions and can play a part in your future professional pursuits. We have found that on the majority of occasions, raw intellect is not the factor that prohibits students from higher grades; it's raw effort.

Preplanning Strategy 4

Build great relationships with your professors and supervisors. From the moment you step on campus, begin considering your relationships with your professors—especially as you choose a major and interact with your major professors. At the time you are ready to apply for a major fellowship, you may need up to ten individuals on your campus to describe in detail your academic performance in the classroom. So, your challenge is not only to perform well in their classes, but also to get to know them in a way in which they feel comfortable writing a strong letter of recommendation for you. This is especially true if you come from a large college or university where professors often have hundreds of students in their classes.

How can you distinguish yourself from other students in a positive way so that your professors can put a face with your name and hopefully write you a solid letter of recommendation? Do you volunteer to help with certain projects? Do you stay after class to ask questions? Do you provide eye contact during lectures and engage in class discussions? Do you take time to go by the professor's office during appointed hours to ask about assignments and even discuss other pertinent matters? These actions may help you break the ice and begin positively interacting with your professors. Don't be afraid to take the first step. In general, most professors are deeply concerned with student learning and respond positively to students who show interest in the subject matter beyond what is required in the course.

It is also important to get to know your professors for another reason. They can often connect you with others within their professional network that can help your application for a competitive fellowship, a research project, or other experiential learning opportunity. For example, if you are applying for a Fulbright grant, one of your professors may have an excellent international contact who will write you a letter of invitation to study. Or a professor on another campus may know which graduate studies program would be the best fit for you given your interests.

Preplanning Strategy 5

If you qualify, join your institution's Honors Program/Honors College and take advantage of everything it offers. Honors programs and honors colleges are unequivocally the domain of high-achieving students. Your achievements in an Honors program will show that you are an ambitious student, deserving of consideration for a certain scholarship. More importantly, Honors will place you around other intelligent and motivated students who will push you to reach your potential. Most Honors programs offer special "Honors" sections of courses. These courses tend to utilize the best professors who will engage and challenge you.

Apart from overall intellectual benefits, look for ways your Honors program can support your specific career ambitions. Say you're enrolled in a business school that offers an Honors track. This is your chance to be instantly identified as part of the top 2 to 5 percent of business students and to be invited to special seminars, retreats, and dinners with visiting experts. Why would you not join? Or suppose you're at a school with a single, university-wide Honors program or Honors college. Ask about getting honors credit for an internship you want to do, or an honors grant for a summer trip abroad, or a seat in an honors seminar that will look great on your resumé.

Be practical. Make your local honors program your tool. Let it help you build credentials and lay the foundation for graduate studies and your professional career.

Preplanning Strategy 6

Plan to study abroad. Time living abroad is transformative. The complexity of living in another culture is challenging; it engenders cultural sensitivity and self-efficacy. A study conducted by the Institute for the International Education of Students found that studying abroad has a positive influence on a student's career path, worldview, and self-confidence. A recent article in the *Economist* highlighted a study conducted by William Maddux and Adam Galinsky that found those who have lived abroad showed higher levels of creativity than those who had not. The article reported that those who lived abroad were more adept at using creativity in problem-solving exercises and in negotiating conflict situations. In addition to this evidence, many students that we have worked with have reported that study abroad has been a defining experience in their lives that impact them throughout their lives.

Success in studying in another culture will shine through in how you write and reason, and the way that you carry yourself with an extra measure of confidence. All of this adds up to helping you be the well-rounded and solid candidate that scholarship programs are looking for in applicants. Study abroad opportunities are not hard to find. Most institutions have offices on campus ready to help students engage in coursework in overseas settings. Study abroad tends to be pricey, but it's an investment of the best kind—an investment in yourself.

Preplanning Strategy 7

Learn about and involve yourself with research as an undergraduate. Opportunities for participating in research as an undergraduate student are growing rapidly on campuses around the country. As educators have seen the benefit of including undergraduate students in the research process, offices coordinating these efforts are popping up on campuses all over the country. The Council for Undergraduate Research (CUR) is a national organization whose purpose is to promote undergraduate research, and numerous opportunities exist to present research findings as an undergraduate through the National Conferences on Undergraduate Research (NCUR).

Participating in research as an undergraduate has numerous benefits for you as a student. First, it situates you in an intimate learning environment, usually either with a team of students led by a professor or one-on-one with a faculty mentor. Here relationships can be created that may lead to future connections in your chosen field and strong letters of recommendation. Undergraduate research also gives you the experience of learning and applying the research process to your particular discipline. Most undergraduates are not granted this opportunity. Finally, often your research projects can be altered or extended to have relevance to a major fellowship for which you're applying. At a minimum, a research experience will demonstrate to major fellowship committees that you are a serious student who desires to go beyond limited classroom learning and engage in higher-level thinking that occurs when engaged in the process of discovery.

Preplanning Strategy 8

Develop your leadership skills by seeking out opportunities to lead. The foundations and organizations that oversee these awards will primarily choose applicants they see as future leaders. Granted, they may believe that the awards they provide help to build future leaders, but our contention is that you need to show them in your application that you already have the ability to lead people. If you are reading this text and you have had numerous leadership opportunities, you are a step ahead. If, however, you have limited leadership experience, you need begin now to seek out opportunities to lead. And this includes high school students reading this book.

Many campuses actively cultivate student leaders by offering courses on leadership skills and leadership theory and by providing opportunities to lead campus organizations. Often student-led initiatives are the most participated in and powerful on a campus. For example, one campus we are familiar with has a yearly student-led program that sends out teams all over the United States during spring break to work on service projects with various organizations. Students sign up to be group leaders, recruit other students, provide predeparture training and logistics information, and manage the actual on-the-ground service project. Many of these group leaders report a transformational leadership experience through the program.

Don't overlook opportunities beyond your campus. Many nonprofits and community organizations are quick to allow talented, eager students to assist and lead. Bear in mind that it's important to a review committee to see evidence of extended involvement whether in a leadership or a volunteer experience. Committees are well-versed in spotting "CV padding."

Seeking out opportunities to develop your leadership skills will not only help you prepare a successful application for a major award, but also prepare you for graduate school applications as well as for your future professional life.

Preplanning Strategy 9

Visit an office dedicated to helping students win major fellowships. More and more campuses are creating offices that are dedicated solely to helping students prepare for and win the major scholarships and experiential opportunities covered in this book. If your school has one of these offices, you're fortunate. Typically, scholarship offices have staff dedicated to providing one-on-one consultation and advice as students prepare their applications. The office will walk you through the process and help you create the most competitive application possible.

If you're in high school and thinking about applying for a major fellowship while you're in college, you may want to choose an institution that has a scholarship office that can help you and that has a track record of producing students who have been successful. If you enroll, or are enrolled, at a school that doesn't offer such help, consider visiting one nearby that does. Also, personnel in an Honors College or Honors Program are often able to provide assistance with scholarship applications.

GREAT SCHOLARSHIP OFFICE WEB SITES

If your school doesn't have a scholarship office, we have found several institutions that have exceptional offices and very thorough and helpful Web sites developed for their students (but you can take advantage of them as well). Here are our top picks:

- University of North Carolina: http://www.unc.edu/scholarships/

- Massachusetts Institute of Technology: http://web.mit.edu/scholarships/index.html

- Stanford University: http://ual.stanford.edu/OO/scholarships_fellowships/FellowshipsScholarships.htm

- Columbia University: http://www.college.columbia.edu/students/fellowships/

- Ohio University: http://www.onca.org/

- Baylor University: http://www.baylor.edu/scholarships/splash.php

- University of Washington: http://www.washington.edu/students/ugrad/scholar/

- Oklahoma State University: http://scholardevelopment.okstate.edu/

Preplanning Strategy 10

Continually seek to build a strong curriculum vitae/resume with an emphasis on service experiences. Look at the biographies of some of the Rhodes and Marshall Scholarship winners, and you will be amazed at how much they have accomplished at such young ages. Sure, to win a Rhodes or Marshall you must be an ultra-achiever, but winners start early to cultivate a strong record of experience, service, and achievement. Compare this strategy to top performing athletes like Michael Phelps and Serena Williams. To become great in their sport, they practiced at young ages and continue even as stars to build their skills and abilities. Their success did not happen overnight, but was intentional and persistently built over many years. The same is true with major award winners. Their records of achievement and service span several years.

You need to start immediately to look for opportunities to build your experience base and to record your achievements in a CV/resume. Some institutions of higher learning help students keep an "official" record of service that serves as a transcript to use for graduate school applications and to show to future employers.

Another smart strategy to use as you build your CV/resume is to involve yourself in activities that may relate in some way to the fellowships that you are interested in. For example, if you are interested in Teach for America, volunteer in a local program that helps disadvantaged children catch up on their reading skills. Activities like this help fellowship sponsors gain a more integrated picture of your interests, skills, and abilities. Many review committees want to see a common thread between your activities and your future goals—and how their particular award fits your trajectory.

Preplanning Strategy 11

Develop a habit of knowing current world events and issues. If you have travelled outside the United States, you will know that as U.S. citizens, we are considered lacking in knowledge about other countries and regions of the world. We truly live in an interconnected world where events in one place impact events in another. As you pursue a competitive fellowship, it is of paramount importance that you become a "citizen of the world." The obvious ways are to take language courses and to make a habit of studying world events by reading scholarly journals, newspapers, and other media. Engagement with global affairs especially becomes critical during the interview phase of a fellowship application. You will need to be ready to answer questions and engage in conversations on a broad scale and not solely focused on your discipline or personal ambitions.

Case in point: As one of our authors was applying for a Fulbright Award as a doctoral student, he ran across a news story that he attributes the success of his application to. The article discussed the struggle of the Roma/Gypsy people in Central and Eastern Europe. Upon further investigation he found parallels to his work with underrepresented students in the United States. These connections and his desire to learn more about Roma/Gypsy education formed the basis of his winning proposal.

GLOBAL NEWS SOURCES

Here is list of news sources to help you learn about the issues in different regions of the world:

- *The Economist:* http://www.economist.com

- *The New York Times:* http://www.newyorktimes.com

- Public Broadcasting Service (PBS): http://www.pbs.org

- National Public Radio (NPR): http://www.npr.org/

- BBC World News: http://news.bbc.co.uk/

- CNN World News: http://www.cnn.com/WORLD/

Preplanning Strategy 12

Take elective courses that prepare you for fellowship applications. Most undergraduates have room in their degree plans for an elective course or two. We think this offers a great opportunity to take a course that may help you in some way to prepare for submitting an application for a fellowship. Here are a few courses that are generally available at all campuses that might help you:

- **A course about interviewing.** Many campuses have courses devoted solely to the theory and practice behind interviewing. A course like this is certain to give you an advantage if you face interviews in your application process. Usually these courses are found in a Communication division.

- **A course on business/professional writing.** This course will further hone your writing skills—especially your ability to articulate your ideas concisely and logically. If you are fortunate, your instructor may even allow you to work on part of your application for course credit.

- **A course on current world events.** As mentioned in Strategy 11, it's important to know what's going on around the world. This course will force you to read deeply and discuss global events thoughtfully, positive assets for anyone aspiring for a major fellowship.

- **A course on advanced public speaking.** The ability to speak confidently is another skill that will come in handy as you enter the world of major fellowships.

- **A course on research methodology.** At its core, research methodology is about using a scientific process to discover something new. A discipline specific course may be required depending on your major, but if it is not, taking a research course could be very useful if your proposal involves a research study.

IN-PROCESS STRATEGIES

As you get closer to starting the actual application process, the following strategies will help you produce the strongest application possible. Many of the strategies deal with managing the entire process, which is often challenging because you will probably be preparing at least part of your application during the busy school year. The following are just suggestions, however; you may other techniques that work well for you. We cannot overemphasize that to create the best picture of yourself as an applicant for any award, you must manage the application process well—and give yourself plenty of time.

In-Process Strategy 1

Start the process early. If you are picking up this book and only have a few weeks until an application deadline is due, there is hope. Fellowship advisors have reported that successful applications have been generated for some competitions in a very short time. However, your best chance for success comes by starting to prepare well in advance of a deadline. Here's why.

As mentioned earlier, you should view your application for a major fellowship as a process. An early start allows you time to think through what you bring to the table, as well as your goals and future opportunities, and how those fit with the purposes of the program you are applying for. Starting the process early will allow you to go through the necessary steps carefully and thoughtfully so that the final product you produce is your best. It is likely that you will develop several drafts of all the documentation needed to support your application and, therefore, it will take a significant amount of time.

Never Too Early

For some of the most competitive programs, like the Rhodes, we believe you should start thinking about your application as early as your senior year in high school.

We recommend that you start the writing pieces of your particular fellowship application at least one year before the deadline. Begin a timeline and set monthly goals for writing and other preparation activities. Many Rhodes winners have reported putting in well over one hundred hours on their applications. With programs like the Rhodes and Marshall, you may find yourself subject to a campus process as well depending on the resources available at your institution.

In-Process Strategy 2

Use a team approach. Most of our achievements in life are not ours alone. The same holds true for winning a prestigious award. You need other people to encourage you, support you, and help you to be better, so it is important to create a team of people to mentor you through the application process. This is a strategy used successfully by several individuals we interviewed for this book. Here is how one winner reported his team-building strategy:

> First, I identified people whom I know well in my campus community. These were people who I felt knew me well and had my best interest at heart. In developing a team, I also looked for people who were not afraid to be critical of my ideas or work. Finally, I tried to choose individuals who were naturally good editors and would take time to review the written work I gave them.

As a student, it may sound difficult at first to build a team like this on your campus, and it may take some work, but we believe campuses are full of quality educators dedicated to helping students pursue their dreams.

In-Process Strategy 3

Break your application tasks down into doable chunks. There is no way around the fact that these applications take time. Some may take more time than others, but the fact remains: To produce your highest quality work you must be devoted to committing serious time to your application. One strategy that we have used successfully with applications as well as with other professional efforts, is to break the task down into smaller parts and then proceed to knit together those smaller parts into the larger product.

The power of this technique is illustrated in a book by Jane Bolker devoted to helping doctoral students finish their dissertation, called *Writing Your Dissertation in Fifteen Minutes a Day: A Guide to Starting, Revising, and Finishing Your Doctoral Thesi*s. Bolker encourages writers to set daily goals, breaking the task of writing a dissertation down into manageable bites. The author also recommends trying to work on the project daily.

The same advice works with fellowship applications, especially the sections that require you to write. For example, your application might require you to write about four different prompts. Set a timeline for when you would like to have each prompt completed. When you finish one, get a friend or professor to look at it while you begin working on the next one. This is just one way of breaking the task into bite-size pieces. After all, almost anything is more manageable when you do it this way.

In-Process Strategy 4

Initiate a series of mock interviews. Many scholarship competitions require applicants to go through an interview. Some competitions even have a student's home university do an initial screening interview. In other competitions, students will not face interviews until they make it to advanced rounds.

If you are applying for a fellowship that requires an interview, we recommend finding some key people on campus that will help you prepare for the interview. Where possible, select people who will challenge you in the interview. What we mean is, don't just pick mock interviewers who will go easy on you; be willing to be pushed. You may have to come up with the questions and organize the interview, but it will be well worth it. Responding in a simulated session will help you when you face the real thing. You may need to set up multiple practice sessions with your interview team to really strengthen your responses.

Hot Tip

For a complete set of interview strategies, see Chapter 10 on interviewing.

In-Process Strategy 5

Revisions, revisions, revisions (or write, revise, rewrite). It is the rare individual who can write something the first time and have it the quality needed to win a prestigious fellowship. As writers, we cannot tell you the countless hours we spend writing and revising our proposals and other professional pieces. Making what you write better over time is a vitally important part of creating a strong application. Also, as mentioned in In-Process Strategy 2, when you utilize a team approach and have other people review and edit your work, your readers become your "trial group" to help you determine if your writing resonates with others. Use their feedback to make your proposals and personal statements stronger. Revising can be tedious and at times appears unending, but trust us: you will find that through the revision process you are crafting a stronger package.

In-Process Strategy 6

Be aware of deadlines. If you are anything like most high school, college, and graduate students we know, your schedule is packed. It is critically important, however, to know the deadline(s) for the fellowship(s) you are applying for and plan to have everything completed at least two weeks in advance of either your campus deadline or the fellowship sponsor's deadline. This window will allow time in case something in the process needs attention, or you decide on a last-minute change. Also, be sure that you have included all of the requested application materials. We recommend that you check and double-check your entire application and the stated deadlines. Late submissions are not considered. Period.

In-Process Strategy 7

If you get a "no" reflect, reevaluate, and if your circumstances permit, reapply. Abraham Lincoln lost his first election; Michael Jordan was cut from his high school basketball team; Bill Gates dropped out of Harvard; yet all of these individuals went on to have an impact on society. These famous failures can help us to realize that a "no" answer doesn't mean we should curl up and retreat from the world, never to take a risk again. One ultimate winner told us:

> In my applications for prestigious scholarships I have put my heart in each application that I have prepared—still only two of my four applications were successful. I received a "no" answer on my first application for a Fulbright student grant and my first application for a Fulbright Scholar grant (as a faculty member). Both times I heard "no" I was crushed—especially the first; however, the "no's" were in many ways a blessing in disguise. They prompted me to reflect on the entire process and reevaluate. This reflection was critically important because it was very clear that I was transformed by the process alone. The reflection also caused me to look critically at where my application might be weak, how it could be improved, and if I had a second chance. I did have a second chance with the Fulbright after my initial failures.

So, our advice if you receive a "no": While it may be difficult—perhaps crushing—acknowledge those feelings and then pull yourself up, reflect, and reevaluate. We think you will come to the conclusion that you have learned much about yourself through the application process. If it fits your life circumstances to apply for the fellowship again, go for it, because success awaits the persistent. Remember: Fall down seven times; get up eight.

In-Process Strategy 8

View the application process as a valuable piece of your collegiate learning. By the time you complete your application, you will have put many hours into producing a potentially successful application. The goal is to win the award, and hopefully that will become reality. But what we want you to realize is that award or no award, if you diligently develop a strong application, you will have compiled something valuable: the story of your personal, intellectual, and academic growth and achievement. This is what makes the application process not just a series of forms to be filled out, but the testimony of your collegiate learning experience. If you can keep this in mind as you journey through your college courses, service activities, extracurricular endeavors, and application processes, you will weave together not only an application to submit, but a road map for your future.

TIMELINE TO SUCCESS

You don't have to do it this way, but college sure works better if you do! This timeline was prepared by collating and condensing timelines like this that we collected from elite colleges and universities all over the country. We encourage you to utilize this timeline to help you plan, but as a tool to help you get the most out of your college experience.

Freshman Year

- Take a wide variety of courses to try to find your major.

- Take a foreign language—whether it's required or not.

- Find and participate in a sport that you can enjoy every week for the rest of your life.

- Learn to see your faculty *outside* of the classroom by stopping by during their open office hours to discuss the class, curriculum, ideas for papers, what's going to be on the test, how best to study, who's who in the department, etc.

- Realize that you can't graduate in four years by taking a minimum load; familiarize yourself *now* with graduation requirements (distribution requirements, minimum credits, major and minor selection, departmental rules). You don't want to become a senior who has to take required freshman-level courses!

- Get by without a car; your grades will be higher.

- Live on campus; your grades will be higher.

- Join at least one academic club.

- Join at least one activity to make the world a better place.

- Join at least one activity solely to pursue an interest.

- Learn that college is not just classes, but also guest speakers, clubs, movies, outdoor recreation, political exploration, social opportunity, etc.

- Go to the career center in the first semester and learn how to (1) register for announcements and notices, (2) write a resume, and (3) get an internship. Competitive internships are selected over the winter/early spring!

- Try to find friends who are going to be successful in life, and conversely, try to avoid those distracting, loud, irresponsible, and sometimes fun people who are ultimately going to fail at college.

- As soon as you can, find the help desk in the library, the writing center or academic support center, the counseling office, the medical clinic, and other sources of help and support.

- Try not to work long hours at a wage job, so you can adjust to college.

- Watch your grades!

- *If, and only if,* you are an engineering major, declare your major and meet with an academic advisor to plan the sequence of courses that will allow you to graduate on time.

- *If, and only if,* you are potentially interested in a career in medicine, find the pre-medical advisor and learn how best to prepare yourself. Do the same if you're interested in law school.

- Begin to plan to study abroad for a semester (or two) during your sophomore year. Stop by the study abroad office and gather information about the programs that it offers.

First Summer

For most students, this is a "free" summer, so:

- Pursue a service opportunity or some big adventure.

- Travel abroad.

- Take any kind of wage job.

- Work at an internship or summer job in an industry or field that you would potentially like to pursue after graduation.

For the most ambitious students:

- Seek an internship or a summer research opportunity. See your internship coordinator *in the first semester* of freshman year to learn about internships. Talk to your faculty to learn about summer research opportunities that would be available to rising sophomores.

Sophomore Year

- Prepare in the first semester to get a summer internship (see "Second Summer" below).

- Test your interest in one or more majors by deepening your class load in those subjects.

- Continue to see faculty outside of the classroom.

- Become involved in departmental activities, such as guest speakers, receptions, symposia, committee work open to students, and especially the informal events such as barbeques, softball Saturdays, whatever they're doing together.

- Continue with an academic activity.

- Begin to think seriously about what you're going to do after college.

- Start going to all career fairs and asking lots of questions.

- Get by without a car; your grades will be higher.

- Live on campus; your grades will be higher.

Second Summer

This summer "counts," and is not free, so try to do one of the following:

- Work at an internship or summer job in an industry or field that you would potentially like to pursue after graduation; if you discover you don't like it, you can still change direction fairly easily.

- Work at an academically related internship that supports your graduate school plans.

- *If, and only if,* you can't find one of the above, go to summer school to beef up your chances of graduating on time and/or to prepare for graduate school.

Junior Year

This is the year that sets up success after graduation!

- Prepare in the first semester to get a summer internship (see "Final Summer" below).

- If you haven't yet settled on a major, decide and meet with an academic advisor to plan the sequence of courses that will allow you to graduate on time.

- Continue to see faculty outside of the classroom.

- Continue to be involved in departmental activities.

- Continue with an academic activity.

- Consider adding to your list of activities (academic, service, sports, interest). Consider seeking a leadership role in one or more *especially* if you're grad-school bound.

- Begin to talk about your future career with fellow students, faculty, alumni, visiting speakers and VIPs, friends of the family, parents of your friends, etc.

- Visit alumni and professionals in your chosen field for a "shadowing" day, or at least an information interview.

- If you're applying for an elite graduate fellowship (Rhodes, Watson, Marshall, etc.), find the scholarship advisor and plan your application strategy. Most successful applicants start first semester of the junior year to prepare their applications.

- Research graduate schools. Look up prominent graduate faculty in your field of interest, read articles in the academic journals for your field, look at Peterson's graduate school guides.

- Begin to correspond with faculty in graduate schools of interest.

- If grad schools on your list require the GRE, plan to take it late in the second semester, or in June of the coming summer.

- If grad schools on your list require a GRE subject test, register in February for an April sitting.

- If headed for medical school, register in March to take the April MCAT. You can take it again in August if you don't like your score.

- If headed for law school, register in November to take the December LSAT, or in January for the February sitting. You can take it again in June or October of the following year if you don't like your score.

- Visit all the graduate schools you can during the school year.

- Try to go to an academic conference in your field.

- Watch your grades! These are the last grades that will show if you plan to apply to graduate school next year.

- Get by without a car; your grades will be higher.

- Live on campus; your grades will be higher.

- If you're applying for scholarships like the Rhodes and British Marshal, they have specific campus deadline, usually late winter term of senior year. Expect to dedicate a significant amount of time to preparing your applications during spring term of junior year.

Final Summer

This is the most important summer of your life; don't fool around!

- Now it's critical to find an internship or summer job in an industry or field that you would potentially like to pursue after graduation. Ask for a letter of recommendation before leaving the internship or job at the end of the summer.

- Work at an academically related internship that supports your graduate school plans.

- Continue to talk about your career goals with everyone you meet; continue to visit professionals in their workplaces whenever you can.

- Try to go to an academic conference in your field. Visit some grad schools if you can. Meet professors who might be mentors in grad school. Correspond with graduate faculty in your area of interest.

- Prepare for and take the GRE or LSAT in June if you still need to (you don't want to have to do this in the fall with classes and applications to graduate school or fellowships hanging over you).

- Prepare for and take the MCAT in June or July if you didn't like your first score.

- *If, and only if,* you're headed for graduate school, consider going to summer school at one of your targeted institutions. Take classes related to your grad school plans, and watch your grades!

- If you're applying to medical school, get all your applications in at the first opportunity on the first round (usually over this summer, with some details possibly running into September and following).

- Prepare for and complete application materials for scholarships and fellowships.

Senior Year

- First week of class, visit your career center and explore all support available to you that will make this transitional year a success. At the very least, get that final resume polish and pursue interview training from the career center.

- Prepare in the first semester to get a career-launching job or post-graduation summer internship. Plot out a year's search activities with your career counselor.

- First week of class, meet with professors about your graduate school plans, seek their advice, and identify potential authors of letters of recommendation.

- Continue to prepare for scholarship and fellowship applications, generally due October through February.

- If selected for nationally prestigious scholarships, prepare for interviews during October and November.

- In September and October, get all your nonmed graduate school applications in (deadlines will vary, but apply at least 30 to 90 days early).

- Schedule any GRE subject tests if you still need to. If grad schools on your list require a subject GRE test, register in September or October for the November sitting.

- Continue to talk about your career goals with everyone you meet; continue to visit professionals in their workplaces.

- Begin to systematically identify alumni who can give you career advice; learn how to conduct an effective information interview.

- Build a networking list of professionals in your targeted field who can help you find a job.

- No matter what your major, participate in the on-campus interview cycle if you're interested in the industries that send recruiters to your campus.

- Get by without a car; your grades will be higher.

- Live on campus; your grades will be higher.

Summer after College

If you're admitted to graduate school, this is a "free" summer:

- Pursue a service opportunity or some big adventure.

- Travel abroad.

- Take any kind of wage job and rest your mind.

- Work at an internship related to your academic interest.

If you land a job before graduation:

- If you want eventually to go to business school, consider taking the GMAT during this summer and applying this fall to enter business school with one year's experience, the following fall to enter with two years' experience, and so on.

- Remember, every August for the rest of your life, ask yourself: "In one year, do I want to be in grad school?" *Watch out for the extensive lead time to get into a graduate program.*

If launching a career, but without a job yet:

- Use the career center to run a systematic search.

- Find a post-baccalaureate internship or summer job in an industry or field that you would potentially like to pursue as a career.

- Stay in touch with professors who may refer you to positions.

- Try hard to find work you're interested in, even passionate about, that requires your college degree and your accumulated skills, and try hard not to panic and settle for any income you can find.

- Remember: "Choose a job you love, and you will never have to work a day in your life."—Confucius

---

This timeline originally appeared in another form in *How to Get Any Job with Any Major,* 1st ed., 2004, and *How to Get Any Job,* 2nd ed., 2008, used with permission. For permission to use this timeline on your campus, request an e-version from Donald Asher, Asher Associates, don@donaldasher.com.

CHAPTER 3
A Selection of Competitive Scholarship Opportunities

Which scholarships are the "best of the best"? Today, there will be plenty of disagreement about which ones are the most prestigious scholarships in the world. Twenty years ago, however, scholarship and fellowship advisers would have almost immediately identified the Rhodes as the most prestigious scholarship in the world. However, in recent years, more and more top-flight opportunities have become available to assist students by supporting graduate studies or other valuable experiential learning opportunities.

By no means are we claiming to have identified every possible prestigious or nationally competitive opportunity. That list is growing all the time. However, we have compiled a selection of first-rate opportunities based on the history of each program, its benefits, and the amount of the award itself. As with any opportunity, these types of distinctions may not, in fact, mean it's the best possible opportunity for you. That is why, throughout this text, we urge you to reflect and "do your homework" to make sure that what may appear to be the most prestigious opportunity is, in fact, the very best fit for you. Any opportunity that supports your ambitions and plans for the future will be the "best" for you.

Having said that, we are confident that from among all the opportunities available, certain scholarships and fellowships stand out because of the level of competition, scope, and benefits provided by each one. Among these are the Rhodes, the British Marshall, the Mitchell, the Truman, the Gates Cambridge, the Churchill, the Jack Kent Cooke, and Fulbright programs. All are similar in that they are highly competitive, nationally prestigious opportunities. In almost all cases, they require an extensive application process that includes, but may not be limited to, an application form, transcripts, exam scores (GRE, ACT, etc.), curriculum vitae (CV), personal statements, research proposal, and extensive reference letters. If your application is successful, most of these nationally prestigious opportunities involve a one- to two-day interview process that results in the final selection of award recipients.

These opportunities provide full funding for a set number of years of graduate study or, like the Rhodes, a second bachelor's degree if preferable. Many also carry a substantial travel stipend. With these scholarships and, arguably, with many of the other opportunities featured in this book, you are truly competing with "the best of the best," and for that reason you should expect to devote a significant amount of time to your application(s) and preparation.

THE APPLICATION PROCESS

Generally speaking, for all of the nationally prestigious opportunities, your best assets are time-management and ambition. Most, if not all of the opportunities mentioned above, require at least a year of advanced planning just to complete the process in such a way as to prove potentially successful. It is important to always keep deadlines and timelines in the back of your mind.

If your institution has a dedicated staff to assist you with your applications, you may in fact go through multiple selection processes. For example, the Rhodes and British Marshall have a nomination process whereby the institution selects a set number of strong candidates for the next step. Often, that selection process happens during winter term, depending on the structure of the institution, with advising and preparation taking place for the entire spring and summer in advance of fall deadlines. The fall deadline for any nationally prestigious opportunity occurs the year before funding actually begins.

So, aside from the reflection and planning that we hope you will begin to do from the very start of your undergraduate career, logistically you need to be thinking a year to a year and a half in advance of the year you seek funding. You will also need to monitor exam dates like the GRE or LSAT, should those be required for a scholarship, fellowship, or graduate school application, and give yourself enough time to prepare for the exam. And you will also need to be sensitive always to the schedules of those helping you with your applications, whether they are advisers, faculty members, family, or friends. You will not garner the reference letters needed for these types of opportunities if you ask for them just weeks before a deadline. Take the time to speak with your support team well in advance and provide them with as much information as possible about the opportunities you are considering.

Finally, you simply need to give yourself enough time to write, rewrite, rewrite again, edit, edit, edit, practice interviewing, and, probably, edit your materials again. Your application for any opportunity is the very first introduction you have to any review committee and the more polished it is, the better.

THE U.S., UK, AND EU SYSTEMS

You will quickly notice as you read this chapter that a significant number of these opportunities are for study in the United Kingdom (UK), the Republic of Ireland, and the European Union. There are increasingly more opportunities becoming available every year to support other kinds of international study such as programs through DAAD (German Academic Exchange Service Scholarships) for study in Germany and for study and/or research at locations around the world through the Fulbright. For the purpose of this book, it may be useful for you to have an understanding of the distinction between higher education in the United States and the United Kingdom because so much of your application for a scholarship like the Rhodes rests on an understanding of the British system.

The point here isn't to provide you with a grand history of the educational system in the United Kingdom versus the United States but to provide you with a few key insights that may help as you look into opportunities as well as funding.

Differences in Organizational Structures

There are increasing numbers of institutions of higher education in the United Kingdom, but, historically speaking, its oldest universities, like the University of Oxford and the University of Cambridge, were built on a monastic system for the training of monks. Aside from the fact that much of the education provided focused on subjects of classical learning, life and learning were interconnected. Students lived, and still do live, with their tutors (faculty) and other college staff. They share meals and, at least at places like Oxford and Cambridge, the institutions have maintained a level of ceremony attached to the educational process. At many UK institutions of higher education, there are multiple levels of organization given that a university was established to govern multiple individual and autonomous colleges. For example, when you apply to Oxford, you are accepted by the University, by the college of your choice, and by your faculty. In the United States, generally speaking, there is a single admissions process, or at least it will appear so to the student applicant.

Newer types of universities now coexist with the oldest in the United Kingdom. Oxford and Cambridge are now joined by schools such the London School of Economics, the University of Leeds, the University of St. Andrews, the University of Aberdeen, the University of York, and many other institutions of higher education that offer strong programs. Schools in the United Kingdom also offer vocational training. The Open University offers learning opportunities on a part-time basis through distance-learning courses to students in many walks of life. Likewise, Ireland's institutions provide a variety of opportunities for students to complete both undergraduate and graduate degrees supported by a variety of fellowships. For example, the University of Limerick has a strong music program, the University of Belfast is known for peace and conflict resolution studies, and 400-year-old Trinity College in Dublin offers degrees in the arts, humanities, social sciences, engineering, math and science, and health sciences.

In the United States, some institutions adopted a similar structure to universities such as Oxford and Cambridge. Princeton, Yale, Sarah Lawrence, and other colleges and universities have intentionally adopted certain social and pedagogical models similar to those in the United Kingdom. By contrast, however, the types of U.S. institutional structures are wide-reaching.

Institutions of higher education may be classified as state, public, or private; nonprofit or for-profit; same sex or coeducational; faith-based or nondenominational; liberal arts, teacher training, or vocational; or four-year or two-year. In reality, U.S. colleges and universities are a mix of these classifications.

Differences in Pedagogy

The pedagogical methods utilized in the United States and the United Kingdom, as well as in other countries in Europe, are also distinct. The primary difference is the tutorial system of teaching used at places like Oxford. In the United States, it is much more common to sit in a large lecture hall or have courses with 20 or more fellow students. In the United Kingdom, it is more common to have one-on-one meetings with your tutor (faculty) and/or participate in very small seminars. This is perhaps the most challenging, but also most rewarding, part of studying in the United Kingdom.

Due, in part, to this type of system, students in the United Kingdom participate more fully in their own education. UK graduate programs are highly research-focused, and far less time is spent on examinations. Graduate students do sit for some type of examination, depending on their course of study, and they usually submit a master's dissertation. Brevity is expected in writing and in study. It is certainly expected that you would have enough research material to write four dissertations, but part of the education is finding a way to indicate the extent of your research without having to include every single quote, scholarly review, journal article, or any other ephemera you've come across after one or two or four years of research.

Higher education in the United States can be a more passive experience, whereas study in the United Kingdom requires an investment in time and preparation for a tutorial experience. Again, these are very general statements and relate specifically to methods still used at Oxford and Cambridge. Newer institutions may have larger class sizes and deviate from the tutorial method slightly, but there remains a commitment to an education supported by smaller class sizes and more one-on-one attention between faculty and students than in the United States.

Differences in Timeframe and Degrees Awarded

The length of time a degree takes in the United Kingdom versus the United States is much shorter. Unlike the seven to eleven years in the United States to earn a doctorate, at institutions such as Oxford or Cambridge, you will be given one to two years to complete a master's degree, depending on your program of choice, followed by two to three years to complete your doctoral dissertation.

It should also be mentioned that there are a number of different kinds of degrees offered in the United Kingdom, and they are shaped by the departmental structure. Students in the humanities can read for a master of studies (MSt, 1 year), a master of philosophy (MPhil, 2 years), and a doctorate of philosophy (DPhil, 2–3 years). Degrees awarded in the sciences follow a similar pattern, but the degrees awarded are described as master of science or doctorate of science.

Differences in Funding

The other significant difference is funding. Aside from the ambitions of programs such as the Rhodes and British Marshall to encourage the diplomatic exchange of ideas between the United States and the United Kingdom, these award programs exist because historically there was very little funding offered to international students. It is a fairly recent phenomenon to have large numbers of international students at universities such as Oxford and Cambridge, in part because of the challenge of securing funding, as well as the fact that these institutions were created to educate British students who did not have to pay any fees if accepted into university.

Going to university was not considered an option or even an expectation for every student in the United Kingdom or generally in Europe. Because of the economic downturn in recent years, fewer U.S. institutions can offer full scholarships for all graduate students, especially those in the humanities, but it is certainly easier to locate funding opportunities in the United States. They sometimes take the form of teaching assistantships or graduate student assistantships. These opportunities may not constitute full rides, but they certainly help students in meeting their tuition costs.

However, the United Kingdom offers a program called the Overseas Research Scheme (ORS) that is available to all international graduate students who submit an accompanying application while applying for admission to graduate schools. The ORS is offered at the national level and is highly selective, but, if awarded, it means that an international student is charged at the same rate as students from the European Union. To attend Oxford, for example, this may mean as much as $16,000 less a year than what an international student would otherwise have to pay.

Visit the pages dedicated to funding international students on the Web sites of UK universities that interest you to find out specific information. It is also worth mentioning that individual colleges offer small awards, and often funding is slightly easier to locate following the first year of any advanced-degree program. For more information, check out the following:

- Overseas Research Scheme: http://www.orsas.ac.uk/
- British Council: http://www.britishcouncil.org/new/
    http://www.britishcouncil.org/usa.htm

A Difference in Completing Your Application

It should also be said that applying for graduate study in the United Kingdom is nuanced as well. Generally speaking, review committees at a place such as Oxford are far less interested in a "personal statement" and far more interested in your research and your ability to use brevity in your writing. In fact, it is common practice in the United Kingdom to limit essays by word count, not page count. Florid, journalistic writing is not especially well-received. Of course, if you're applying for a Rhodes or something similar, you will be expected to submit a personal statement—but it will have a very different flavor from anything that you submit as part of your undergraduate or graduate admissions materials.

Once You're Accepted: A Word of Advice

Perhaps the most important bit of advice is to find a "champion." You will want to be sure that you have identified faculty and resources useful to you as you work toward your master's and perhaps a doctorate. As mentioned above, the timeframe for earning a degree is much shorter than in the United States, so it is critical to find someone to support your work, not just read a draft here or there.

DO YOUR HOMEWORK

The advice in the previous paragraph ties into what we discussed in Chapters 1 and 2 and will discuss again in following chapters: the importance of giving yourself enough time to conduct research on programs, resources, and faculty prior to making application to any of these opportunities and, in fact, to any graduate school you may be considering. Funding opportunities like the Overseas Research Scheme and Clarendon Bursaries, which assist international students with tuition in the United Kingdom, are particularly keen on seeing an applicant make a clear, supported case for why he or she must be at a particular institution. For example, if you're interested in nineteenth-century art and literature, why would Oxford's library and archival resources be so critical to the success of your work? Could you do your work anywhere else in the world? These are the types of questions to be asking yourself as you move through these kinds of processes.

> ### Changes Underway in European Higher Education
>
> For a description of changes occurring in higher education in greater Europe, review The Bologna Process and Declaration: http://www.ond.vlaanderen.be/hogeronderwijs/bologna. An attempt is under way to standardize degrees across much of Europe; however, it remains to be seen how long it will take to accomplish this and whether the United Kingdom is going to fully align its practices.

COMPETITIVE SCHOLARSHIP OPPORTUNITIES

The scholarships, fellowships, and grants presented in this chapter are not a comprehensive listing, but a sampling of some of the more popular, prestigious, and lucrative opportunities available. The information presented is adapted from the program Web sites and summarized in a form that allows for quick reference and comparison between programs. Many of the elements of each application process are similar, namely, transcripts, letters of recommendation, a CV, a personal statement, and/or a research proposal. But it is important to pay close attention to the specific requirements for each opportunity. All will vary slightly, but it doesn't hurt to have the above-mentioned pieces available for reference, regardless of the opportunity. For more information, it is critical that you visit and thoroughly examine the official Web site of each fellowship, grant, or program that you are considering.

The profiles are divided into the following five topic areas:

1. A Selection of the Most Elite Scholarships in the World

2. Scholarships and Fellowships for Students Enrolled at Any U.S. Institution of Higher Education

3. Scholarships and Fellowships Limited to Students Enrolled at Invited Institutions

4. Discipline-Specific Scholarships and Fellowships for the Arts, Humanities, and Social Sciences

5. Discipline-Specific Scholarships and Fellowships for the Sciences

Please note that like all taxonomies, this is an imperfect one. Some scholarships and fellowships are classified according to their typical award focus, but some programs have exceptions or small, ancillary programs that are outside their known, primary focus. So, some exploration on your own is in order before deciding that a program is *not* appropriate for you. We recommend browsing through these sections, even the ones that seemingly don't apply to you.

While we have set forth the notion that ambition, perseverance, and preparation are at the heart of the scholarship and fellowship process, many of the programs detailed in this section are *merit-based* awards. Take minimum GPAs listed on program Web sites seriously. There is always a chance that you will receive an award without meeting that minimum, but you can expect to be competing against other applicants who meet and/or exceed the minimum GPA. On average, a minimum GPA is 3.6. The expectation for many of the programs listed, especially the most elite, is as close to a 4.0 as possible. This is not meant to discourage you, but rather encourage you to do your research and make sure your profile and academic history match the expectation of the program(s) that interest you.

Also, we remind you that this is an *idea book,* not in any sense an exhaustive listing of scholarships and fellowships. See the companion guide to this book, *Peterson's Scholarships, Grants & Prizes* for millions of awards worth billions of dollars.

A SELECTION OF THE MOST ELITE SCHOLARSHIPS IN THE WORLD

In our research for this book, we set out to identify a handful of very elite scholarships. The following listings are the result of that labor. Based on interviews with fellowship advisers, winning students, and the broader academic community, these awards rose to the top as the most difficult and most valuable to win. We realize that others might add some specific favorite to this list, but we are confident that people who know about these fellowship programs will agree that all of the following belong on any list of "the best of the best":

- Rhodes Scholarships
- Marshall Scholarships
- The Gates Cambridge Scholarships
- The George J. Mitchell Scholarship
- Harry S Truman Scholarships
- The Barry M. Goldwater Scholarship and Excellence in Education Program
- The Morris K. Udall Scholarship
- Fulbright Grants

> **You Can't Go It Alone**
>
> We once again call your attention to the fact that successful applicants to these types of awards will usually have the backing, coaching, and full endorsement of faculty, fellowship advisers, and, in some cases, top officers of their undergraduate institutions.

One might reasonably ask why these awards are so prestigious, so here are a few reasons:

- Take a quick glance at the numbers: Rhodes has thirty-two awards for approximately 900 applicants and Marshall awards forty scholarships annually out of approximately 1,000 applicants. The other scholarship programs are similarly daunting. These programs have built a reputation for selecting "the best of the best."
- These programs have robust histories and recognizable names. They are well-publicized at the most elite U.S. institutions and are sought after by the most talented U.S. students.
- They offer a fantastic set of tangible and intangible benefits that have the potential to open doors for recipients throughout their lives.
- The applicants and winners have backgrounds that exude achievement. Take a look at the biography pages of winners of these awards. These young people are

super-achievers and began preparation for these awards well before they hit college campuses.

Rhodes Scholarships

Cecil Rhodes, an Oxford alumnus and South African colonist, was the first to consolidate the De Beers mines, which at one time controlled 90 percent of the world's known diamond reserves. At his death in 1902, the will of Cecil Rhodes established the Rhodes Trust so that high-achieving foreign students could be educated at Oxford.

The Rhodes Scholarship is one of the oldest and most prestigious awards and was the first internationally based scholarship competition. In addition to thirty-two Rhodes Scholars chosen from the United States each year, Rhodes Scholars are selected from Australia, Bermuda, Canada, the nations of the Commonwealth Caribbean, Germany, India, Jamaica, Kenya, New Zealand, Pakistan, South Africa, Botswana, Lesotho, Malawi, Namibia, Swaziland, Zimbabwe, and Zambia. Over eighty Rhodes Scholars are selected worldwide each year.

Benefits

The Rhodes Scholarship covers tuition and fees for two years of study at Oxford University. An optional third year is possible. Students are also provided travel to and from England and a maintenance scholarship to cover living expenses: a total value of approximately $45,000. Students may choose almost any area of study offered at Oxford and will affiliate with a residential college. Although students are permitted to choose undergraduate degrees, most winning applications propose master's or doctoral-level work. Once at Oxford, students also have the benefit of access to the Rhodes House, an early-twentieth-century mansion containing part of the Bodleian Library.

General Eligibility Requirements

According to the Rhodes Scholar Web site, Rhodes applicants from the United States must meet the following criteria to be considered:

- be a citizen of the United States
- be between 18 and 23 years of age at the time of application
- complete the bachelor's degree before October 1 of the grant year

Application Process

Interested applicants must first secure an endorsement from their undergraduate or graduate institution. Institutional endorsements are no guarantee, however. Usually each institution has a process in place for choosing the students whom they wish to endorse. Once a student is endorsed by his/her institution, the application is forwarded to one of sixteen regionally based review committees. These committees will select candidates for a round of personal interviews before the final awards are announced.

Application materials include:

- an application form
- a personal statement describing academic and personal interests
- a list of activities and honors in college
- college transcripts
- up to seven letters of recommendation

Deadline

The Rhodes Scholarship application is due annually in October. Campus deadlines will be earlier. Please check with your campus representative.

For More Information

http://www.rhodesscholar.org

MARSHALL SCHOLARSHIPS

The Marshall Scholarships were created in 1953 by an act of the British parliament and named in honor of General George C. Marshall. Marshall served as primary military adviser to President Franklin D. Roosevelt during World War II. After the war, Marshall was named Secretary of State by President Harry S Truman. Marshall developed the postwar plan to rebuild the allied countries of Europe, which came to be known as the Marshall Plan. For his efforts, Marshall earned the Nobel Peace Prize in 1953.

The British Marshall Scholarships were created to continue the work of the Rhodes Scholarships by providing young American leaders the opportunity to study in Britain. Distinct from Rhodes Scholarships, however, the Marshall Scholarships expanded study opportunities beyond Oxford University. Approximately forty Marshall Scholarships are awarded annually.

Marshall himself wrote a message to the first 12 scholars in 1954, and in this letter he states, "A close relationship between our two countries is essential to the good of mankind in this turbulent world to today, and that is not possible without the intimate understanding of each other."

Benefits

The Marshall Scholarship covers tuition and fees for two years of study at a British university. Students are also provided travel to and from England and a maintenance scholarship to cover living expenses. The total amount of the award varies based on the university, but the average award is valued at approximately $42,000.

General Eligibility Requirements

According to the Marshall Web site, applicants must meet the following criteria to be considered:

- must be a citizen of the United States
- must have earned a bachelor's degree at an accredited U.S. university before beginning study in Britain
- must have earned at least a 3.7 GPA as an undergraduate

Application Process

Applicants begin the process by filling out the online application form located on the Marshall Scholarship Web site. The application must be authorized by the institutional representative, who will secure the institutional endorsement from the school's president, provost, or academic dean. After receiving the institution's endorsement, the application is forwarded to one of eight regionally based review committees. These committees select candidates for a round of personal interviews before the final awards are announced.

Additional application materials include:

- the applicant's college transcripts
- four letters of recommendation

Deadline

The application is due annually in October. Campus deadlines will be earlier. Please check with your campus representative.

For More Information

http://www.marshallscholarship.org/

THE GATES CAMBRIDGE SCHOLARSHIPS

In 2000, Bill Gates, the founder of Microsoft, and his wife Melinda established the Bill and Melinda Gates Foundation. The Foundation's primary interests include global health, poverty and development, and education and information.

In 2000, the Bill and Melinda Gates Foundation donated $210 million to Cambridge University to establish the Gates Cambridge Trust. This donation created a scholarship for outstanding graduate students from outside the United Kingdom to attend Cambridge University. Each year, the Foundation Trustees award about 100 scholarships that cover the total cost of studying at Cambridge. Usually about half of these awards go to U.S. citizens. Awards are made ". . . on the basis of the candidate's academic excellence, a good fit between the Scholar and the University of Cambridge, evidence of leadership potential and a commitment to improving the lives of others."

Benefits

The Gates Cambridge Scholarship covers the entire cost of studying at Cambridge. Benefits include University Composition Fees and College fees, a maintenance allowance, airfare, and possible support for dependents. Once at Cambridge, students may apply for assistance to help with activities related to professional development.

General Eligibility Requirements

To apply for the Gates Cambridge Scholarships, the following requirements must be met:

- may be citizens of any country except the United Kingdom
- may apply for study in any field available at Cambridge
- must have a strong record of academic achievement and meet the criteria for the academic degree program for which they are applying
- nonnative-English speakers must prove language proficiency

Application Process

Applicants must first apply to the University of Cambridge Board of Graduate Studies using the Graduate Admission and Scholarship Application Form (GRADSAF). By filling out the GRADSAF, applicants will be considered for:

- admission to study on the graduate level at Cambridge University
- admission to one of the Cambridge Colleges
- the Gates Cambridge Scholarship and other awards offered by the Cambridge Trusts

The GRADSAF can be filled out online and is usually due in mid-October. The candidates selected as finalists for the Gates Cambridge Scholarship will be interviewed in the United States in mid-February.

Deadline

The application is due annually in October.

For More Information

http://www.gatesscholar.org/

THE GEORGE J. MITCHELL SCHOLARSHIP

The George J. Mitchell Scholarship, created in 1998, is named in honor of former U.S. Senator George J. Mitchell. Senator Mitchell played a leading role in creating a lasting peace accord in Northern Ireland with the Good Friday Peace Agreement, signed in 1998. He has also taken a leading role in representing the United States in negotiations in the Middle East.

The George J. Mitchell Scholarships are sponsored by the U.S–Ireland Alliance and are ". . . designed to introduce and connect generations of future American leaders to the Island of Ireland, while recognizing and fostering intellectual achievement, leadership, and a commitment to public service and community."

The Mitchell Scholarship funds one year of graduate study for U.S. citizens at universities in the Republic of Ireland and Northern Ireland, part of the United Kingdom. Each year, the selection committee receives approximately 250 applications. From these applications, the committee names 20 national finalists and selects 12 of these finalists as scholarship recipients.

Benefits

The Mitchell Scholarship covers the entire cost of one year of graduate study at a university in the Republic of Ireland or Northern Ireland. This includes tuition and fees, accommodations, a living stipend of $12,000, a travel stipend, and round-trip transportation between the United States and the university.

General Eligibility Requirements

According to the program Web site, Mitchell applicants must meet the following criteria:

- be U.S. citizens
- be between 18 and 30 years of age at the time of application

- hold a bachelor's degree from an accredited institution before they begin a graduate program in Ireland
- have a strong record of academic achievement; however, the Mitchell Scholarship does not have a minimum GPA requirement

Application Process

The application process for the Mitchell Scholarship is entirely online. The application consists of:

- a completed online application
- institutional endorsement letter
- five letters of recommendation
- proof of U.S. citizenship
- academic transcripts
- a thousand-word personal essay.

Once applications are submitted, they are evaluated by the Mitchell Selection Committee. Finalists are notified and required to participate in a personal interview in Washington, DC.

Deadline

The application is due annually in October. Campus deadlines will be earlier. Please check with your campus representative.

For More Information

http://www.us-irelandalliance.org/

HARRY S TRUMAN SCHOLARSHIPS

The Harry S Truman Scholarship Foundation was created by congressional approval in 1975 as a living memorial to the thirty-third president of the United States.

The mission of the Foundation is "to find and recognize college juniors with exceptional leadership potential who are committed to careers in government, the nonprofit or advocacy sectors, education or elsewhere in the public service; and to provide them with financial support for graduate study, leadership training, and fellowship with other students who are committed to making a difference through public service."

This is the premier scholarship program for students interested in public service careers. Each year, this federal scholarship program selects 70 to 75 Truman Scholars.

Benefits

Truman Scholars are provided up to $30,000 for graduate study in public service areas. Upon completion of a Truman Foundation–funded graduate degree, Scholars are required to work in public service for at least three of the first seven years after graduation. In addition to the monetary benefits, award winners are eligible to participate in leadership training held at Jewell College in Liberty, Missouri, a Summer Institute held in Washington, DC, and a legal-based conference.

General Eligibility Requirements

According to the program Web site, Truman applicants must meet the following criteria:

- be a full-time student at a four-year institution of higher education
- have junior-level standing at the time of application
- be a U.S. citizen or a U.S. national from American Samoa or the Commonwealth of the Northern Mariana Islands
- rank in the upper-half of their class
- be committed to a career in public service

The Truman Foundation's definition of public service is the following:

The Foundation defines public service as employment in government at any level, uniformed services, public-interest organizations, nongovernmental research and/or educational organizations, public and private schools, and public service–oriented nonprofit organizations such as those whose primary purposes are to help needy or disadvantaged persons or to protect the environment.

Application Process

Similar to other major fellowships, the Truman Scholarship program requires that applicants be nominated by their institution. Information and deadlines can be obtained from the school's faculty representative. Once a student is endorsed by his/her institution, the application is forwarded to the Harry S Truman Foundation for review. The Foundation announces finalists on its Web site, and these finalists are invited for interviews.

Generally, the application includes:

- an institutional nomination form and letter
- three letters of recommendation
- an academic transcript

- an application
- a policy proposal

A sample application can be viewed online.

Deadline

The application is due annually in February. Campus deadlines will be earlier. Please check with your campus representative.

For More Information

http://truman.gov/

THE BARRY M. GOLDWATER SCHOLARSHIP AND EXCELLENCE IN EDUCATION PROGRAM

The Barry M. Goldwater Scholarship and Excellence in Education Program was established in 1986 to honor Barry Goldwater, the five-term U.S. Senator from Arizona and 1964 Republican Party Presidential nominee.

The Goldwater Scholarships are designed to assist college juniors and seniors interested in careers in mathematics, the natural sciences, and engineering. The Foundation expects scholarship recipients will go on to pursue graduate-level degrees.

The Goldwater Scholarship is widely considered the most prestigious award bestowed upon undergraduates pursuing careers in the sciences. Each year, the Goldwater Foundation funds approximately 300 students from institutions across the United States. Applicants must be nominated by their schools. Four-year institutions may nominate up to 4 students and two-year institutions may nominate up to 2 students.

Benefits

The Goldwater Scholarship funds up to a maximum of $7,500 per academic year. Junior-level applicants are eligible to receive funding for two years. Seniors are only eligible for one year of funding. Although the only direct benefit of winning a Goldwater Scholarship is financial, many Goldwater recipients go on to be admitted to some of the top graduate programs in the nation.

General Eligibility Requirements

According to the program Web site, Goldwater applicants must meet the following criteria:

- be a U.S. citizen, U.S. national, or permanent resident
- be full-time students at the time of application
- be sophomore- or junior-level status at the time of application
- have at least a "B" average and be ranked in the top 25 percent of their class

Application Process

The application process for the Barry Goldwater Scholarship is entirely online. The application consists of:

- an institutional nomination submitted by the institution's Goldwater Faculty Representative
- an application
- an essay
- three letters of recommendation addressing the applicant's potential for a career in the sciences

Supporting documents include:

- academic transcripts from all undergraduate institutions attended
- a high school/secondary school transcript (home-schooled applicants should contact the Goldwater Foundation)

Applicants who are U.S. permanent residents must submit a copy of their Permanent Resident card.

A committee reviews all applications submitted by schools and sends recommendations from each state to the Goldwater Foundation Board of Trustees, which names up to 300 scholarship winners annually.

Deadline

Information about the Goldwater Scholarship deadline is posted annually in September.

For More Information

http://www.act.org/goldwater/

THE MORRIS K. UDALL SCHOLARSHIP

The Morris K. Udall Foundation, established in 1992 by the U.S. Congress, was named in honor of Morris K. Udall, who served in the U.S. Congress for thirty years, from 1962 to 1992. He left a legacy of concern for the environment and advocacy for Native Americans. The focus of the Foundation reflects this commitment.

The Udall Foundation ". . . seeks future leaders across a wide spectrum of environmental fields, including policy, engineering, science, education, urban planning and renewal, business, health, justice, and economics. The Foundation also seeks future Native American and Alaska Native leaders in public and community health care, tribal government, and public policy affecting Native American communities, including land and resource management, economic development, and education."

One of the primary programs of the Udall Foundation is the Udall Scholarship Program. This program provides scholarships for sophomore- and junior-level college students. Each year, the Udall Foundation funds approximately 80 students from institutions across the United States.

Benefits

The Udall Scholarship provides winners a $5,000 scholarship that may be used for tuition, room and board, or other related educational expenses. In addition to this funding, all expenses are paid for winners to attend a four-day orientation held in Arizona annually. Networking opportunities with other Udall Scholars is also encouraged.

General Eligibility Requirements

According to the program Web site, Udall applicants must meet the following criteria:

- be nominated by their respective institutions
- have at least a "B" average
- have sophomore- or junior-level status
- be enrolled as a full-time student at a two- or four-year institution of higher education
- be a U.S. citizen, U.S. national, or permanent resident
- must demonstrate a firm commitment to a career related to the environment

Native American and Alaska Native nominees must plan to pursue careers related to tribal public policy or Native American health care.

Application Process

To apply for a Udall Scholarship, interested students must contact their faculty representative, who serves as a liaison between the Udall Foundation and the student's institution. Each school may nominate up to 6 students. Institutional nominations are sent to the Udall Foundation for review by region. The selection committee then identifies approximately 80 winners as Udall Scholarship recipients. Fifty additional candidates are named honorable mentions.

Students must prepare their entire application package and submit it to their faculty representative for review. This application package consists of the following documents:

- completed application form
- three letters of recommendation
- an 800-word essay
- transcripts from all institutions attended

Additional documentation is required from Native American and Alaska Native nominees.

Deadline

The application is due annually in March. Campus deadlines will be earlier. Please check with your campus representative.

For More Information

http://www.udall.gov/OurPrograms/MKUScholarship/MKUScholarship.aspx

FULBRIGHT GRANTS

U.S. Senator J. William Fulbright, a Rhodes Scholar himself, was instrumental in creating the largest international exchange program in the United States. After seeing the devastation caused by World War II, Senator Fulbright desired to create a program that would help to engender world peace.

The Fulbright program was created in 1946 by the U.S. Congress and is funded by Congress and administered through the U.S. Department of State. It is designed to "enable the government of the United States to increase mutual understanding between the people of the United States and the people of other countries." According to the program's Web site, since the program began in 1946, "more than 46,000 students from the United States and 150,000 students from other countries have benefited from the Fulbright experience."

The Fulbright program for students remains one of the most prestigious awards for U.S. undergraduate and graduate students studying abroad, as well as foreign students desiring to study in the United States. Each year, the program gives approximately 1,300 awards to students from the United States to study and conduct research in over 140 countries. In addition, the Fulbright Foreign Student Program annually brings approximately 1,800 students to U.S. institutions of higher education (more about this program in Chapter 6).

Benefits

Students may apply for grants to study in over 140 countries. Grants are usually categorized as a full grant or a travel grant. Specialized grants, such as the Fulbright Teaching Assistantship, Business Grants, Fulbright Journalism Grants, Fulbright Critical Language Enhancement Award, and the Fulbright mtvU awards, are also available. Most of these specialized grants fall under the full-grant category.

Most full grants include transportation, a living expenses stipend, research/book allowance, and medical insurance. Some countries also cover tuition costs if a student is enrolled in one of their academic programs.

General Eligibility Requirements

The criteria to apply for a Fulbright grant are:

- be a U.S. citizen
- be a graduating senior, recent graduate, or graduate student

Individuals who do not hold a bachelor's degree, but have significant specialized study and/ or experience in the field to which they are applying, may be considered as well.

Application Process

Students enrolled as undergraduate or graduate students in the United States must apply through their campus Fulbright Program Advisors. Individuals not enrolled are considered "At-Large" applicants and must submit documentation directly to the Institute for International Education (IIE), which is an organization that collaborates with the U.S. government to administer the Fulbright Program (see the Web site listed below). Students must prepare extensive application packets that include:

- a project proposal
- a personal essay
- a language report
- transcripts
- reference letters

Applicants are interviewed at the institutional level before being sent to the IIE in Washington, DC. A board appointed by the IIE reviews each application and makes a decision to "recommend" or "not recommend." If the applicant is recommended, the application is forwarded for further review to a Fulbright selection committee in the country to which the student is applying. The committee then decides on the final slate of applicants, and the presidentially appointed Fulbright board makes a final decision on the applications.

Deadline

The Fulbright Scholarship application is due annually in October. Campus deadlines will be earlier. Please check with your campus representative.

For More Information

http://us.fulbrightonline.org/home.html

SCHOLARSHIPS AND FELLOWSHIPS FOR STUDENTS ENROLLED AT ANY ACCREDITED U.S. INSTITUTION OF HIGHER EDUCATION

Our list of scholarships and fellowships continues with a variety of competitive awards that are available for undergraduate and graduate students who are enrolled at any accredited institution in the United States. Many of the awards in this section are just as lucrative and competitive as those listed in our top tier. The only difference is that they may not carry the name recognition of those awards. The awards listed and described in this section vary in both scope and purpose, yet all provide winners outstanding benefits and experiences. Happy browsing!

- American Association of University Women (AAUW) American Fellowships
- Benjamin A. Gilman International Scholarship
- Boren Undergraduate Scholarships: National Security Education Program (NSEP)
- Boren Graduate Fellowships: National Security Education Program (NSEP)
- The Carnegie Endowment for International Peace Junior Fellows Program
- Clarendon Fund Scholarship for Study at Oxford University
- DAAD: German Academic Exchange Service Undergraduate Scholarship
- DAAD: German Academic Exchange Service Graduate Study Scholarship
- The Department of Homeland Security Undergraduate Scholarships
- Harvey Fellows Program (Mustard Seed Foundation)
- The Hertz Foundation Graduate Fellowships
- Howard Hughes Medical Institute (HHMI) Research Training Fellowships for Medical Students

- Jack Kent Cooke Undergraduate Transfer Scholarship Program
- Jacob K. Javits Fellowships Program
- The James Madison Graduate Fellowships
- Killam Fellowships Program
- Knowles Science Teaching Foundation (KSTF) Teaching Fellowship
- National Geographic Young Explorers Grants
- National Institutes of Health (NIH)-Oxford-Cambridge Scholars Program
- National Science Foundation (NSF) Graduate Research Fellowship Program
- The Paul and Daisy Soros Fellowships for New Americans
- The Roothbert Fund Scholarships
- Rotary Ambassadorial Scholarships
- Saint Andrews's Society of the State of New York Scholarship Program
- The Science, Mathematics and Research for Transformation (SMART) Scholarship for Service Program
- ThinkSwiss Research Scholarships
- William E. Simon Fellowship for Noble Purpose (Intercollegiate Studies Institute)

AMERICAN ASSOCIATION OF UNIVERSITY WOMEN (AAUW) AMERICAN FELLOWSHIPS

"For more than a century, the American Association of University Women has helped more than 10,000 women from more than 130 countries break through barriers and pursue their dreams of obtaining graduate degrees or making an impact in their communities."

The American Association of University Women (AAUW) offers American Fellowships through which the organization awards fellowships for women in their final year of writing their doctoral dissertation or women seeking postdoctoral research leave from accredited institutions. The fellowship is designed to offset living expenses during this period to allow for full-time work on the dissertation or research. According to the program Web site, "Fellowship and grant recipients undergo a highly competitive selection process. Academic excellence, commitment to improving the human condition, and the promise of continued impact are cornerstones of the rigorous criteria."

Benefits

Recipients of the dissertation fellowships receive $20,000 for the fellowship year, and post-doctoral-leave fellows receive $30,000.

General Eligibility Requirements

Applicants for American Fellowships must be U.S. citizens. Applicants must take an eligibility quiz on the program Web site.

Application Process

Applications may be submitted online. A completed application contains the following:

- an application (including a budget, narrative autobiography, and project statement)
- letters of recommendation
- supporting documentation (including academic transcripts, institution certification form, and institution letter)

Deadline

Applications are due annually in November.

For More Information

http://www.aauw.org/learn/fellowships_grants/american.cfm

Cross Pollination

AAUW has other grants and fellowships. Check out AAUW's Summer/Short-Term Research Publication Grants, International Fellowships, Career Development Grants, Community Action Grants, and Special Professions Fellowships. More information is available at http://www.aauw.org/learn/fellowships_grants/.

BENJAMIN A. GILMAN INTERNATIONAL SCHOLARSHIP

The Gilman Scholarship Program was established by the International Academic Opportunity Act of 2000 to enable U.S. undergraduate students receiving Federal Pell Grants to study abroad. The program is administered by the Bureau of Educational and Cultural Affairs in the U.S. Department of State.

The Congressionally funded Benjamin A. Gilman International Scholarship program provides funding for undergraduate study abroad for students with limited financial means. Approximately 820 Gillman Scholarships are awarded annually. An additional twenty-five Critical Need Language Supplements are awarded to Gilman Scholarship recipients. Students may use the awards to defray the costs of their study-abroad experience and may choose any study-abroad program worldwide that offers academic credit that their home institution will accept.

Benefits

The Gilman Scholarship maximum award is $5,000 that may be applied to study-abroad expenses. Grants are awarded based on need, and the average award is $4,000. Gilman recipients are eligible to receive another $3,000 Critical Need Language Supplement for language study.

General Eligibility Requirements

According to the Gilman program Web site, applicants must meet the following criteria to be considered:

- be receiving a Federal Pell Grant or provide proof that they will be receiving a Pell Grant during the study-abroad term
- are applying to or have been accepted into a study-abroad program eligible for credit by their school
- will study abroad for at least four weeks in one country; programs going to more than one country are eligible if the student will be studying in one country for at least four consecutive weeks

Applicants can study abroad in any country except Cuba or a country on the U.S. Department of State's current travel warning list. Check www.travel.state.gov/travel and click on International Travel Information, which will take you to Travel Warnings.

Application Process

To apply for a Benjamin A. Gilman International Scholarship, applicants must fill out an online application located on the program Web site. In order to do this, applicants must first create a password and log in to the site.

Deadline

Check program Web site for deadline information.

For More Information

http://www.iie.org/en/Programs/Gilman-Scholarship-Program

Boren Undergraduate Scholarships: National Security Education Program (NSEP)

David L. Boren served in the U.S. Senate from 1979 to 1994. He was influential in passing legislation creating the National Security Education Program (NSEP) established in 1991 as part of the National Security Education Act.

One of the primary programs offered by the NSEP is the Boren Scholarship for international study, which is given on both the undergraduate and graduate levels. The undergraduate awards are available to students seeking to study abroad in regions critical to U.S. interests. The Boren Web site lists the eligible countries and languages for student study. The program is administered by the Institute for International Education (IIE) located in Washington, DC.

Benefits

The Boren Scholarship provides up to $20,000 for a full-year study-abroad program and up to $10,000 for a semester study-abroad program. A full academic year of study is encouraged.

General Eligibility Requirements

According to the program Web site, applicants must meet the following criteria:

- be U.S. citizens at the time of application
- be enrolled in an accredited institution of higher education in the United States
- must complete the study-abroad experience prior to graduation

A service commitment is required of all Boren award recipients. The duration varies based on the award received. Service must take place ". . . in the Federal Government in a position with National Security responsibilities."

Application Process

Applicants for the Boren Scholarship fill out an online application. The application is forwarded to the Boren institutional representative. Other materials required to complete the application packet include:

- transcripts from all higher education institutions attended (freshman applicants must provide a high school transcript)
- three reference letters
- information about the study-abroad program or individually arranged international experience (see Web site for details)
- preliminary language report

Deadline

The application is due annually in February.

For More Information

http://www.borenawards.org/

BOREN GRADUATE FELLOWSHIPS: NATIONAL SECURITY EDUCATION PROGRAM (NSEP)

David L. Boren was influential in passing legislation creating the National Security Education Program (NSEP) established in 1991 as part of the National Security Education Act. The National Security Education Act is designed to assist U.S. citizens in acquiring language skills in foreign languages that are deemed by the U.S. government to be critical to national security.

The Boren Awards for International Study are given on both the undergraduate and graduate levels. The graduate awards are available to graduate students desiring an international experience that entails language study in an area critical to U.S. interests. The Boren Web site lists countries and languages that are considered critical to the United States. The program is administered by the Institute for International Education (IIE) located in Washington, DC.

Benefits

The Boren Fellowships provide up to $30,000. These awards may entail both domestic and foreign components and may span from one semester to two academic years.

General Eligibility Requirements

According to the program Web site, applicants must meet the following criteria:

- be U.S. citizens at the time of application
- be admitted to, or enrolled in, a graduate program at an accredited institution of higher education in the United States
- be continuously enrolled in the same graduate program throughout the duration of their grant

A service commitment is required of all Boren award recipients. The service duration varies based on the award received. Service must take place ". . . in the Federal Government in a position with National Security responsibilities."

Application Process

Applicants for the Boren Fellowship must begin by filling out an online application. A completed application includes:

- three essays
- a detailed budget
- three letters of recommendation
- a letter of overseas affiliations (not required at the time of application)
- an online language proficiency form (optional)
- official academic transcripts from all higher education institutions attended

Deadline

The application is due annually in January.

For More Information

http://www.borenawards.org/

THE CARNEGIE ENDOWMENT FOR INTERNATIONAL PEACE JUNIOR FELLOWS PROGRAM

"The Carnegie Endowment for International Peace is a private, nonprofit organization dedicated to advancing cooperation between nations and promoting active international engagement by the United States. Founded in 1910, its work is nonpartisan and dedicated to achieving practical results."

The Carnegie Endowment for International Peace awards eight to ten Junior Fellowships each year to talented undergraduates and students who have recently graduated with a bachelor's degree. Junior Fellows are selected from approximately 400 participating universities in the United States. Fellows work as research assistants for senior associates.

Benefits

Fellows are paid an annual stipend of approximately $35,000. A benefits package is also offered.

General Eligibility Requirements

According to the Carnegie Endowment for International Peace Junior Fellows Program Web site, applicants must meet the following criteria to be considered:

- Applicants must be graduating seniors or students who have graduated during the last academic year. No one who has started graduate studies is eligible for consideration. The Carnegie Endowment accepts applications only from designated nominating officials of participating universities.
- International students may apply if they attend one of the participating universities. However, all applicants must be eligible to work in the United States for a full twelve months from August 1 through July 31 following graduation. Students on F-1 visas who are eligible to work in the United States for the full year (August 1 through July 31) may apply for the program.

Application Process

Applicants must work through their university's nominating official to begin the application process. The program Web site has a link to participating universities and nominating officials.

Deadline

The application is due annually in January. Campus deadlines will be earlier. Please check with your campus representative.

For More Information

http://www.carnegieendowment.org/about/index.cfm?fa=jrfellows

CLARENDON FUND SCHOLARSHIP FOR STUDY AT OXFORD UNIVERSITY

The Clarendon Scholarship is the premier scholarship for graduate study at the University of Oxford available only to non-UK residents. In the 2009–10 academic year, there were 298 Clarendon scholars from thirty-five nations at Oxford.

According to the Clarendon Fund Scholarship Web site, "Scholarships are awarded to academically excellent students with the best proven and future potential. Clarendon Scholarships are highly competitive, with less than 10 percent of applicants selected for the scholarship." The scholarships are open to students starting a new course at Oxford. Scholarships are awarded on the basis of prior academic record, potential success in the chosen discipline, and student motivation.

Benefits

The Clarendon Scholarship covers tuition and fees in full, and a grant is provided for living expenses.

General Eligibility Requirements

According to the program Web site, applicants must meet the following criteria:

- applying to start a new graduate course at Oxford, including students who are currently studying for a master's degree at Oxford, but who will be reapplying for a DPhil. Students who will continue to study for the same degree at Oxford in the next year are not eligible for this scholarship.
- enrolled in any degree-bearing course at the graduate level, which encompasses all full-time and part-time master's courses (MSt, MSc, BCL/MJur, MBA, MFE, MPhil, BPhil, MSc by Research, MTh) and all DPhil programs.

All subjects can be funded by a Clarendon Scholarship. There is no quota by subject or preference for any particular course type.

Applicants liable to pay the overseas fee rate at the University of Oxford are eligible. If you are unsure whether you count as an "overseas" or international student for fee purposes, the Fee Status page on the Clarendon Web site should answer your question.

Application Process

Applicants must apply for a Clarendon Scholarship when they are applying for admission to Oxford University.

Deadline

The deadline for the Clarendon Scholarship is annually in January.

For More Information

http://www.clarendon.ox.ac.uk/

DAAD: GERMAN ACADEMIC EXCHANGE SERVICE UNDERGRADUATE SCHOLARSHIP

The New York office of the DAAD (German Academic Exchange Service) was founded in 1971 to support academic exchange between the United States and Canada and Germany.

DAAD offers a variety of programs and funding aimed at supporting undergraduate and graduate students to engage German culture, society, and education. DAAD provides financial support to over 50,000 students each year, divided between undergraduate and graduate students. This program is designed specifically for undergraduates and includes opportunities for internships, language training, and higher education course work (including study-abroad programs). One of the primary programs offered is the undergraduate scholarship for study, research, or internship in Germany for a four- to ten-month period. Knowledge of the German language is not necessary to apply. Preference is given to students whose project or study program is connected with a German university.

Benefits

DAAD Undergraduate Scholarship recipients receive 650 euros per month plus additional funding to offset travel and research expenses. Scholarship recipients also receive health insurance.

General Eligibility Requirements

According to the DAAD Web site, applicants must meet the following criteria to be considered:

- possess outstanding academic records and personal integrity, as evidenced by both their grades and letters of recommendation.
- be U.S. or Canadian citizens or permanent residents of their country. Foreign nationals are eligible if they have been full-time students at an accredited U.S. or Canadian university for more than one year at the time of application and will return to the U.S. or Canada after the scholarship period to complete their bachelor's degrees.
- have well-defined study, research, or internship plans for their stay in Germany.
- submit the DAAD language evaluation form with their application, although German language competency is not mandatory.
- demonstrate an interest in contemporary German and European affairs and explain the significance of their project in Germany to their future studies, research, or professional goals.
- be enrolled, full-time students in an undergraduate degree–granting program at an accredited North American college or university.

Second- and third-year undergraduate students may apply. Applicants must be in their third or fourth years during their stay in Germany.

Application Process

Applicants begin the process by filling out an outline application form. Supplemental documents include:

- a resume
- a project proposal
- two letters of recommendation
- a language evaluation form
- statement of support and credit eligibility
- transcripts
- one of the following: acceptance into a study-abroad program or exchange program, a letter from a mentor, or an invitation from a German university

Deadline

Applications are due annually in January.

For More Information

http://www.daad.org/

DAAD: German Academic Exchange Service Graduate Study Scholarship

DAAD (German Academic Exchange Service) is a national agency funded by the German government. DAAD is designed to support international academic cooperation and promote German higher education.

DAAD offers a variety of programs—at the graduate and undergraduate levels—aimed at supporting students to engage German culture, society, and education. The programs designed specifically for graduate students include opportunities for internships, language training, research, and higher education course work. DAAD provides financial support to over 50,000 students a year, divided between graduate and undergraduate students. One of the primary programs offered is the graduate scholarship for study in Germany.

Benefits

DAAD Graduate Study Scholarship recipients receive 750 euros per month plus additional funding to offset travel and research expenses. Scholarship recipients also receive a rent subsidy and health insurance.

General Eligibility Requirements

According to the DAAD Web site, applicants must meet the following criteria:

- be graduating seniors (fourth-year students in Canada), graduate students, or recent graduates who have completed their bachelor's degrees no longer than six years before the application deadline
- be enrolled full-time at an accredited North American university at the time of application if graduating seniors (last year of undergraduate studies) or graduate students (those who have already completed an undergraduate degree do not need to be currently enrolled)
- be in the first year of a full master's degree program in Germany and seeking to fund their second year of the master's program
- be enrolled in any academic field (for study in the fields of dentistry, medicine, pharmacy, or veterinary medicine, contact DAAD)
- be U.S. or Canadian citizens or permanent residents (foreign nationals are eligible if they have been full-time students at an accredited U.S. or Canadian university for at least two years at the time of application)

Application Process

If your school is a DAAD partner, you must submit your application through your institution's DAAD representative. If your school is not a DAAD partner, see program Web site for appropriate instructions.

A completed application includes the following:

- a signed application form
- supplemental materials (for music, fine arts, dance only)
- CV/resume
- study proposal
- two letters of recommendation
- evidence of contact with a German institution
- DAAD language evaluation form
- official academic transcripts

Deadline

National deadlines vary. Check program Web site for complete information.

For More Information

http://www.daad.org/

THE DEPARTMENT OF HOMELAND SECURITY UNDERGRADUATE SCHOLARSHIPS

The Department of Homeland Security was created in response to the September 11, 2001, terrorist attacks in New York City and Washington, DC. This federal agency is designed to ". . . lead the unified national effort to secure the country and preserve our freedoms."

The Department of Homeland Security Scholarship Program was created as a way to attract top students into the Department of Homeland Security. This program ". . . is intended for students interested in pursuing the basic science and technology innovations that can be applied to the DHS mission."

Applicants must have academic backgrounds that match the homeland security–related areas of science, technology, engineering, and mathematics (HS-STEM) designated by the Department of Homeland Security. These include biological threats and countermeasures, border security, food and agriculture security, and infrastructure protection. For a list of the seventeen areas, visit www.orau.gov/dhsed/.

Benefits

The DHS Undergraduate Scholarships cover full tuition and fees as well as $1,000 per month for the academic year. An additional $5,000 stipend is provided for a 10-week summer internship. This funding is available for two years based on satisfactory academic progress. Upon graduation, scholarship recipients are required to serve for one year at the Department of Homeland Security.

General Eligibility Requirements

To be eligible, according to the Department of Homeland Security, students must meet the following requirements:

- be U.S. citizens at the time of application
- be enrolled in an accredited institution of higher education in the United States

Application Process

The DHS Undergraduate Scholarship is an online application. Other materials required to complete the application packet include:

- transcripts from all higher education institutions attended
- two reference letters
- standardized test scores (ACT and/or SAT)
- essays

Deadline

Deadline is announced annually in the fall.

For More Information

http://www.orau.gov/dhsed/

HARVEY FELLOWS PROGRAM (MUSTARD SEED FOUNDATION)

The Mustard Seed Foundation is a Christian family foundation established in 1983 under the leadership of Dennis W. Bakke and Eileen Harvey Bakke. In addition to grants to churches and Christian organizations worldwide engaged in ministry that includes outreach, discipleship, and economic empowerment, the Foundation awards scholarships to Christians pursuing advanced degrees in preparation for leadership roles in both the Church and society.

The Harvey Fellows Program supports Christian graduate students in elite graduate programs at premier U.S. universities. Specifically, the program is designed to provide funding for Christian students pursuing disciplines underrepresented by individuals espousing a Christian worldview.

Benefits

Harvey Fellows are awarded a stipend of approximately $16,000 for a broad variety of educational expenses. Fellowships are renewable.

General Eligibility Requirements

Based on the foundation's requirements, applicants must meet the following requirements:

- demonstrate personal faith in Jesus Christ and desire to serve and witness in His name
- be enrolled in or have applied to a full-time graduate program

- be applying to or be attending a premier university—typically those with an internationally recognized reputation as a "top five" program in the specific discipline, or studying with an adviser (and/or team) who is an internationally recognized expert in his or her field
- demonstrate that intended vocational field has a significant impact on society and yet appears to be underrepresented by Christians

Application Process

Applicants must begin the application process by registering for an online application system. A completed application contains the following:

- complete contact information
- current resume or CV
- vocational goal statement
- affirmation of the Lausanne Covenant
- six essays
- school and degree program information
- recommendation letters
- test scores
- official transcripts
- a sample of academic work

Deadline

The application materials are released in August with a deadline of November 1.

For More Information

http://msfdn.org/harveyfellows/

THE HERTZ FOUNDATION GRADUATE FELLOWSHIPS

Born into a poor family in Austria in 1879, John Daniel Hertz immigrated to the United States as a young child. He became a successful businessman in a variety of areas, including the transportation industry, investment banking, and horse-breeding.

With a vision to give back to the country that had given him so much, John Daniel Hertz and his wife Fannie created the Hertz Foundation in 1953. Hertz believed that for the United States to continue in its role of global leadership, talented young students needed to be cultivated in the areas of science and technology. Thus, the enduring mission of the Foundation is ". . . to build America's capacity for innovation by nurturing remarkable applied scientists and engineers who show the most promise to change the world."

Today, the Hertz Foundation annually awards between sixty and eighty fellowships for Ph.D. students in applied physical, biological, and engineering sciences.

Benefits

Hertz Graduate Fellowships provide $31,000 per academic year, renewable for up to five years. Fellows with dependent children receive an extra $5,000 a year. Fellowships also cover full tuition and fees for the duration of the award.

General Eligibility Requirements

According to the Hertz Foundation Web site, applicants must meet the following requirements:

- be U.S. citizens or permanent residents
- pursue an academic discipline in applied physical, biological, or engineering sciences (see the list of approved areas on the Hertz Foundation Web site)
- apply during their senior year of college or as graduate students currently pursuing the Ph.D. degree
- be willing to ". . . morally commit to make their skills available to the United States in time of national emergency."

These awards may be used only at schools identified by the Hertz Foundation. These are schools that lead the nation in applied physical, biological, and/or engineering sciences. A comprehensive list is available on the Foundation's Web site.

Application Process

To apply for a Hertz Foundation Graduate Fellowship, applicants must first create a password and log in to fill out an online application. The application period usually begins in August and winners are announced in March of the following year.

Deadline

The application is due annually in October.

For More Information

http://www.hertzfoundation.org/

Howard Hughes Medical Institute [HHMI] Research Training Fellowships for Medical Students

According to its Web site, "HHMI, a nonprofit medical research organization that ranks as one of the nation's largest philanthropies, plays a powerful role in advancing biomedical research and science education in the United States. The Institute spent $730 million for research and distributed $101 million in grant support for science education in fiscal year 2009."

The Howard Hughes Medical Institute offers approximately sixty-six fellowships annually to medical, dental, or veterinary school students. The fellowships are for one year and must be completed before a student graduates. Fellowships are designed to ". . . strengthen and expand the nation's pool of medically trained researchers."

Benefits

Fellows receive a stipend of approximately $27,000 over a working term of twelve consecutive months. Health insurance is also provided. A research allowance of $5,500 is provided that may be used for research-related expenses. Loans may be deferred during a fellowship year.

General Eligibility Requirements

To be eligible, according to HHMI, students must meet the following requirements:

- Applicants must be currently enrolled in medical, dental, or veterinary school in the United States
- International applicants may apply if they are enrolled in a U.S. institution and have and maintain an appropriate visa

Students enrolled in dual-degree programs (e.g., M.D./Ph.D.) are not eligible to apply.

Application Process

Applicants must complete an online application. A complete application includes:

- the applicant's portion
- the mentor's endorsement
- letters of reference

Deadline

Applications are due annually in January.

For More Information

http://www.hhmi.org/grants/individuals/medfellows.html

JACK KENT COOKE UNDERGRADUATE TRANSFER SCHOLARSHIP PROGRAM

The Jack Kent Cooke Foundation was established in 2000. The mission of this private foundation is "to help young people of exceptional promise reach their full potential through education."

To help fulfill its mission, the Jack Kent Cooke Foundation provides scholarships to community college students as they transfer to some of our nation's most elite four-year schools. The Jack Kent Cooke Foundation awards approximately fifty transfer scholarships each year to academically talented students who demonstrate financial need.

Benefits

The transfer scholarship pays up to $30,000 per year and covers tuition, room, board, fees, and books. The duration of the scholarship is two to three years.

General Eligibility Requirements

According to the Foundation, to be eligible, applicants must:

- be a current student at an accredited U.S. community college or two-year institution with sophomore status by December of the academic year in which the student is applying or a recent graduate
- plan to enroll full-time in a baccalaureate program at an accredited college or university in the coming fall
- have a cumulative undergraduate GPA of 3.50 or better on a scale of 4.0 (or the equivalent)
- be nominated by his/her two-year institution
- have unmet financial need
- have not previously been nominated for the Jack Kent Cooke Foundation Undergraduate Transfer Scholarship

Application Process

Applicants must first fill out an online application form and work with their institutional representative to be nominated by their home institution. Applicants should meet with their institutional representative early in the fall semester, as the application period begins annually in October.

Applicants are required to submit the following documents to their institutional representative:

- official high school transcripts, GED scores, or letter from home-school instructor
- official college transcripts from all undergraduate institutions attended
- personal tax forms and parents' tax forms
- parent financial information forms (downloadable from the Foundation Web site)
- two letters of recommendation, submitted online

Deadline

The application is due annually in January. Campus deadlines will be earlier. Please check with your campus representative.

For More Information

http://www.jkcf.org/

JACOB K. JAVITS FELLOWSHIPS PROGRAM

The Jacob K. Javits Fellowships Program is a federally funded scholarship program administered through the U.S. Department of Education. The program is named in honor of Jacob K. Javits, a U.S. Senator from New York who served from 1957 to 1981.

The purpose of the Jacob K. Javits Fellowship program is to provide ". . . fellowships to students of superior academic ability—selected on the basis of demonstrated achievement, financial need, and exceptional promise—to undertake study at the doctoral and Master of Fine Arts level in selected fields of arts, humanities, and social sciences."

The program provides approximately sixty-five fellowships a year, renewable up to three additional years.

Benefits

Javits Fellowships provide a maximum of $30,000 a year for a total of forty-eight months or to the completion of the degree. Javits Fellows may also have their tuition and fees waived because the award pays the institution $13,000 to cover tuition and fees.

General Eligibility Requirements

According to the Javits Fellowships Program Web site, applicants must meet the following criteria:

- be U.S. citizens, U.S. nationals, or permanent residents
- be pursuing an academic discipline in the arts, humanities, or social sciences (see approved list on Javits Fellowships Web site)
- be enrolled in graduate-level education at an institution that is accredited by an agency approved by the U.S. Department of Education

Applicants are eligible for an award if they are entering a doctoral program or have not completed the first year of doctoral studies at the time of application; or they are beginning a terminal master's program.

Application Process

The competition is announced each year in the *Federal Register* and on the U.S Department of Education Web site. Applicants download an application packet and must fill out the FAFSA (Free Application for Federal Student Aid) to be eligible for a Fellowship. In addition to the FAFSA, the application packet includes the following documents:

- general information form
- GRE scores
- transcripts from all undergraduate institutions
- evidence-of-eligibility form
- list of honors and awards
- statement of purpose

Deadline

Applications are usually due at the beginning of October.

For More Information

http://www.ed.gov/programs/jacobjavits

THE JAMES MADISON GRADUATE FELLOWSHIPS

"The James Madison Memorial Fellowship Foundation was established by Congress in 1986 for the purpose of improving teaching about the United States Constitution in secondary schools."

The James Madison Graduate Fellowship is designed to help secondary teachers become outstanding teachers of the U.S. Constitution. The Fellowship provides funding for study toward a master's degree in one of the following areas:

- American history
- American government
- social studies

Applicants for Junior Fellows may apply if they are finishing or have finished their bachelor's degrees and are planning on pursuing full-time graduate study. Applicants for Senior Fellows may apply for part-time master's programs if they plan on continuing to work as teachers while studying. After earning their master's degree, Fellows are required to teach one full year for each year they received funding under the Fellowship. At least one Madison Fellow is selected from each state.

Benefits

The maximum award available to fellowship recipients is $24,000. This can be used to cover tuition, room and board, books, and fees, but must be distributed over the entire time it takes to complete the master's degree. Madison Fellows are also given the opportunity to participate in a four-week summer institute on the Constitution, held at Georgetown University in Washington, DC.

General Eligibility Requirements

According to the Foundation Web site, applicants must meet the following criteria to be considered:

- be a U.S. citizen or U.S. national
- be a teacher, or plan to become a teacher, of U.S. history, U.S. government, or social studies at the secondary school level (grades 7 to 12)
- possess a bachelor's degree or plan to receive a bachelor's degree no later than August 31 of the year in which they are applying
- have waited at least three years from the time that any previous graduate degree was awarded before applying for a James Madison Fellowship

Application Process

To apply for the James Madison Graduate Fellowship, applicants must fill out an online application located on the program Web site.

Deadline

The application is due annually in March.

For More Information

http://www.jamesmadison.com

KILLAM FELLOWSHIPS PROGRAM

The Foundation for Educational Exchange Between Canada and the United States sponsors the Killam Fellowships Program. This organization "is a bi-national, treaty-based, nongovernmental, not-for-profit organization which was established in 1990 with a mandate to identify the best and brightest minds in both countries and engage them in residential, academic, and professional exchange. The Foundation provides support to students, graduate students, scholars, teachers, and independent researchers through a variety of programs."

The Killam Fellowships Program is an exchange program between the United States and Canada for undergraduate students. The Killam Fellowships Program allows for both direct exchange arrangements (registering at the home university, paying the home university fees, but attending the host university as an exchange visitor) or self-placed visiting students (registering at the host university and paying host tuition fees). The program is available to both U.S. and Canadian students and can be undertaken for a semester or academic year.

Benefits

Killam Fellows (Americans heading to Canada) receive a $10,000 academic stipend, health insurance, orientation session, professional development seminar, and travel grant. Canadian Fellows heading to the United States receive a similar benefits package.

General Eligibility Requirements for U.S. students

Based on the program's requirements, applicants must meet the following criteria:

- be a citizen of the United States
- be a full-time undergraduate student in good standing at a degree-granting institution in the United States
- meet the eligibility requirement of their home university (as they relate to the participation in international exchange programs)
- be fluent in English (and/or French, where appropriate)
- have a superior academic record

- in the case of the direct exchange applicants, be nominated by his/her university to receive a Killam Fellowship

Application Process

Interested applicants may apply either for the direct exchange program or the open competition. Applicants for the direct exchange must attend a participating university and be nominated. A completed application contains the following:

- a completed cover sheet and checklist
- a completed, signed, and dated Killam Fellowships Program application form
- a personal statement (one single-spaced page maximum)
- a course selection for each institution for which the applicant wishes to be considered, approved by a student adviser at the applicant's home university
- an official university transcript
- a photocopy of applicant's passport (preferable), birth certificate, or other documentation that verifies citizenship
- two reference forms (at least one should be from a professor familiar with the student's work)
- a curriculum vitae (maximum three pages)

In addition, applicants must submit a report on English-language proficiency if their first language is not English and they are not currently studying at an English-language institution. If applicant's first language is not French and they plan to study at a French-language institution, they must submit a French-language proficiency report.

Deadline

Applications open annually in September with a deadline usually in December or January of the following year.

For More Information

http://www.killamfellowships.com/

KNOWLES SCIENCE TEACHING FOUNDATION (KSTF) TEACHING FELLOWSHIP

"The Janet H. and C. Harry Knowles Foundation was established in 1999 to strengthen the quality of science and mathematics teachers teaching in grades 9–12 in United States schools. The Knowles Science Teaching Foundation supports individuals and programs designed to encourage and sustain young scientists and mathematicians as they dedicate their lives to teaching other young people and to becoming leaders in the field of education."

The Knowles Science Teaching Foundation Teaching Fellowship is a five-year fellowship designed to help grow outstanding math and science teachers. This fellowship is aimed at creating "educational leaders" and "change agents" to strengthen math and science education in U.S. high schools. KSTF Teaching Fellows are selected based on their strengths in four primary areas:

1. science or mathematics content knowledge

2. commitment to teaching

3. ability to teach

4. leadership potential

Annually, the Foundation awards nine to fourteen new Science Teaching Fellowships and nine to fourteen new Math Teaching Fellowships.

Benefits

The Knowles Science Teaching Fellowship provides students significant financial and professional support over a five-year period. The award covers tuition assistance, a monthly stipend, professional development, and teaching materials. The award per Fellow is valued at approximately $150,000.

General Eligibility Requirements

According to the Foundation's requirements, students must meet the following criteria:

- have earned, or are in the process of earning, a degree in science, mathematics, or engineering from a recognized institution of higher education
- are committed to teaching high school mathematics, physical sciences, or biological sciences (see the Knowles Foundation Web site for a list of approved subjects)
- have received their most recent content (i.e., science, mathematics, or engineering) degree within five years of the start of the Fellowship (June 1 of the application year)

An individual who is in the final year of an undergraduate, master's, combined B.S. with MAT or M.Ed program, or near the completion of a doctoral program in a content area may also be eligible.

Application Process

Applicants must begin the application online. Required documentation includes:

- the applicant's contact information
- three essays
- a resume or curriculum vitae
- contact information for three references
- official transcripts for all postsecondary course work

Deadline

Applications are due annually in January.

For More Information

http://www.kstf.org/about/about.html

NATIONAL GEOGRAPHIC YOUNG EXPLORERS GRANTS

The National Geographic Web site states, "An initial grant from National Geographic helped launch the careers of many of the Society's, and our planet's, most renowned explorers. We are committed—as we have been for more than a century—to supporting new generations of archaeologists, anthropologists, astronomers, conservationists, ecologists, geographers, geologists, marine scientists, adventurers, storytellers, and pioneers."

The Young Explorers Grants program funds creative proposals for research, conservation, and exploration-related projects. It supports a variety of projects—and an age range of applicants—that are generally not covered by other sources of funding. Past projects range from uncovering a mummified dinosaur to kayaking through Bolivia.

Benefits

Young Explorers Grants vary in amount; most range between $2,000 and $5,000. Many successful applicants have arranged supplemental funding from other sources.

General Eligibility Requirements

According to the program Web site:

- Applicants are not required to have advanced degrees. However, a record of prior experience in the fields of research, conservation, or exploration should be submitted as it pertains to the proposed project.
- Funding is not restricted to U.S. citizens; foreign nationals are invited to apply. Researchers planning work in countries abroad should make great effort to include at least one local collaborator as part of their team.

Application Process

To apply for a Young Explorers Grant, interested applicants must first go through an online pre-application process. Invited applicants will then be asked to fill out the entire application.

Deadline

The Young Explorers Grant Program accepts applications throughout the year.

For More Information

http://www.nationalgeographic.com/field/grants-programs/young-explorers/

NATIONAL INSTITUTES OF HEALTH (NIH)-OXFORD-CAMBRIDGE SCHOLARS PROGRAM

The National Institutes of Health (NIH) is a branch of the U.S. Department of Health and Human Services. The mission of the NIH is ". . . science in pursuit of fundamental knowledge about the nature and behavior of living systems and the application of that knowledge to extend healthy life and reduce the burdens of illness and disability."

The program's Web site states that "The National Institutes of Health-Oxford-Cambridge Scholars Program is an accelerated, individualized doctoral training program for outstanding science students committed to biomedical research." Started in 2001, this elite program allows participants to gain significant experience in biomedical research at world-class institutions. The program culminates in doctoral-level degrees at Oxford or Cambridge.

M.D./Ph.D. combinations are also possible through partnerships that the NIH maintains with several U.S. medical schools.

Benefits

Funding for the Ph.D. option includes tuition for Oxford or Cambridge, a living stipend, health insurance, and a travel allowance.

General Eligibility Requirements

According to the NIH Graduate Partnerships Program, students must:

- be U.S. citizens or U.S. permanent residents
- hold an undergraduate degree
- be pursuing a Ph.D. in the biomedical sciences

Application Process

To apply for the National Institutes of Health (NIH)-Oxford-Cambridge Scholars Program, students must apply through the Graduate Partnerships Program (GPP) Web site at http://gpp.nih.gov.

Deadline

Applications are due annually in January.

For More Information

http://oxcam.gpp.nih.gov

NATIONAL SCIENCE FOUNDATION (NSF) GRADUATE RESEARCH FELLOWSHIP PROGRAM

"The reputation of the GRFP follows recipients and often helps them become life-long leaders that contribute significantly to both scientific innovation and teaching. Past fellows include numerous Nobel Prize winners; U.S. Secretary of Energy, Steven Chu; Google founder, Sergey Brin; and Freakonomics co-author, Steven Levitt."

The National Science Foundation Graduate Research Fellowship is designed to ". . . ensure the vitality of the human resource base of science and engineering in the United States and reinforces its diversity." The program attracts top students from across the nation who are studying in science, technology, engineering, and math disciplines. The Fellowship provides generous support for research-based master's and doctoral-level degrees. Approximately 1,000 new three-year fellowships are awarded annually.

Benefits

The NSF Graduate Research Fellowship recipients receive a $30,000 annual stipend, a $10,500 educational allowance, and a $1,000 international travel allowance.

General Eligibility Requirements

To be eligible according to the NSF, students must:

- be a U.S. citizen, U.S. national, or permanent resident alien
- be in a research-focused master's or Ph.D. program in an NSF-supported field
- have completed no more than twelve months of full-time graduate study (or the equivalent)

The "no more than twelve months" limit applies to an applicant's entire postbaccalaureate career, not just the current program.

Application Process

Applicants must begin the application online. The application requires:

- a personal statement essay
- a previous research experience essay
- a proposed plan of research essay
- three reference letters
- academic transcripts
- GRE scores (recommended, but not required)

Deadline

The deadline is annually in September.

For More Information

http://www.nsfgrfp.org/

Cross Pollination

For similar awards, see also: http://www.nsf.gov/funding/education.jsp?fund_type=2 and http://www.nsf.gov/funding/education.jsp?fund_type=1.

THE PAUL AND DAISY SOROS FELLOWSHIPS FOR NEW AMERICANS

Paul and Daisy Soros both emigrated from Hungary and have made outstanding philanthropic contributions to U.S. society. To encourage and support the development of other new Americans aspiring to make significant contributions, they founded the Paul and Daisy Soros Fellowships for New Americans in 1997.

According to its Web site:

> "The purpose of The Paul and Daisy Soros Fellowships for New Americans is to provide opportunities for continuing generations of able and accomplished New Americans to achieve leadership in their chosen fields. The Program is established in recognition of the contributions New Americans have made to American life and in gratitude for the opportunities the United States has afforded the donors and their family."

Thirty Fellowships are awarded each year and may be used for up to two years of graduate study. All academic disciplines are eligible to apply.

Benefits

The Paul and Daisy Soros Fellowships for New Americans provide recipients a maintenance grant of $20,000 a year, plus half of their tuition costs up to a maximum of $16,000 a year. The tuition grant is paid directly to the institution.

General Eligibility Requirements

To be eligible to receive a fellowship, applicants must be considered new Americans. The Foundation's Web site defines this as an individual who "(1) is a resident alien, i.e., holds a Green Card; or, (2) has been naturalized as a U.S. citizen, or (3) is the child of two parents who are both naturalized citizens."

In addition, the following requirements apply to all applicants:

- must hold a bachelor's degree or be in the final year of undergraduate education
- must not be older than 30 at the time the application is submitted

Application Process

To apply for a Paul and Daisy Soros Fellowship, applicants must fill out an online application form located on the Foundation's Web site. Supporting documents include:

- academic transcripts from undergraduate and graduate institutions attended
- two essays
- three letters of recommendation

- resume
- if still enrolled in a baccalaureate-degree program, applicants must submit a form of completion certified by the institution
- documents proving "new American" status (see definition above)
- test scores required by discipline/graduate program (GRE, LSAT, MCAT, or GMAT)

Applications are due around the first of November every year. After an initial screening, approximately eighty-four individuals are chosen for interviews that are held in New York City. All travel expenses are covered for interviewees. Thirty winners are announced each February.

Deadline

The application is due annually in November.

For More Information

http://www.pdsoros.org

The Roothbert Fund Scholarships

"The Roothbert Fund was created in 1958 by Albert and Toni Roothbert to help men and women in need of financial aid to further their education. . . . The Fund seeks candidates who are motivated by spiritual values."

The Roothbert Fund Scholarships are need-based awards designed to support undergraduate and graduate students at accredited institutions in the United States. The scholarships are open to all in the United States regardless of sex, age, color, nationality, or religious background. About twenty awards are given each year.

Benefits

Roothbert Scholarships average between $2,000 and $3,000 and are renewable depending on academic performance.

General Eligibility Requirements

According to the Scholarship Web site:

- While the Fund does not emphasize any particular form of religious practice or worship, it seeks to provide support to persons motivated by spiritual values.

- The Fund has awarded grants to persons entering a wide range of careers. However, preference is given to those who can satisfy high scholastic requirements and are considering careers in education.
- Scholarships funds are awarded only to students with current or permanent addresses in the following states: Maine, New Hampshire, Vermont, Rhode Island, Massachusetts, Connecticut, New York, New Jersey, Pennsylvania, Ohio, Delaware, Maryland, District of Columbia, Virginia, West Virginia, or North Carolina. (See program Web site for complete details.). International students living in the United States are welcome to apply.

Application Process

Applicants must request an application form from The Roothbert Fund, Inc. Application packets consist of:

- two essays
- transcripts
- three letters of recommendation

A limited number of finalists will be called for an interview at one of the following locations: New York City; Washington, DC; New Haven, Connecticut; or Philadelphia.

Deadline

Applications are made available in November with a deadline of January 31 most years.

For More Information

http://www.roothbertfund.org/scholarships.php?PHPSESSID=2bfa6f358e9673231c21e20 0680cb445

ROTARY AMBASSADORIAL SCHOLARSHIPS

Started in 1905, Rotary International is a global service organization operating worldwide in the form of local Rotary Clubs. The purpose of the organization ". . . is to bring together business and professional leaders to provide humanitarian service, encourage high ethical standards in all vocations, and help build goodwill and peace in the world."

One of the major efforts in achieving the goals of the Rotary International is the Rotary Ambassadorial Scholarships, offered annually to undergraduate as well as graduate students. The following three types of Ambassadorial Scholarships are available:

1. Academic-Year Ambassadorial Scholarships, given for one year of study/research at a foreign institution of higher education

2. Multi-Year Ambassadorial Scholarships, given for two years of study/research at a foreign institution of higher education

3. Cultural Ambassadorial Scholarships, awarded for either three or six months of intensive language study and cultural immersion

Benefits

Benefits vary depending on the type of Ambassadorial Scholarship:

- Academic-Year Ambassadorial Scholarships provide $25,000 for a full academic year
- Multi-Year Ambassadorial Scholarships provide $12,500 per year for two years of study
- Cultural Ambassadorial Scholarships provide $17,000 for six months of study or $12,000 for three months of study

General Eligibility Requirements

To apply for any of the Ambassadorial Scholarships, applicants must meet the following requirements:

- be undergraduate or graduate students or professionals pursuing vocational studies
- must demonstrate language proficiency in non-English-speaking countries if applying for Academic-Year or Multi-Year Ambassadorial Scholarships
- must be admitted to foreign institutions of higher education

Country and regional preferences are taken into consideration, but Rotary International has the right to place scholarship winners where they deem appropriate.

Application Process

Applications must be made through a local Rotary Club. The Rotary International Web site has a helpful search function. It is recommended that applicants first check with the Rotary Club in their hometown, but they may also apply through the Rotary Club where they are full-time students. Not all local clubs will have Ambassadorial Scholarships available in a given year. Online application materials are available once a local Rotary Club has been identified.

Generally, the following materials are requested as part of the application:

- letter of intent
- essays

- letters of recommendation
- language-ability forms
- transcripts

Deadline

Local Rotary Clubs have scholarship and local deadline information in November/December of each year.

For More Information

http://www.rotary.org

SAINT ANDREWS'S SOCIETY OF THE STATE OF NEW YORK SCHOLARSHIP PROGRAM

In recognition of the benefits of higher education, the Society provides significant funding for two Scottish graduate students to study in the United States and two Scottish-American students to study in Scotland.

The scholarship program was initiated by the Saint Andrews's Society at its 200th anniversary in 1956. The program "has consistently attracted top students from the most competitive institutions of learning including Harvard University, St. Andrews University, Edinburgh University, New York University, University of Glasgow, Oxford University, Cambridge, Columbia University, and similar institutions in both countries."

Benefits

Each of the four scholarships awarded annually currently provides funds of $20,000 to $30,000 to be used initially for tuition and then board, transportation, and other expenses.

General Eligibility Requirements

According to the Web site, U.S. applicants must meet the following criteria:

- will obtain a bachelor's degree from an accredited college or university in the spring of the year in which they are applying
- demonstrate the significance of studying in Scotland
- possess the qualifications that will enable them to be good ambassadors for the United States while in Scotland
- outstanding academic achievement

- breadth of extracurricular activities
- show financial need
- be of Scottish descent
- be U.S. citizens

Finalists will need to show proof of application to their selected school.

In addition, preference will be given to candidates who have not previously studied in the United Kingdom, and candidates must reside or attend school within 250 miles of New York State. An appropriate official, with knowledge of the applicant's financial status, must certify that assistance would be required for a year of graduate study in Scotland.

Application Process

Interested students should request application forms through their institution. Only one applicant shall be considered from each institution per year.

It is the scholarship committee's usual practice to invite 6 finalists to a luncheon in New York City during February or early March. Following this meeting, two of these finalists will be awarded a scholarship for graduate study in Scotland.

Deadline

The deadline is December 15 of a student's senior year at an institution of higher education.

For More Information

http://www.standrewsny.org/standrews/content/scholarship-program

Specific Guidance for U.K. Students

The Carnegie Trust for the Universities of Scotland administers the selection process on behalf of the Society. Scottish students who wish to apply for a scholarship for a year of graduate study in the United States should contact:

Carnegie Trust for the
   Universities of Scotland
Andrew Carnegie House
Pittencrieff Street
Dunfermline
Fife
SCOTLAND KY12 8AW

THE SCIENCE, MATHEMATICS AND RESEARCH FOR TRANSFORMATION (SMART) SCHOLARSHIP FOR SERVICE PROGRAM

The Science, Mathematics and Research for Transformation (SMART) Scholarship for Service Program was created by the U.S. Department of Defense and is administered by the American Society for Engineering Education (ASEE) and the Naval Postgraduate School.

The SMART Scholarship for Service Program is available to both undergraduate and graduate students pursuing majors in science, technology, engineering, and math (STEM). The SMART Scholarship for Service Program is designed to help prepare a talented pool of civilian scientists and engineers to work at Department of Defense laboratories. SMART Scholarship recipients receive immediate postgraduation job placement within the Department of Defense.

Benefits

The SMART Scholarship covers full tuition and education-related fees and a cash award paid at a rate of $25,000 to $41,000, depending on prior educational experience (may be prorated depending on award length). The award also provides health insurance, a book allowance, job placement, and mentoring for scholarship recipients. The Department of Defense and sponsoring organizations also arrange paid summer internships for scholarship recipients.

General Eligibility Requirements

According to Department of Defense requirements, students must meet the following criteria:

- be a U.S. citizen
- be 18 years of age or older as of August 1 of the application year
- be able to participate in summer internships at DoD laboratories
- be willing to accept postgraduate employment with the DoD
- have a minimum cumulative GPA of 3.0 on a 4.0 scale (as calculated by the SMART application) and be a student in good standing
- be pursuing an undergraduate or graduate degree in one of the approved disciplines
- be currently enrolled as an undergraduate in a regionally accredited U.S. college or university and have a high school diploma/GED. Current high school students are not eligible to apply.
- be either currently enrolled as a graduate student in a regionally accredited U.S. college or university or awaiting notification of admission

Application Process

Applicants must complete the application online. The application requires:

- academic and professional information
- standardized test scores
- at least two letters of reference
- transcripts
- a statement of future goals

Deadline

The SMART Scholarship deadline is annually in December.

For More Information

http://smart.asee.org

THINKSWISS RESEARCH SCHOLARSHIPS

ThinkSwiss offers fifteen scholarships for a research stay in Switzerland. It supports highly motivated and qualified U.S. undergraduate and graduate students to conduct research at a public Swiss university or research institute for two to three months. The scholarship is open to students in all fields.

By accepting this scholarship, a recipient agrees to participate in a blog to share experiences during his or her research stay in Switzerland. After returning to the United States, the recipient also agrees to carry out at least one activity as student "ambassador" to promote Swiss research.

While German, French, or Italian language skills are not required for the research stay in Switzerland, knowledge of any of these languages will be helpful in daily life. The working language will generally be English.

Benefits

The ThinkSwiss Research Scholarship program provides a monthly scholarship of CHF 1,050 (approximately USD 1,000) for a period of two to three months (CHF 3,150 maximum), which covers two thirds of the student's average living costs. Half of the scholarship will be paid at the beginning and half at the end of the research stay, after the awardee's final report has been received.

This program does not provide health, accident, or liability insurance. Applicants must make sure that they have insurance coverage applicable for their stay in Switzerland.

General Eligibility Requirements

According to the Web site, applicants must meet the following criteria:

- be currently enrolled at an accredited U.S. university/college
- be a graduate or an undergraduate student who will have completed his/her sophomore year by the time the research stay in Switzerland begins
- provide a written confirmation from a professor at a Swiss university that he/she will accept the applicant for a research stay in his/her group

Application Process

The application packet must include a cover letter with information about the applicant's educational and professional background, goals for the research stay in Switzerland, why the applicant has chosen that particular Swiss university, one reason why the applicant would make an excellent student "ambassador," and suggest an activity that the recipient could do to promote Swiss research at the applicant's U.S. university. In addition, the application must include:

- a resume
- a letter of acceptance by a professor at a Swiss university into his/her research group
- a current official university/college transcript
- a letter of reference from a senior academic in the applicant's field of study

Deadline

The deadline is March 31 of the year a student wants to take up a research experience.

For More Information

http://www.thinkswiss.org/us-swiss-exchange/research-scholarship

WILLIAM E. SIMON FELLOWSHIP FOR NOBLE PURPOSE (INTERCOLLEGIATE STUDIES INSTITUTE)

William E. Simon (1927–2000) was the sixty-third Secretary of the Treasury with a distinguished history as public servant, businessman, and philanthropist.

The Intercollegiate Studies Institute (ISI) established the William E. Simon Fellowship for Noble Purpose to "recognize graduating college seniors who are pursuing lives dedicated to and distinguished by honor, generosity, service, and respect." Three candidates a year are selected for the fellowship, which is funded by the John Templeton Foundation. Sir John Templeton was a noted investor and wished to use his wealth "to encourage a fresh appreciation of the importance of the moral and spiritual dimensions of life for all peoples and cultures."

Benefits

The Simon Fellowship is a $40,000 unrestricted grant awarded to those graduating college seniors who have demonstrated passion, dedication, a high capacity for self-direction, and originality in pursuit of a goal that will strengthen civil society. In addition, awards of $20,000 and $10,000 are made to two other outstanding students.

According to the award's Web site, some examples of how recipients may use the award include:

- engage directly in the civic life of their community
- help to create opportunity for others, including job creation
- advance their expertise
- fund the ultimate realization of their noble purpose

General Eligibility Requirements

According to the Web site, applicants must meet the following criteria:

- be members of the Intercollegiate Studies Institute who receive The Intercollegiate Review
- engage in graduate studies for the purpose of teaching at the college level
- cannot be attending preprofessional (medical, law, divinity, business, etc.) schools
- be U.S. citizens
- will be enrolled in a full-time graduate program for the academic year for which they are submitting an application

Application Process

Applicants are evaluated on the basis of the mature conception of and passion for what they hope to accomplish as well as their academic records, extracurricular activities, and letters of recommendation. Students must provide completed applications that include:

- an application form
- a five- to ten-page narrative essay detailing past efforts, future plans, and individual philosophy for living a life of noble purpose
- one-page outline of prior education, awards, fellowships, and internships
- official transcripts of all undergraduate course work
- a letter of recommendation relevant to the applicant's noble purpose

Applicants may apply for more than one fellowship in any given academic cycle. For each fellowship sought, applicants must submit separate copies of all components of the application. Previous recipients may compete for future ISI Graduate Fellowships without restriction.

ISI notifies each applicant by mail.

Deadline

Applications should be postmarked by January 16. However, monitor deadlines closely as they may shift by a day or two depending on the year.

For More Information

http://www.isi.org/programs/fellowships/simon.html

SCHOLARSHIPS AND FELLOWSHIPS LIMITED TO STUDENTS ENROLLED AT INVITED INSTITUTIONS

The list of awards that follows continues to highlight competitive awards that offer students outstanding experience and lucrative funding. However, these awards are only available to students who attend certain institutions of higher education in the United States. Most awards listed include a broad array of schools. All of the awards have a clearly identifiable link on their Web sites that indicate participating institutions. Check carefully to make sure you're eligible before you get too far into the application process.

- Beinecke Scholarship
- The Luce Scholars Program
- Thomas J. Watson Fellowship Program
- Winston Churchill Foundation Scholarship

BEINECKE SCHOLARSHIP

In 1971, the Board of Directors at the Sperry Hutchinson Company created the Beinecke Scholarship to honor Edwin, Frederick, and Walter Beinecke. The Beinecke brothers assumed the leadership of The Sperry and Hutchinson Company in the 1920s and built if from a small enterprise to one with revenues exceeding $350 million by 1970.

The Beinecke Scholarship is available to students at over 100 institutions of higher education in the United States. According to its Web site, "The program seeks to encourage and enable highly motivated students to pursue opportunities available to them and to be courageous in the selection of a graduate course of study in the arts, humanities, and social sciences." Twenty Scholarships are awarded annually.

Benefits

The Beinecke Scholarship provides students $4,000 prior to entering graduate school and $30,000 throughout their time in graduate school. Students may also take advantage of assistantships and other aid they receive for graduate-level studies.

General Eligibility Requirements

According to the foundation's requirements, an applicant must:

- have demonstrated superior standards of intellectual ability, scholastic achievement, and personal promise during his or her undergraduate career

- be a college junior pursuing a bachelor's degree during the academic year of application
- plan to enter a master's or doctoral program in the arts, humanities, or social sciences; students in the social sciences who plan to pursue graduate study in neuroscience should not apply for a Beinecke Scholarship
- be a U.S. citizen or a U.S. national from American Samoa or the Commonwealth of the Northern Mariana Islands
- have a documented history of receiving need-based financial aid during his or her undergraduate years. Primary evidence of meeting this criterion is a student's history of receiving need-based institutional, state, or federal grants-in-aid. An institutional financial aid officer will be required to complete a Financial Data Sheet certifying that the student meets this criterion.

Application Process

Students must be nominated by a participating institution of higher education. For a complete list of "nominating" institutions, see the official list on the program Web site: http://foundationcenter.org/grantmaker/beinecke/nominating.html.

Students must submit several documents as part of their application packet. These include:

- a certificate of eligibility (verifying a history of financial need)
- an application form
- resume
- personal statement
- three letters of recommendation
- official transcripts
- a letter from the Dean or Administrating Officer summarizing the reasons for nominating the student

Deadline

Nominations are due from participating institutions in February of each year. Check with institutional representatives for institutional deadlines.

For More Information

http://foundationcenter.org/grantmaker/beinecke

THE LUCE SCHOLARS PROGRAM

The Henry Luce Foundation was created in 1936 by Henry Luce, a prominent U.S. publisher and owner of Time, Inc. Luce was born and raised in China where his parents served as missionaries and educators.

In 1974, the Luce Foundation began the Luce Scholars Program, which is designed to ". . . provide an awareness of Asia among potential leaders in American society." Each year, the Foundation selects 18 Luce Scholars who participate in an eleven-month internship program in one of several Asian countries.

Benefits

The Luce Scholarship provides a stipend that is large enough to cover general living expenses. Roundtrip transportation is also provided.

General Eligibility Requirements

Applicants must be enrolled in and nominated by one of the seventy-five participating institutions. For a complete list visit the Foundation's Web site.

In addition, the following requirements apply to all applicants:

- be U.S. citizens
- have earned a bachelor's degree before beginning the program
- be no more than 29 years old on September 1 of the year they enter the program
- be in good physical health
- have any academic background except Asian Studies
- be excellent students with outstanding leadership ability
- have specific career goals and evidence of ability within that field

Application Process

To apply for a Luce Scholarship, interested students should contact their designated institutional Luce liaison. Each institution is allowed to nominate two graduating seniors, graduate students, or recent alumni. Once nominations are received, applicants are interviewed by a representative of the Luce Foundation. Approximately 45 finalists are chosen, and additional panel interviews take place at three regional locations throughout the United States. The selection committee then identifies 18 winners as Luce Scholars.

For More Information

www.hluce.org/lsprogram.aspx

THOMAS J. WATSON FELLOWSHIP PROGRAM

The Thomas J. Watson Fellowship is a great grant. Students who receive it are funded for a year of travel outside the United States for practically any purpose whatsoever! However, it is only available to students from specific undergraduate institutions.

The Watson is a one-year grant for independent study and travel outside the United States awarded to graduating seniors by specific nominating campuses. The mission of the Thomas J. Watson Fellowship Program is to "offer college graduates of unusual promise a year of independent, purposeful exploration and travel outside of the United States in order to enhance their capacity for resourcefulness, imagination, openness, and leadership and to foster their humane and effective participation in the world community."

Benefits

The stipend for the fellowship year is $25,000 ($35,000 for fellows accompanied by a spouse or dependent child).

General Eligibility Requirements

Based on the foundation's requirements, students must:

- attend a participating college or university
- be eligible to graduate with a bachelor's degree by the end of the academic year for which the student is nominated. If awarded, the applicant must graduate from that institution before the fellowship can begin.
- be nominated by their undergraduate institution

For the complete list of participating institutions, see the program Web site.

Application Process

Begin the application process by contacting your campus Watson Liaison about the nomination process. If nominated by a participating college, you must create the following for your application packet:

- a proposal
- a personal statement

- an application form
- a personal photo
- official transcripts
- letters of recommendation

Materials are submitted electronically. An interview with a representative of the Fellowship Program will follow.

Deadline

The deadline is annually in March.

For More Information

http://www.watsonfellowship.org/site/what/what.html

Winston Churchill Foundation Scholarship

"Churchill College is the national and Commonwealth memorial to Sir Winston Spencer Churchill (1874–1965), best known for his courageous leadership as British Prime Minister during World War II. He was a formidable political thinker, soldier, historian, bricklayer, painter and orator, and he won the Nobel Prize for literature in 1953."

It was Winston Churchill's desire that Americans attend a new college named in his honor at Cambridge University. This scholarship helps to carry out his wishes. Students at over 100 U.S. institutions of higher education are eligible to apply. The award covers one year of study that leads to a master's degree at Churchill College. Fourteen scholarships are awarded annually.

Benefits

The Churchill Scholarship covers tuition and fees at Churchill College, a living allowance, and a travel stipend. The total award package is valued at between $44,000 and $50,000.

General Eligibility Requirements

Based on the Foundation's list of requirements, students must meet the following criteria:

- be citizens of the United States
- be a senior who is enrolled in one of the institutions participating in the Scholarship Program competition or a student who has recently graduated from one of those institutions

- be between the ages of 19 and 26 upon taking up the scholarship
- hold a bachelor's degree or its equivalent but may not have attained a doctorate

Application Process

Students must be nominated by a participating institution of higher education. For a complete list of participating institutions, see the official list on the program Web site: http://winstonchurchillfoundation.org/.

As part of the application process, students must first apply to be admitted to Cambridge University. Then students may apply for the Churchill Scholarship.

The application consists of:

- a comprehensive application form (including essays)
- four letters of recommendation
- official transcripts from all institutions that students have attended
- GRE scores

The completed application packet must be sent by a representative of the student's nominating institution.

Deadline

Applications are due annually in November. Participating institutions may have earlier deadlines.

For More Information

http://winstonchurchillfoundation.org

DISCIPLINE-SPECIFIC SCHOLARSHIPS AND FELLOWSHIPS FOR THE ARTS, HUMANITIES, AND SOCIAL SCIENCES

This set of opportunities, ranging from language study to peace studies, highlights awards that require you to be in specific disciplines related to the Arts, Humanities, and Social Sciences. Like applying for other awards, these applications require a careful, well-thought-out game plan.

- American-Scandinavian Foundation Awards for Americans
- Andrew W. Mellon Foundation Fellowship in Conservation at the Huntington Library
- Davis-Putter Scholarship Fund
- Herbert Scoville Jr. Peace Fellowship
- Institute for International Public Policy Undergraduate Fellowship (PPIA)
- Japanese Government (Monbukagakusho) Scholarship for Japanese Studies
- Leonore Annenberg Teaching Fellowship
- Rotary World Peace Fellowship
- The Thomas R. Pickering Undergraduate Foreign Affairs Fellowship
- The Thomas R. Pickering Graduate Foreign Affairs Fellowship
- U.S. Department of State Critical Language Scholarship
- The Woodrow Wilson Doctoral Dissertation Fellowship in Women's Studies

AMERICAN-SCANDINAVIAN FOUNDATION AWARDS FOR AMERICANS

In 1910, Danish-American industrialist Niels Poulson founded the American-Scandinavian Foundation (ASF) to promote cultural and educational exchange between the United States and Denmark, Sweden, Finland, Norway, and Iceland. Since its inception, the ASF has supported the work of over 27,000 Americans and Scandinavians who have participated in international exchange programs, as well as in research and professional development opportunities.

The ASF awards approximately $800,000 a year in fellowships/grants for study and research abroad. There are two separate opportunities for U.S. students, professionals, and artists, including the Fellowship/Grants program and the Translation Prize.

Benefits

Both the Fellowship/Grants program and the Translation Prize have their own unique benefits. The ASF Fellowships and Grants program provides fellowships of up to $23,000 and grants of $5,000 to pursue study or research in one or more Scandinavian countries. Awards are made in all disciplines. Fellowships are available for the support of yearlong study experiences, and preference is given to graduate students for assistance with dissertation-related study. Grants are available for postgraduate scholars, professionals, and artists to carry out research for one to three months.

The Translation Prize awards $2,000 for the best translation of poetry, literary prose, fiction, or drama by a Scandinavian author born before 1800. The Leif and Inger Sjöberg Award of $1,000 is given to an individual who has not previously published a literary translation.

General Eligibility Requirements

According to the Foundation's Web site, applicants must meet the following criteria:

- be U.S. citizens or permanent residents
- have completed their undergraduate education prior to the start of their study experience in Scandinavia
- have arranged their academic or professional affiliations as early as possible. Applicants are solely responsible for securing such placements; ASF cannot assist in making such connections.
- are expected to devote themselves full-time to their course of study or research
- have some proficiency in the language of their host country, even if this is not essential to their specific research interest

Application Process

Applicants are required to submit a paper copy and an electronic copy of their application. A complete application includes:

- a signed application form
- a project summary (not to exceed 200 words)
- a budget form
- a project statement (not to exceed 1,200 words) and bibliography
- curriculum vitae (not to exceed ten pages, including publications listing)
- invitation and other relevant correspondence confirming the availability of overseas resources

Recipients of fellowships and grants are notified by mid-March of the year following application.

Deadline

The application deadline is in early November. Entries for the translation awards must be submitted by June 1.

For More Information

http://www.amscan.org/grants_americans.html

ANDREW W. MELLON FOUNDATION FELLOWSHIP IN CONSERVATION AT THE HUNTINGTON LIBRARY

The Huntington is one of the largest and most comprehensive research libraries in the United States in the areas of British and American history and literature. Many historians utilize the Huntington for its exceptional materials on the American West.

The Andrew Mellon Foundation offers a fellowship in conservation at the Huntington Library each year. The fellowship is offered in the conservation of either books or works on paper. Applicants must have a bachelor's degree and "demonstrate a commitment to working in conservation or a related field." Fellows work directly with the Preservation Department's Conservators to learn conservation treatment techniques. They learn the underlying principles of conservation as well as the tools and techniques used in the conservation of library/museum collections materials.

Benefits

Fellowship recipients receive $5,000 for work over a three-month period.

General Eligibility Requirements

Applicants must have received their bachelor's degrees and show future desire to work in conservation.

Application Process

Applicants must prepare and send:

- a cover letter
- a resume
- contact information for three references to the Head of Conservation at Huntington Library

For More Information

http://www.huntington.org/huntingtonlibrary.aspx?id=2976

DAVIS-PUTTER SCHOLARSHIP FUND

This scholarship was originally established in 1960 as the Marian Davis Scholarship Fund in honor of the teacher, political activist, and advocate of racial justice and the rights of labor. Norton S. Putter, an immigrant from Poland and activist for justice and member of the civil rights movement, became an active supporter of the scholarship fund and today shares the honor of having it named for him as well.

Since its establishment, the fund has awarded scholarships to over 1,200 students who embody the peace and justice principles of the Davis and Putter families. Davis-Putter Scholarships are need-based opportunities dedicated to those working at the university level and participating in progressive movements on their campuses and within their communities. Davis-Putter Scholars may be either undergraduate or graduate students.

Benefits

The Davis-Putter Scholarship Fund contributes up to $10,000 toward education at any accredited institution of higher education in the United States. This includes community colleges, provided they are accredited, and there are provisions available for study abroad if it complements a student's course of study in the United States. The scholarship is renewable.

General Eligibility Requirements

According to its Web site, applicants must meet the following criteria:

- provide financial information indicating the level of their financial need
- have a strong academic background at the college level, focused on issues of peace and justice
- live in the United States
- be enrolled in an accredited institution

Students who have completed their undergraduate degrees and who are working toward a master's, doctoral, or professional degree (law, medicine, architecture, journalism, etc.) are eligible to receive scholarship funding.

Application Process

This particular scholarship application process involves completing the required application form as a PDF, collating all additional required materials, and mailing it by post to the Davis-Putter Scholarship Fund organization. The application includes:

- the application forms

- transcripts
- two letters of reference
- a personal statement
- a copy of the Student Aid Report (SAR)
- a current photograph

Applicants are notified of decisions by the end of July in either a letter or an e-mail.

Deadline

The deadline is April 1.

For More Information

http://www.davisputter.org/

HERBERT SCOVILLE JR. PEACE FELLOWSHIP

Herbert "Pete" Scoville helped to develop nuclear weapons and military strategies before he turned into a staunch arms-control advocate.

The Herbert Scoville Jr. Peace Fellowship is designed to give applicants experience in Washington, DC, working with an organization focused on peace and security issues. Scoville Fellows are placed at one of twenty-five Washington organizations as junior staffers and provided with a monthly stipend for a six- to nine-month period. Most Fellows continue working with their host organization, work for other public interest organizations, work for the federal government, or pursue graduate studies in the area of international relations or related fields. Since 1987, the program has awarded 128 fellowships.

Benefits

Scoville Fellows receive a monthly stipend of $2,300, health insurance, and travel expenses to Washington, DC. They are also given $500 for conference travel. Fellows are matched with mentors throughout their professional experience.

General Eligibility Requirements

According to the Web site, applicants must meet the following criteria:

- have obtained a bachelor's degree by the time they begin their fellowship. Graduate students and professionals are eligible to apply.

- be a U.S. citizen or a non-U.S. citizen living in the United States with the proper work visa

Application Process

While there is no formal application form for the Scoville Peace Fellowship, students must develop a packet of information that contains the following:

- cover sheet
- signed letter indicating desire to apply and contact information
- curriculum vitae
- personal essay
- policy/opinion essay
- official transcripts
- two letters of reference

Documents are to be e-mailed as attachments to the Herbert Scoville Jr. Peace Fellowship organization.

Deadline

Applications for a fellowship starting in the spring are due in October. Applications for a fellowship starting in the fall are due in January.

For More Information

http://www.scoville.org/

INSTITUTE FOR INTERNATIONAL PUBLIC POLICY UNDERGRADUATE FELLOWSHIP (PPIA)

The Public Policy and International Affairs Program (PPIA) focuses on students from groups who are underrepresented in leadership positions in a number of professional sectors, including government, nonprofits, international organizations, and other similar programs. For over twenty years, PPIA has been promoting diversity in public service and encouraging the potential of students to serve as active, engaged citizens.

PPIA is a national program designed to prepare young adults for advanced degrees and eventually for careers serving the public good. The PPIA Junior Summer Institutes (JSI) are the hallmark of the PPIA Fellowship Program. For seven weeks during the summer between the junior and senior years, JSI Fellows focus on preparation for graduate programs in public and international affairs, careers as policy professionals, and other leadership opportunities in public service.

The JSI provide students with training and financial support for graduate school and further professional development. JSI are administered by a consortium of top public and international affairs graduate programs in the United States, including the University of California at Berkeley, the University of Michigan, Carnegie Mellon University, the University of Maryland, and Princeton University. The JSI also provide an alumni association of approximately 3,000 PPIA Fellows from across the nation for networking.

Benefits

PPIA Fellows receive full tuition to attend a PPIA Junior Summer Institute to prepare them for entrance into top graduate programs in public policy and foreign affairs, plus a minimum stipend of $1,000. They also receive a minimum of $5,000 toward graduate school tuition. Often, PPIA Fellows go on to receive additional financial offers above the stated minimums and also become eligible for paid internships.

General Eligibility Requirements

According to the PPIA Web site, applicants must meet the following criteria:

- be interested in a career in public service
- be a U.S. citizen or legal permanent resident to apply to the JSI hosted by UC Berkeley, Maryland, and Michigan. International applicants who are pursuing an undergraduate degree in the United States will be considered by Carnegie Mellon and Princeton.
- have completed their junior year of college prior to the start of a JSI and have at least two quarters or one full semester of course work to complete prior to graduation
- may not hold a bachelor's degree prior to the start of a JSI
- show a clear commitment to completing a master's degree in public and/or international affairs at one of the PPIA Consortium graduate schools
- demonstrate a genuine interest in pursuing a career associated with public service and contribute to the diversity of perspectives in such organizations as the government, nonprofits, and other related programs

All academic majors are welcome to apply, and some consideration is given to economic need. There are additional institution-specific requirements and options for PPIA Fellows at UC Berkeley and Maryland.

Application Process

Applicants must complete an online application. Other materials required to complete the application include:

- a personal statement
- a resume
- transcripts
- two letters of reference
- Student Aid Report (SAR) and current financial aid award letter

There is no minimum GPA; however, transcripts and the application should demonstrate an applicant's ability to succeed in graduate school. GPA is considered, as are other factors, such as the classes taken, the difficulty of course work, and overall academic progress. PPIA applicants will be impressive academically but, more important, they will demonstrate a keen sense of cultural awareness, social sensitivity, and a commitment to public service.

Deadline

The application deadline is generally during the early part of November prior to the year of the Junior Summer Institute.

For More Information

http://www.ppiaprogram.org/about/

JAPANESE GOVERNMENT (MONBUKAGAKUSHO) SCHOLARSHIP FOR JAPANESE STUDIES

The Japanese Government Scholarship was started in 1954. "The purpose of these scholarships is to promote mutual understanding and deepening friendly ties between Japan and other countries through the application of advanced knowledge regarding Japan's language and culture."

The Japanese government's Ministry of Education, Culture, Sports, Science, and Technology provides scholarships for study in Japan to foreign students interested in further study of the Japanese language, Japanese affairs, and Japanese culture. Some 79,000 students from approximately 160 countries and world regions have studied in Japan through this program.

Benefits

The actual Scholarship amount changes each year depending on funding. For 2010, the scholarship amount was 125,000 yen per month (approximately US$1,380 per month). Roundtrip transportation is also provided.

General Eligibility Requirements

According to the Web site, applicants must meet the following criteria:

- be a national of a country that has diplomatic relations with Japan. Selection is conducted at facilities such as the Japanese Embassy/Consulate General located in the country of the applicant's nationality.
- be under 35 years of age
- be an undergraduate at foreign (non-Japanese) universities and majoring in fields related to the Japanese language or Japanese culture at the time of arriving in and leaving Japan
- have Japanese language ability sufficient for receiving education in Japanese at a Japanese university
- be free from any mental or physical disabilities that would be an impediment to the pursuit of university study
- be able to arrive in Japan within two weeks counted from the starting day of the study course set by the university in Japan (usually October) and the period set by the accepting university. (If the applicant arrives in Japan before the period for personal reasons, travel expenses to Japan will not be paid. If the applicant cannot arrive in Japan during the designated period, the applicant must resign.)

Applicants are required to acquire a "College Student" (*ryugaku*) visa when they come to Japan.

Application Process

Applicants must work through the Japanese embassy or consulate. Applicants must submit:

- an application form
- digital image
- certificate of university enrollment from current university
- academic transcripts
- academic recommendation from current university
- proof of Japanese language ability
- medical form

The initial interview is carried out by a Japanese legation in the applicant's home country. Those who pass this interview process are recommended to the scholarship committee.

For More Information

http://www.studyjapan.go.jp/en/toj/toj0302e.html and then click on http://www.studyjapan.go.jp/en/toj/pdf/nikken_e.pdf

LEONORE ANNENBERG TEACHING FELLOWSHIP

The Leonore Annenberg Teaching Fellowship is considered the equivalent of the Rhodes Scholarship for teaching. It is one of three recently launched programs by the Woodrow Wilson National Fellowship Foundation to address challenges to improving the teacher work force. Through these fellowships, the Foundation seeks to improve the rigor of teacher selection and demonstrate what effective teacher preparation and retention look like, especially in high-need schools.

Funded by a $5 million grant from the Annenberg Foundation and a $1 million grant from the Carnegie Corporation of New York, the Leonore Annenberg Fellowship provides funding for exceptionally capable candidates to complete a yearlong master's program at one of four of the nation's top schools: Stanford University, the University of Pennsylvania, the University of Virginia, and the University of Washington.

Benefits

The Leonore Annenberg Teaching Fellowship includes a $30,000 stipend and guidance toward a teaching certificate. Fellows are prepared to teach in a high-need urban or rural secondary school and receive support and mentoring throughout their three-year teaching commitment. Upon completion, they receive lifelong membership in the national network of Woodrow Wilson Fellows.

General Eligibility Requirements

According to the Web site, eligibility requirements vary slightly depending on the individual institution, but all maintain an interest in applicants who are strong academically as well as able to show a genuine commitment to teaching as a profession. Fellows are selected from a diverse pool of candidates who hold baccalaureate degrees in arts and sciences fields or related professions, such as finance and engineering. Candidates must show a commitment to high-need communities and public schools. College seniors, recent graduates, and midcareer professionals are encouraged to apply.

Selected candidates must be willing to complete a three-year teaching commitment following their fellowship period.

Application Process

Applicants apply through one of the four participating institutions and are encouraged to visit the individual Web sites for additional information and application forms.

- Stanford University: http://ed.stanford.edu/suse/admissions/admissions-financial-aid-step.html
- University of Pennsylvania: http://www.upenn.edu/ccp/view-complete-list/267.html?task=view
- University of Virginia: http://curry.edschool.virginia.edu/n_curryadmissions/latf.html#application
- University of Washington: http://education.washington.edu/funding/wilson/

For More Information

http://www.woodrow.org/teaching-fellowships/annenberg/index.php

ROTARY WORLD PEACE FELLOWSHIP

According to the Rotary Club International, "Rotary Peace Fellows are leaders promoting national and international cooperation, peace, and the successful resolution of conflict throughout their lives, in their careers, and through service activities."

The Rotary Club International is a worldwide service organization that is active in over 200 countries with approximately 1.2 million members. The Rotary World Peace Fellowships are part of the Rotary Club Foundation's Educational Program. Every year, up to 100 Peace Fellows are chosen from around the world to work on a master's degree in international relations, public administration, sustainable development, peace studies, conflict resolution, or a related field or a professional development certificate in peace and conflict resolution.

Benefits

Rotary Fellows study at one of six Rotary Centers for International Studies in peace and conflict resolution. The Rotary World Peace Fellowship covers tuition, room and board, roundtrip transportation, and expenses needed to cover internship and field work experiences.

General Eligibility Requirements

According to the Web site, applicants must meet the following criteria:

- be committed to international understanding and peace, demonstrated through professional and academic achievements and personal and community service activities
- hold a bachelor's degree or equivalent in a related field with strong grades at the time of application
- have a minimum of three years' combined paid or unpaid full-time relevant work experience for the master's degree program
- have a minimum five years' relevant work experience with current full-time employment in a mid- to upper-level position for the certificate program
- be proficient in a second language for the master's program or proficient in English for the certificate program
- have excellent leadership skills

Application Process

The Rotary selection process is completely localized, and applications must be made through a local Rotary Club. The Rotary International Web site has a helpful search function. Online application materials are available and are to be submitted once a local Rotary Club has been identified.

Generally, the following materials are requested as part of the application:

- letter of intent
- essays
- letters of recommendation
- language-ability forms
- transcripts

Deadline

Your nearest Rotary Club will have scholarship information and local deadline information for each year.

For More Information

http://www.rotary.org/en/StudentsAndYouth/EducationalPrograms/
RotaryCentersForInternationalStudies/Pages/ridefault.aspx

THE THOMAS R. PICKERING UNDERGRADUATE FOREIGN AFFAIRS FELLOWSHIP

Thomas R. Pickering enjoyed a long and distinguished career in the U.S. Foreign Service. He served as ambassador to Russia, India, Israel, El Salvador, Nigeria, Jordan, and the United Nations.

The Woodrow Wilson National Fellowship Foundation annually awards the Thomas R. Pickering Undergraduate Foreign Affairs Fellowship. The goal of the undergraduate foreign affairs fellowship is ". . . to recruit talented students in academic programs relevant to international affairs, political and economic analysis, administration, management, and science policy." Approximately 20 undergraduate fellowships are awarded each year.

Benefits

The program provides generous funding (up to $50,000 annually) to cover tuition, room and board, and other related educational expenses. The program also provides internship opportunities and mentoring. Recipients must agree to a three-year term of service as a Foreign Services Officer upon completion of their degree and testing requirements.

General Eligibility Requirements

According to the program's official Web site, applicants must meet the following criteria:

- be a U.S. citizen at the time of application
- be in the junior year of undergraduate study
- have a cumulative grade point average of 3.2 or higher on a 4.0 scale at the time of application

A cumulative grade point average of 3.2 or higher on a 4.0 scale must be maintained throughout participation in the program.

Application Process

To begin the application process, applicants must register and fill out an online application form. Additional materials to be submitted include:

- a certification of U.S. citizenship
- a copy of SAT or ACT scores
- two letters of recommendation
- official academic transcripts for all undergraduate institutions attended
- a two-page resume
- verification of financial aid received (if applicable)

Deadline

The application is due annually in February.

For More Information

http://www.woodrow.org/higher-education-fellowships/foreign_affairs/index.php

THE THOMAS R. PICKERING GRADUATE FOREIGN AFFAIRS FELLOWSHIP

Thomas R. Pickering holds the distinction of Career Ambassador in the U.S. Foreign Service, having served in various ambassadorial positions since 1974. He was also Under Secretary of State for Political Affairs from 1997 to 2000.

The Woodrow Wilson National Fellowship Foundation awards the Thomas R. Pickering Graduate Foreign Affairs Fellowship to approximately 20 applicants annually. According to the program's Web site, its goal is ". . . to attract outstanding students who enroll in two-year master's degree programs in public policy, international affairs, public administration, or academic fields such as business, economics, political science, sociology, or foreign languages, who represent all ethnic, racial, and social backgrounds and who have an interest in pursuing a Foreign Service career in the U.S. Department of State."

Benefits

The program provides generous funding (up to $50,000 annually) to cover tuition, room and board, and other related educational expenses. The program also provides internship opportunities and mentoring. Recipients must agree to a three-year term of service as a Foreign Services Officer upon completion of their degree and testing requirements.

General Eligibility Requirements

According to the program's official Web site, applicants must meet the following criteria:

- be U.S. citizens at the time of application
- have a minimum undergraduate grade point average of 3.2 or higher on a 4.0 scale. (A cumulative grade point average of 3.2 or higher on a 4.0 scale must be maintained throughout participation in the program.)
- be seeking admission to graduate school for the following academic year

Winners are expected to enroll in a two-year, full-time master's degree program in public policy, international affairs, or public administration, or in an academic field such as business, economics, political science, sociology, or foreign languages (U.S. graduate institutions only).

Application Process

To begin the application process, applicants must register and fill out an online application form. Additional materials to be submitted include:

- a certification of U.S. citizenship
- a copy of GRE or GMAT scores
- two letters of recommendation
- official academic transcripts for all undergraduate institutions attended
- a two-page resume
- verification of financial aid received (if applicable)

Deadline

The application is due annually in February.

For More Information

http://www.woodrow.org/higher-education-fellowships/foreign_affairs/pickering_grad/index.php

U.S. DEPARTMENT OF STATE CRITICAL LANGUAGE SCHOLARSHIP

According to the program's Web site, "The Critical Language Scholarship Program is part of a U.S. government effort to expand dramatically the number of Americans studying and mastering critical need foreign languages." These languages are considered critical to the nation's security and future.

The Bureau of Educational and Cultural Affairs of the U.S. Department of State offers intensive summer language institutes overseas through the Critical Language Scholarship (CLS) Program. These institutes focus on thirteen critical-need languages. Critical Language Scholarship (CLS) institutes provide fully funded, group-based intensive language instruction and structured cultural enrichment experiences for seven to ten weeks for undergraduate, master's, and Ph.D. students who are also U.S. citizens. Languages and levels available for each language are as follows:

- Arabic, Persian: beginning, intermediate, or advanced level
- Azerbaijani, Bangla/Bengali, Hindi, Indonesian, Korean, Punjabi, Turkish, Urdu: beginning, intermediate, or advanced level
- Chinese, Japanese, Russian: intermediate or advanced level

Countries where students may study are Azerbaijan, Bangladesh, China, Egypt, India, Indonesia, Japan, Jordan, Morocco, Oman, Russia, South Korea, Tajikistan, Tunisia, Turkey, or others where the target languages are spoken.

Students of diverse disciplines and majors are encouraged to apply. Students who participate in the program are expected to continue their language study beyond the scholarship period and eventually apply their critical-language skills in their future professional careers.

Benefits

All CLS Program costs are covered, including travel to and from the student's U.S. home city and program location; a mandatory Washington, DC, pre-departure orientation; applicable visa fees; room and board; group-based intensive language instruction; program-sponsored travel within the study country; and all entrance fees for CLS Program cultural enhancement activities.

General Eligibility Requirements

According to the program's Web site, applicants must meet the following criteria:

- be U.S. citizens
- be currently enrolled in a U.S. degree-granting program at the undergraduate or graduate level. Undergraduate students must have completed at least one year of general college course work by program start date.
- submit a satisfactory Medical Information Form and Physician's Statement
- be 18 before beginning a CLS Program
- have a U.S. passport valid with at least two blank visa pages by early March of the year they are selected

Students in all disciplines, including business, engineering, law, medicine, sciences, and humanities, are encouraged to apply.

Application Process

The CLS Program application is an online process, and applicants must register to start the process. Applicants are encouraged to consult very specific materials provided online about the language levels and prerequisites. The selection process is administered by the Council of American Overseas Research Centers (CAORC) with awards approved by the U.S. Department of State, Bureau of Educational and Cultural Affairs. Program administration is also supported by the American Councils for International Education.

Recipients will be selected on the basis of merit as indicated by their academic record and potential to succeed in rigorous academic environments. They will also be assessed on their ability to adapt to different cultural situations and on their commitment to further study of the language and its eventual use in their future profession. Applicants will be notified of the results of their application to the CLS Program in mid- to late-March. After notification, selected participants will be required to complete a language evaluation that will determine their particular CLS institute assignment. Assignments are given in mid- to late-April.

Deadline

The CLS Program application deadline is generally mid-December, prior to the year a selected applicant will begin the course of study.

For More Information

http://www.clscholarship.org/

THE WOODROW WILSON DOCTORAL DISSERTATION FELLOWSHIP IN WOMEN'S STUDIES

Counted among Woodrow Wilson Fellowship recipients are 13 Nobel Laureates, 35 MacArthur Fellows (known popularly as genius awards), 14 Pulitzer Prize winners, and hundreds of other distinguished individuals.

As part of the Woodrow Wilson National Fellowship Foundation, the Doctoral Dissertation Fellowship in Women's Studies "... encourages original and significant research about women that crosses disciplinary, regional, or cultural boundaries." The fellowships are designed to assist applicants in completing their doctoral dissertations and thus making future contributions in the area of Woman's Studies.

Benefits

Fellows receive $2,000 toward costs associated with their dissertations. Fellows must complete their dissertations during the year they are awarded funding.

General Eligibility Requirements

According to the program's official Web site, before deciding to apply for a Women's Studies Fellowship, applicants need to consider the following questions to be certain that they are eligible:

- Have they completed all pre-dissertation requirements?
- Are they writing on issues related to women, gender, women's studies, or feminist/gender/LGBTQ theory?
- Are they enrolled in a graduate school in the United States?
- Do they expect to complete the Ph.D. by the following summer?

Application Process

Applicants must:

- fill out an online application form
- supply two letters of recommendation
- supply a current transcript

The online application requires the applicant to include significant information about the dissertation project.

Deadline

Not given each year; check the Web site.

For More Information

http://www.woodrow.org/higher-education-fellowships/women_gender/index.php

DISCIPLINE-SPECIFIC SCHOLARSHIPS AND FELLOWSHIPS FOR THE SCIENCES

As you will notice in the pages that follow, significant funding is available for students interested in science-related careers. The scholarships and fellowships in this section are, for the most part, attempting to provide outstanding academic, research, and professional opportunities to the best and brightest minds interested in careers involving various science, technology, engineering, and mathematics disciplines.

- Department of Health and Human Services Emerging Leaders Program
- Doris Duke Conservation Fellows Program
- Environmental Protection Agency (EPA): Greater Research Opportunities (GRO) Fellowships for Undergraduate Students
- Ernest F. Hollings Undergraduate Scholarship Program
- International Max Planck Research School for Molecular and Cellular Biology (IMPRS-MCB) International Summer Internships
- International Research and Education in Engineering Program (IREE)
- KAUST Fellowship: King Abdullah University of Science and Technology Fellowship Program
- Math for America Fellowship Program
- National Defense Science and Engineering Graduate (NDSEG) Fellowships
- National Institutes of Health Undergraduate Scholarship Program

DEPARTMENT OF HEALTH AND HUMAN SERVICES EMERGING LEADERS PROGRAM

The Emerging Leaders Program of the Department of Health and Human Services (HHS) offers an excellent opportunity to begin a professional career with the HHS.

The U.S. Department of Health and Human Services Emerging Leaders Program (ELP) is a two-year, paid, federal internship with HHS. It is a competitive program that provides interns with the opportunity to develop leadership skills in one of the largest federal agencies. The HHS recruits talented and highly motivated individuals with a significant commitment to public service.

Benefits

The internship carries with it a salary of up to $50,408, depending on location. Interns are placed in Washington, DC; Baltimore, Maryland; or Atlanta, Georgia.

Interns are provided with the opportunity to rotate through eleven divisions within the HHS. Promotions are granted during the two-year internship program, and interns receive significant training in both leadership and other areas of professional development. Mentoring is provided by senior executives and renowned experts within the HHS. Networking opportunities exist with both HHS leaders and fellow interns.

General Eligibility Requirements

According to the ELP Web site, applicants must meet the following criteria:

- be a citizen of the United States
- meet the GS-09 federal employment requirements
- have a master's or equivalent graduate degree, or have two full years of progressively higher-level graduate education leading to such a degree, or an LL.B. or a J.D., if related. The major field of study must be related to the career track for which the applicant is being considered. One year of full-time graduate education is considered to be the number of credit hours that the school attended considers one year of full-time study. If that information cannot be obtained from the school, 18 semester hours will satisfy the one year of full-time study requirement.

Full details about the employment requirements and requisite job descriptions can be found at http://hhsu.learning.hhs.gov/elp/qualifications.asp.

Application Process

The DHHS ELP program requires:

- an application for the internship program
- a completed online Occupational Questionnaire
- a resume documenting any specialized experience
- undergraduate and graduate transcripts
- "accomplishment record narratives" detailing capabilities in accountability, problem-solving, written communication, customer service, and oral communication

Applications are submitted using an online application process.

Deadline

The DHHS ELP program requires that complete applications be submitted in December following an annual call for interns in November of that same year. Deadlines vary slightly and are contingent on government funding for the internship program.

For More Information

http://hhsu.learning.hhs.gov/elp/

DORIS DUKE CONSERVATION FELLOWS PROGRAM

The Doris Duke Conservation Fellows Program is one of many fellowship programs offered by the Woodrow Wilson National Fellowship Foundation, whose motto reads "identifying and developing the best minds for the nation's most important challenges." Doris Duke was an extremely wealthy woman who had a great interest in nature and conservation.

The Doris Duke Conservation Fellows Program was created in 1997 by the Environment Program of the Doris Duke Charitable Foundation. The fellowship supports students enrolled in multidisciplinary master's programs at partner universities. Fellows are committed to careers as practicing conservationists. The program currently supports students at eight universities: Yale, Duke, Cornell, Florida A&M, Northern Arizona, and the Universities of Michigan, Wisconsin, and California at Santa Barbara.

Benefits

The Doris Duke Conservation Fellowship provides financial assistance for tuition and cultivates leadership skills through internships, professional and career development programs, and ongoing alumni networking activities. The program has supported over 300 Fellows, many of whom are already making their mark in environmental and conservation fields. Several have been employed by organizations such as the World Wildlife Fund, the federal Environmental Protection Agency, Nature Conservancy, and the federal Office of Management and Budget.

General Eligibility Requirements

According to the Program Web site, applicants must meet the following criteria:

- be enrolled in a master's program at a participating institution
- intend to pursue a career related to conservation and the environment

Application Process

Each of the eight institutions that awards this fellowship has its own application and selection process. Each also has a contact person to advise interested applicants. Those contacts are listed at http://www.woodrow.org/higher-education-fellowships/conservation/contacts.php

Deadline

Deadlines are specific to each campus application process. Contact your campus representative for deadline details.

For More Information

http://www.woodrow.org/higher-education-fellowships/conservation/index.php

ENVIRONMENTAL PROTECTION AGENCY (EPA): GREATER RESEARCH OPPORTUNITIES (GRO) FELLOWSHIPS FOR UNDERGRADUATE STUDENTS

The EPA offers a variety of opportunities for undergraduate and graduate students that include internships, professional development opportunities, employment, and fellowships, including the National Network for Environmental Management Studies.

The Greater Research Opportunities (GRO) program helps provide the opportunity for research at colleges and universities with limited funding by awarding undergraduate fellowships to students in environmental fields. The fellowship program aims to encourage promising students to pursue advanced degrees, and eventually careers, in environmental fields.

Benefits

Eligible students receive financial support for their junior and senior years of undergraduate study and for an internship at an EPA facility during the summer between their junior and senior years. The fellowship provides up to $17,000 per year of academic support and up to $7,500 of internship support for the three-month summer period.

General Eligibility Requirements

According to its Web site, applicants must meet the following criteria:

- attend a fully accredited U.S. college or university (located in the United States or its territories) for their undergraduate studies
- be citizens of the U.S. or its territories or possessions, or be lawfully admitted to the United States for permanent residence. Resident aliens must include their green card number in their application (students must have their green card at the time of application to be eligible for this Fellowship opportunity). EPA may verify this number with the U.S. Citizenship and Immigration Service of the Department of Homeland Security.

- must be entering the last two years of study before obtaining a bachelor's degree. Students who have already earned one bachelor's degree and are pursuing additional degrees are not eligible.
- have at least a "B" average overall

The schools that applicants attend must be among those that are not highly funded for the development of environmental research capacity. For the purposes of this solicitation, EPA considers as *ineligible* those institutions receiving more than $35 million in annual federal research and development funding. Check the EPA Web site to make sure that you are enrolled in a qualified institution.

Application Process

To apply for the EPA's GRO program, applicants must submit the following:

- an application for Federal Assistance (Standard Form (SF) 424 or 424-1 Individual)
- EPA key contacts form
- information data sheet
- front page
- personal statement
- background information (CV)
- transcripts
- letters of recommendation

Submission can be done electronically or on paper, but only one submission format is acceptable.

Deadline

The deadline for the EPA's GRO program is generally in December following a call for applicants sent in September of that same year.

For More Information

http://epa.gov/ncer/fellow/
http://epa.gov/ncer/guidance/faqs.html

Cross Pollination

Graduate students also have a variety of opportunities with the EPA and should refer to the following for further details: http://www.epa.gov/careers/stuopp.html#coll.

ERNEST F. HOLLINGS UNDERGRADUATE SCHOLARSHIP PROGRAM

Ernest F. Hollings was a U.S. Senator from South Carolina from 1966 to 2005. He also served as governor of South Carolina from 1959 to 1963.

The National Oceanic and Atmospheric Administration (NOAA) annually offers the Ernest F. Hollings Scholarship Program, which is designed to increase undergraduate training in oceanic and atmospheric science, technology, research, and education. Other goals are to increase public understanding and support for the stewardship of the oceans and the atmospheres and to improve environmental literacy. NOAA, through the Hollings program, recruits and prepares students for public service careers with NOAA and other science agencies at the federal, state, and local levels of government as well as for careers as teachers and educators in oceanic and atmospheric science.

Benefits

The Hollings Scholarship provides successful undergraduate applicants with awards that include financial assistance up to $8,000 a year for full-time study during a 9-month academic year and a 10-week, full-time internship position at $650 a week during the summer at a NOAA facility. If reappointed the following year, $8,000 will again be awarded for academic assistance. Awards also include travel funds to attend a mandatory Hollings Scholarship Program orientation, conferences where students present a poster or paper about their research, and a housing subsidy for scholars who do not reside at home during their summer internships.

General Eligibility Requirements

According to the Web site, applicants must meet the following criteria:

- be a U.S. citizen
- have full-time status as a college sophomore at an accredited college or university within the United States or U.S. territories
- have a cumulative and semester/quarter GPA of 3.0 (based on a 4.0 scale) in all completed undergraduate courses and in the major field of study
- be majoring in a discipline area related to oceanic and atmospheric science, research, technology, or education and be supportive of the purposes of NOAA's programs and mission, e.g., biological, social, and physical sciences; mathematics; engineering; computer and information sciences; and teacher education

Application Process

To apply for a Hollings Undergraduate Scholarship, applicants download an application at http://www.oesd.noaa.gov/Hollings_info.html. The application is available from November until the January deadline.

Applicants must submit all of the following items to be considered for the scholarship:

- a completed scholarship application form
- two essays
- official college transcripts sent directly to NOAA by the granting institution
- two academic references.

Deadline

Applications are available in November with a deadline at the end of January of the following year.

For More Information

http://www.oesd.noaa.gov/Hollings_info.html

Cross Pollination

Also note NOAA's many other opportunities, such as NOAA's Sea Grant Awards, Eight Climate Engagement Mini-Grants, and similar awards. This grant profile is just the tip of the iceberg of NOAA opportunities. To spark ideas, see http://www.magazine.noaa.gov/stories/mag201.htm.

INTERNATIONAL MAX PLANCK RESEARCH SCHOOL FOR MOLECULAR AND CELLULAR BIOLOGY (IMPRS-MCB) INTERNATIONAL SUMMER INTERNSHIPS

According to its Web site, the International Max Planck Research School for Molecular and Cellular Biology (IMPRS-MCB) is a joint international Ph.D. program of the Max Planck Institute of Immunobiology (MPI-IB) and the Albert-Ludwigs-University Freiburg. The program provides outstanding students state-of-the-art, research-oriented, interdisciplinary training in biochemistry, cell biology, developmental biology, genetics, immunobiology and molecular biology at the highest levels.

The Max Planck Institute of Immunobiology offers three-month summer internships in Freiburg, Germany, for undergraduate students. Undergraduates gain valuable lab experience at the institute while experiencing German culture and society. According to the program Web site, placements are available in a wide variety of fields, including immunology, developmental biology, epigenetics, cell biology, etc.

Benefits

Students are provided a living stipend and housing for the duration of their internship.

General Eligibility Requirements

According to the program Web site, applications are invited from undergraduate students in their third or fourth year of study toward a degree in immunobiology, genetics, molecular biology, cell biology, developmental biology, bioinformatics, or related fields.

Application Process

Applications may be e-mailed or sent through regular mail. A completed application consists of the following:

- an application form
- a letter of motivation
- a CV that includes a photograph
- academic transcripts
- proof of previous lab experience
- evidence of English proficiency if not a native English-speaker
- passport copy
- certificate of current undergraduate enrollment
- letters of recommendation

Deadline

Applications are due annually in January.

For More Information

http://www.imprs-mcb.mpg.de/home/imprs/summer_internship/index.html

INTERNATIONAL RESEARCH AND EDUCATION IN ENGINEERING PROGRAM (IREE)

The Web site explains that "[t]he International Research and Education in Engineering (IREE) Program was initiated by the National Science Foundation (ENG/EEC) in 2006 to promote enhancement of global competency of 21st century engineering professionals, development of collaborations with engineering researchers abroad, and providing students with opportunities to experience the life and culture of another country."

The International Research and Education in Engineering Program is designed to send approximately 20 undergraduates and 30 graduate engineering students to China each year. The goals of the program are ". . . to support international travel by U.S. early-career researchers to enable them to gain international research experience and perspective, and to enable closer research interaction between U.S. institutions and their foreign counterparts."

Benefits

Undergraduates receive a $3,000 stipend, and graduate students receive a $4,000 stipend. In addition, participants receive a $1,000 housing allowance, health insurance, travel allowance, and an orientation and re-entry program.

General Eligibility Requirements

According to the program Web site, applicants must meet the following criteria:

- be currently enrolled as a degree-seeking undergraduate or graduate student at a U.S. institution of higher education
- be in good academic standing and not currently under any academic or other disciplinary action at one's home university
- be able to express both a demonstrated interest in a field of engineering-related research and a desire to work in China

In addition, women, underrepresented groups, and students from schools with limited research opportunities are particularly encouraged to apply.

Application Process

Applicants must create an account on GlobalHUB to submit their application online. A completed application includes:

- a personal statement
- a resume/CV
- official transcripts
- two letters of recommendation

Deadline

Applications are due annually in February.

For More Information

http://globalhub.org/iree

KAUST FELLOWSHIP: KING ABDULLAH UNIVERSITY OF SCIENCE AND TECHNOLOGY FELLOWSHIP PROGRAM

The King Abdullah University of Science and Technology, KAUST, is an international, graduate-level research university that is dedicated to inspiring a new age of scientific achievement within Saudi Arabia, the region, and the world.

The KAUST Fellowship is a scholarship program offered by the King Abdullah University of Science and Technology in Jeddah, Saudi Arabia. It provides full support and a monthly stipend to students pursuing an M.S., M.S. to Ph.D., or Ph.D. degree for the duration of their graduate studies. KAUST-relevant fields of study include applied math and computational science, bioscience, materials science, and engineering. For a complete list, check the university's Web site.

Benefits

In addition to the opportunity to study at KAUST and work with a world-class faculty, students awarded the KAUST Fellowship will receive full tuition support, a monthly stipend, free housing, and travel costs to the KAUST campus.

General Eligibility Requirements

According to the Web site, applicants must meet the following requirements:

- have completed the bachelor's or master's degree in a KAUST-relevant field of study prior to the semester of enrollment
- be enrolled in a current field of study in a KAUST-relevant area, such as·engineering, mathematics, or the physical, chemical, and biological sciences
- have a minimum cumulative GPA of 3.5 on a 4.0 scale or equivalent in other international grading systems
- be able to enroll at KAUST for the upcoming academic year
- submit a minimum TOEFL score of 79 on the IBT (Internet-Based Test) or 6.0 on the IELTS (International English Language Testing System)
- Only official TOEFL or IELTS scores will be accepted. TOEFL or IELTS scores for tests administered by an educational institution for admission to that particular institution are not acceptable.
- A TOEFL or IELTS score is not required if the applicant is a native speaker of English or received a degree from a university in the United States, Canada, United Kingdom, Ireland, Australia, or New Zealand.
- KAUST's university code for the TOEFL exam is 4107.
- submit official GRE scores
- The university code for the GRE exam is 4139. Please use this code to request that test scores be sent to KAUST.
- submit official university transcript from every institution previously attended

Application Process

There are five requirements for a KAUST Fellowship application:

- a statement of purpose included within the student application form
- official university transcripts
- three letters of recommendation
- an official TOEFL or IELTS English language proficiency score
- official GRE scores. A scan of the official transcript must be uploaded into the online application form, and an official document must also be sent directly from the university in a university-sealed envelope.

Deadline

Applications are generally released in September with an application deadline of mid-January.

For More Information

http://www.kaust.edu.sa/admissions/tokaust/fellowship.html

MATH FOR AMERICA FELLOWSHIP PROGRAM

Math for America Fellows are mathematically sophisticated individuals who are new to teaching and use their talents to make a difference in students' lives.

The Math for America (MfA) Fellowship is a five-year program in which recent college graduates and mid-career professionals make a commitment to teach math in public secondary schools. The program includes one year earning a master's degree in education and four years of teaching math in public secondary schools. During the fifth year, Fellows may apply to become Master Teachers.

Benefits

MfA Fellows receive a full-tuition scholarship to a master's degree or teacher credentialing program in mathematics education. Up to $100,000 in stipends are awarded in addition to a full-time teacher's salary. Fellows become members of a national corps of highly qualified secondary school mathematics teachers and receive mentoring, job-search support, and access to ongoing professional development opportunities.

General Eligibility Requirements

According to the Web site, applicants must meet the following criteria:

- be a U.S. citizen or permanent resident of the United States
- be new to teaching
- hold a bachelor's degree from an accredited college or university. An applicant's bachelor's degree must be conferred by June of the academic year for which the candidate is applying.
- have completed substantial course work in mathematics. All of the pre-service training programs require strong quantitative preparation.
- achieve a competitive score on the ETS Praxis Exams

Application Process

Applicants must submit:

- the online application form
- a resume

- unofficial transcripts
- three letters of recommendation
- a personal statement
- a mathematics course credit list

In addition, all applicants are required to take the Praxis II Math Content Exams. Some sites require additional testing based on state and university requirements; check the site-specific application pages for more information. Information on the exams can be found at www.ets.org.

Deadline

The deadline is January.

For More Information

http://www.mathforamerica.org/benefits

NATIONAL DEFENSE SCIENCE AND ENGINEERING GRADUATE (NDSEG) FELLOWSHIPS

Since it established the National Defense Science and Engineering Graduate Fellowship in 1988, the Department of Defense has awarded more than 3,200 fellowships. The award does not entail any military or other service obligation.

The purpose of the National Defense Science and Engineering Graduate (NDSEG) Fellowships is to support more U.S. citizens and nationals training for careers in science and engineering disciplines that have military importance. The Department of Defense (DoD) expects to award approximately 200 new three-year graduate fellowships each year. NDSEG Fellowships are awarded to applicants who will pursue doctoral degrees in an area of interest to the DoD. Among the areas of interest are aeronautical and astronautical engineering; chemical engineering; cognitive, neural, and behavioral sciences; and naval architecture and ocean engineering. For a complete list, check the program's Web site.

Benefits

The NDSEG Fellowship is a competitive, portable fellowship awarded to individuals for graduate study in one of fifteen supported disciplines. Awardees can attend any U.S. institution of choice. NDSEG Fellowships last for three years and pay for full tuition and mandatory fees, a monthly stipend, and up to $1,000 a year in medical insurance.

General Eligibility Requirements

According to the Web site, applicants must meet the following criteria:

- be U.S. citizens or nationals of the United States. The term "nationals" refers to native residents of a possession of the United States, such as American Samoa. It does not refer to citizens of another country who have applied for U.S. citizenship. Persons who hold permanent resident status are not eligible. Proof of citizenship will be required upon formal offer.
- be enrolled in an area of study that fits under one (or more) of the fifteen supported disciplines
- meet the academic-status requirements of the Fellowship program
- be enrolled at a U.S. institution in a full-time program leading to a graduate degree

Fellowships are awarded only to applicants who intend to pursue a doctoral degree. A student doesn't have to be accepted into a program at the time the application is submitted; however, should the applicant be selected, the award is contingent upon admission to a suitable program.

Application Process

The NDSEG application is an online process that requires the following:

- general GRE score from the last 5 years
- official transcripts from both undergraduate and graduate institutions
- contact information for at least three references
- a detailed CV
- contact information for supervisors of a student's research, leadership, community, and volunteer work

Deadline

Applications are due in early January.

For More Information

http://ndseg.asee.org/

NATIONAL INSTITUTES OF HEALTH UNDERGRADUATE SCHOLARSHIP PROGRAM

"The NIH, or the National Institutes of Health, is the world's largest biomedical research institution. NIH seeks to improve health by conducting research in its own laboratories and by funding the research of other scientists throughout the United States and around the world."

The National Institutes of Health (NIH) Undergraduate Scholarship Program (UGSP) offers competitive scholarships to students from disadvantaged backgrounds who are committed to careers in biomedical, behavioral, and social science health-related research. Fifteen scholarships are awarded each year.

Benefits

The benefits include both scholarship support and research training at NIH. The NIH UGSP will pay up to $20,000 per academic year in tuition, educational expenses, and reasonable living expenses to scholarship recipients. Scholarships are awarded for one year and can be renewed for up to four years.

For each full- or partial-scholarship year, recipients are committed to two NIH service obligations. The obligations themselves are benefits of the UGSP—providing invaluable research training and experience at the NIH. The first is the ten-week Summer Laboratory Experience. After each year of scholarship support, recipients train for ten weeks as paid summer research employees in an NIH research laboratory. This employment occurs after the receipt of the scholarship award. Each scholar will be assigned to an NIH researcher and an NIH postdoctoral fellow, who will serve as mentors. Recipients also attend formal seminars and participate in a variety of programs.

The second benefit/obligation is employment at NIH after graduation. Scholarship recipients continue their training as full-time employees in an NIH research laboratory. This is a one-year, full-time employment obligation for each year of scholarship funding.

General Eligibility Requirements

The NIH Undergraduate Scholarships are awarded on a competitive basis to students who show a commitment to pursuing careers in biomedical, behavioral, and social science health-related research. According to the program Web site, applicants must also meet the following basic requirements:

- be a U.S. citizen, national, or qualified noncitizen
- be enrolled or accepted for enrollment as a full-time student at an accredited four-year undergraduate institution

- be from a disadvantaged background, meaning that the financial aid office has certified the applicant as having "exceptional financial need"
- have a 3.5 GPA or higher (on a 4.0 scale) or be within the top 5 percent of the class

Application Process

Students are encouraged to apply online at https://ugsp.nih.gov. In addition to the online application, the NIH Web site contains detailed information on the UGSP.

Deadline

The applications are due the end of February.

For More Information

https://ugsp.nih.gov/overview_faqs/overview_faqs.asp?m=01&s=01

CHAPTER 4
A Selection of Access and Equity-Based Programs

Access and equity programs help people succeed in the U.S. educational system and in society. They are designed to provide the types of experiences that lead to success, such as opportunities for undergraduates to work closely with faculty on research projects or opportunities for young people to get experience in elite settings in business, industry, and government. That's the "access" part of the name for these programs.

These programs are often designed to help underrepresented groups gain exposure to experiences that will prepare them for success in environments where they may not have enough connections and/or resources of their own to facilitate that success. For this reason, many of these programs are restricted to certain groups, such as first-generation college students, people who live or grew up in low-income homes or areas, people from certain states, underrepresented groups, women interested in STEM (science, technology, engineering, and mathematics), veterans returning to civilian society, and even people who belong to certain faith traditions or who have certain sexual orientations. That's the "equity" part of the name for these programs.

> **Cross Pollination**
>
> Be sure to check out experiential opportunities that focus on access and equity in Chapter 5 such as the Washington Center or the Getty Museum Internship Program.

HOW THESE PROGRAMS BENEFIT RECIPIENTS

According to the research we've been reading, one of the heaviest burdens to overcome in this country is poverty. Poverty in the United States is multigenerational, pervasive, insidious, and resistant to intervention. Education is one of the best avenues out of multigenerational poverty. But low-income students beginning college are disadvantaged in ways that are significant and mostly invisible. There are things that many students take for granted that low-income students may not know. For example, it's better to withdraw from a class than to fail it; why it's important to take prerequisites before taking classes that require them; working too much in college means it will take longer and, ultimately, cost more to finish; study groups help all students, including the brightest and best-prepared, to do better in college; internships are critical to prepare for professional employment; it's possible to go to graduate school for free; and government-backed student loans are deferred while one is in graduate school. A good access and equity program guides students through the educational process, so that when it comes time to look for professional employment or to apply for a prestigious graduate program, "graduates" of these programs are highly successful.

IF YOU'RE NOT A CANDIDATE FOR ACCESS AND EQUITY PROGRAMS

We encourage *all* students to browse this chapter. If you're attracted to an access and equity program like the ones described in this chapter, but you don't qualify to apply, seek out similar programs that are not designed to support underrepresented students. There are plenty of undergraduate research programs, business internships, and summer research opportunities that all types of students can seek. Of course, students who qualify for these programs should also be vigorously applying for all those other programs as well.

Read the other chapters in this book to identify promising opportunities that match your qualifications. Be sure to talk to faculty and staff about opportunities that would be right for you! Find the scholarships and fellowships committees on your campus, and get them to help you build an exciting list of targets.

This chapter contains profiles on the following access and equity-based programs:

- AT&T Labs Fellowship Program
- The Carter G. Woodson Institute at the University of Virginia: Predoctoral and Postdoctoral Fellowships in African-American and African Studies
- Consortium of Graduate Study in Management Fellowship Program
- The Ford Foundation Predoctoral Diversity Fellowships
- Hispanic Scholarship Fund Scholarships
- INROADS
- The Posse Foundation
- La Unidad Latina Foundation Scholarship
- Leadership Alliance Summer Research Early Identification Program (SR-EIP)
- National Institute of General Medical Sciences Division of Minority Opportunities in Research (NIGMS-MORE)
- The PhD Project
- Project 1000
- CIC FreeApp

- Ronald E. McNair Postbaccalaureate Achievement Program (McNair Scholars Program)
- Society for Advancement of Chicanos and Native Americans in Science (SACNAS)
- Summer Research Opportunities Program (SROP)
- United Negro College Fund (UNCF)
- The William Randolph Hearst Endowed Fellowship for Minority Students
- Xerox Technical Minority Scholarship Program

AT&T LABS FELLOWSHIP PROGRAM

"The AFLP fellowship, in existence since 1972, was one of the first programs aimed at women and minorities underrepresented in sciences and technology. The completion rate is approximately 75 percent, making it one of the most successful fellowship programs."

The AT&T Labs Fellowship Program is a three-year fellowship program designed to provide support for underrepresented students in pursuing Ph.D. studies in computing and communications-related fields. AT&T Labs Fellows receive financial support for graduate school and participate in a research internship with AT&T Labs.

Benefits

AT&T Labs Fellows receive full financial support and mentoring for three years of doctoral study. The financial support includes tuition, books and fees, a living allowance, support for conference travel, and support for summer school. In addition, Fellows receive an internship at AT&T Labs Research after their first year of study.

General Eligibility Requirements

According to the program Web site, to be eligible, applicants must meet the following criteria:

- be a U.S. citizen or permanent resident
- be a female or member of a minority underrepresented in science fields (Hispanic, African American, or Native American)
- be a senior graduating in the current academic year or be in the first or second year of graduate school
- be currently enrolled, or planning to enroll, in a graduate school program leading to a Ph.D.

- major in computer science, math, statistics, electrical engineering, operations research, systems engineering, industrial engineering, or related fields

Application Procedure

Interested applicants must begin the process by filling out an application online. In addition to the online application, applicants must provide supplemental materials through regular mail. Completed applications include:

- an application form
- resume
- letters of recommendation
- personal statement
- official transcripts
- select standardized test scores

Deadline

Applications open annually in September and are due in January.

For More Information

http://www.research.att.com/internships

Cross Pollination

See also AT&T Labs Summer Internships, listed in Chapter 5.

THE CARTER G. WOODSON INSTITUTE AT THE UNIVERSITY OF VIRGINIA: PREDOCTORAL AND POSTDOCTORAL FELLOWSHIPS IN AFRICAN-AMERICAN AND AFRICAN STUDIES

"University of Virginia's Carter G. Woodson Institute for African-American and African Studies is named in honor of Carter Godwin Woodson. Born in 1875 in Buckingham County, Virginia, to parents who were formerly enslaved, Woodson went on to earn a Ph.D. in history at Harvard University in 1912, only the second African-American to receive a Harvard doctorate, his predecessor being the eminent scholar, W.E.B. DuBois." Woodson founded the Journal of African-American History and was instrumental in gaining recognition for Black History Month, first known as Negro History Week.

The Woodson Fellowships are designed to assist researchers who have completed all or a substantial proportion of their research and could benefit from institutional support for writing and dissemination of their ideas.

Benefits

The Predoctoral Fellowship is given for two years and has an annual stipend $20,000, plus health insurance. The Postdoctoral Fellowship is also for two years with an annual salary of $45,000, plus benefits.

General Eligibility Requirements

Candidates for the Woodson Fellowships may be citizens of any country and do not have to have any prior affiliation with the University of Virginia. The residency requirement should not be confused with a requirement to have attended the University of Virginia. Students who have attended any institution are eligible, but during the period of the award, they may be required to reside at the University of Virginia.

Applicants for the Predoctoral Fellowship must:

- have completed all requirements for the Ph.D. except the dissertation prior to August of the year of application
- be in residence at the University of Virginia for the duration of the award period

"Fellows are expected to participate in the series of workshops held during the academic year and to present their work periodically to the larger academic community. Fellows may accept no employment, fellowships, or consulting obligations during the Woodson fellowship period without the approval of the Director."

Applicants for the Postdoctoral Fellowship must:

- have been awarded their Ph.D. by the time of application or furnish proof from the relevant registrar that all documentation required for the Ph.D. has been submitted by mid-July in the year of application
- be in residence at the University of Virginia for the duration of the award period
- agree to teach one course per year in the African-American and African Studies program

"Woodson fellows are expected to participate in the series of workshops (about twice monthly) and to make at least one formal presentation of their work to the University community."

Deadline

The deadline for each of these Fellowships is December 1.

For More Information

http://artsandsciences.virginia.edu/woodson/fellowship

Consortium of Graduate Study in Management Fellowship Program

"The mission of The Consortium for Graduate Study in Management, an alliance of leading American business schools and some of our country's top corporations, is to enhance diversity in business education and leadership by helping to reduce the serious underrepresentation of African Americans, Hispanic Americans, and Native Americans in both our member schools' enrollments and the ranks of management."

The goal of The Consortium of Graduate Study in Management is to promote diversity in U.S. business. Each year, The Consortium holds a competition that awards merit-based, full-tuition fellowships to students who apply to and are accepted into The Consortium. These fellowships are for study at one of fifteen member higher education institutions. These member-institutions are among the top business schools in the United States. The list of member-institutions is available at http://www.cgsm.org/universities/index.asp.

Benefits

To be eligible to apply for The Consortium of Graduate Study in Management Fellowship Program, students must first apply to be members of The Consortium. To become a member, visit http://www.makeyourcareermove.com. Fellowship awards cover tuition and related fees. Additional benefits of Consortium membership include:

- a common application designed to save members time and money
- networking opportunities
- early access to corporate recruiters at an annual Orientation Program and Career Forum
- access to job postings at top companies through an online database

General Eligibility Requirements

According to The Consortium's requirements, students must:

- be a U.S. citizen or permanent resident
- demonstrate a commitment to The Consortium's mission
- hold a four-year bachelor's degree from an accredited college or university

Application Process

Students who apply through The Consortium common application are applying for three key decisions. They include:

- membership in The Consortium
- acceptance into The Consortium-member business schools
- a two-year fellowship that covers tuition and fees
- tiered application fees

Deadline

The early application deadline is annually in November. The traditional application deadline is annually in January.

For More Information

http://www.makeyourcareermove.com

THE FORD FOUNDATION PREDOCTORAL DIVERSITY FELLOWSHIPS

The purpose of the Ford Foundation Predoctoral Diversity Fellowships is ". . . to increase the diversity of the nation's college and university faculties by increasing their ethnic and racial diversity, to maximize the educational benefits of diversity, and to increase the number of professors who can and will use diversity as a resource for enriching the education of all students."

The National Academies administer the Ford Foundation Predoctoral Diversity Fellowships. Each year, approximately sixty awards are granted to applicants who are entering or have recently started Ph.D. programs at accredited U.S. institutions of higher education.

Benefits

Predoctoral Fellowships provide $20,000 per year for up to three years. Ford Fellows also may have their tuition and fees waived because the Ford Foundation provides the institution a $2,000 payment ". . .in lieu of tuition and fees." Ford Fellows receive funding to attend one Conference of Ford Fellows, which provides networking and career-development opportunities.

General Eligibility Requirements

According to the Web site, applicants must meet the following criteria:

- be committed to pursuing a Ph.D. or Sc.D. degree that leads to a career in teaching and/or research
- be a U.S. citizen or U.S. national
- demonstrate an outstanding academic record
- not already holding a terminal degree

The selection committee will view as positive the following:

- membership in an underrepresented group
- the ability to integrate the "diversity of the human experience" into pedagogy and research interests
- have "sustained personal engagement with communities that are underrepresented in the academy and an ability to bring this asset to learning, teaching, and scholarship at the college and university level"

Application Process

Applicants must begin by filling out an online application. Materials required to complete the application include:

- a personal statement
- a description of previous research
- essay describing future educational plans and career plans
- four reference letters from professors

Deadline

Applications are usually due annually in the middle of November.

For More Information

http://www7.nationalacademies.org/FORDfellowships

HISPANIC SCHOLARSHIP FUND SCHOLARSHIPS

The Hispanic Scholarship Fund (HSF) supports a successful path for Latinos to attain a college degree—creating an increasingly valuable asset for a stronger, more competitive nation in the twenty-first century.

The Hispanic Scholarship Fund's (HSF) mission is to strengthen the nation by advancing the college education of Hispanic Americans. HSF delivers a range of programs to Hispanic families and students through community outreach and education, scholarships, college retention, and career opportunities. Since its inception, the HSF has awarded over $300 million and close to 100,000 scholarships to students in need.

Benefits

Benefits vary according to each of the opportunities supported by the HSF:

- College Scholarship Programs: http://www.hsf.net/innerContent.aspx?id=424
- Community College Transfer Scholarship Programs: http://www.hsf.net/innerContent.aspx?id=428
- Gates Millennium Scholars (GMS): http://www.gmsp.org/
- Scholarship Programs for Graduating High School Seniors: http://www.hsf.net/innercontent.aspx?id=426
- University Alliance Scholarship Programs: http://www.hsf.net/innercontent.aspx?id=434

General Eligibility Requirements

According to the Web site, applicants for the various scholarships must meet the following criteria:

- have a minimum 3.0 cumulative GPA on a 4.0 scale (or the equivalent)
- be a U.S. citizen or legal permanent resident with a valid permanent resident card or passport stamped I-551
- be pursuing or plan to pursue a first undergraduate or graduate degree
- apply for federal financial aid using the Free Application for Federal Student Aid (FAFSA)
- plan to enroll full-time as an undergraduate or graduate student in a degree-granting program at a U.S.-accredited institution in the United States, Puerto Rico, U.S. Virgin Islands, or Guam in the upcoming academic year

Application Process

Each opportunity has its own application materials and process, but all opportunities require an online application that can be found at https://apply.hsf.net/applications/.

Deadline

Deadlines vary according to the opportunity.

For More Information

http://www.hsf.net/

INROADS

"The mission of INROADS is to develop and place talented minority youth in business and industry and prepare them for corporate and community leadership."

INROADS provides underrepresented youth access to career-related professional paid internships, the type of experience that is necessary to launch a professional career after graduation from college. By providing the skills, support, and network that students need to obtain an internship at a top company, INROADS prepares students to lead and contribute from day 1 of their employment. INROADS can deliver a life-launching experience and pay students while they gain it.

INROADS is more than a summer internship program. It requires a multiyear commitment to prepare for success and leadership, with mentoring processes that go on year-round. Attendance at regularly scheduled INROADS training and coaching sessions is mandatory.

Benefits

INROADS offers the following:

- a paid, multiyear internship with a top company
- customized skills-development training
- unparalleled networking opportunities with career-minded peers, corporate executives, and INROADS alumni
- community involvement
- year-round professional and personal coaching and guidance from an INROADS advisor
- a corporate mentor who will take a personal interest
- access and advising for scholarship opportunities

- free tutoring
- potential for a full-time career after graduation

According to its Web site, "With INROADS, you can literally walk from the classroom to the boardroom with the confidence and experience you need to succeed."

General Eligibility Requirements

INROADS is for high-performing minority students, "only the best and the brightest are selected." Applicants must meet the following qualifications:

- be a graduating high school senior or college or university freshman or sophomore
- have a GPA of 3.0 or better
- have a combined SAT score of 1000 or ACT score of 20 or better
- demonstrate leadership ability
- indicate an interest in pursuing a bachelor's degree in business, accounting, actuarial science, engineering, computer and information sciences, sales, marketing, allied health, health-care management, or retail store management

Application Process

The process begins with submission of an online application that includes a resume in compliance with INROADS' specific instructions. Applicants then have to pass a telephone screening and participate in mandatory program training *before* they can interview with potential corporate sponsors.

Deadline

Applications are due by March 31.

For More Information

http://www.inroads.org/

Cross Pollination

See also the profile on the Xerox College Experiential Learning Programs (XCEL) in Chapter 5.

THE POSSE FOUNDATION

"The Posse Foundation has identified, recruited and trained thousands of public high school students with extraordinary academic and leadership potential to become Posse Scholars. These students— many of whom might have been overlooked by traditional college selection processes—receive four-year, full-tuition leadership scholarships from Posse's partner institutions of higher education."

The Posse Foundation was formed when founder Deborah Bial noticed that unusually high numbers of talented underrepresented students were dropping out of college in spite of being academically prepared. She asked them why they didn't thrive at college, and one student replied, "If I only had my posse with me, I never would have dropped out." Thus was born the idea that underrepresented students could be sent in a cohort group to elite colleges and universities, so they would have friends with them every step of the way to support and encourage them.

> **Best-Kept Secret!**
> A high school student can nominate himself or herself to be a Posse Scholar.

Posse Scholars report that there is tremendous group cohesion in being a Posse Scholar and a great sense of responsibility to the group. A Posse Scholar who begins college as a freshman has a 90 percent chance of graduating.

Posse Scholars are selected to join groups of 10 to attend specific colleges and universities. Posse Scholars are selected individually using the Dynamic Assessment Process, a technique that looks at more than grades and scores. Evidence of leadership, drive, and special talents of all sorts are considered in the Posse selection process. Most colleges and universities do not have the time, or the means, to assess these personal attributes.

Benefits

Posse Scholars receive full-tuition scholarships. They have dedicated academic counselors and tutors on campus and access to a dedicated Career Program to help them get internships and jobs. All Posse Scholars participate in an eight-month Pre-Collegiate Training Program, and they have a graduation rate of 90 percent.

General Eligibility Requirements

At this time, public high school seniors who live in Atlanta, Boston, Chicago, Los Angeles, Miami, New York City, and Washington, DC are eligible to become Posse Scholars. Scholars have also been chosen from parochial and private high schools, on occasion.

For More Information

http://www.possefoundation.org

Cross Pollination

If the Posse program is of interest to you, check out the Harlem Children's Zone, a pre-college program; Making Waves Education Program in California; and Say Yes to Education Program in Syracuse, New York.

LA UNIDAD LATINA FOUNDATION SCHOLARSHIP

The La Unidad Latina Foundation was established in 1999 to serve as an independent, non-profit, charitable organization dedicated to educational achievement and civic empowerment in the Latino community.

The objectives of the La Unidad Latina Foundation are:

- to award scholarships and grants to worthy and needy Latino students for the pursuit of higher education
- to encourage participation of Latinos in educational programs and activities
- to support community programs that aid in the civic empowerment and educational improvement of the Latino community

Benefits

Educational scholarships are awarded to Hispanic students on a competitive basis and range from $250 to $1,000.

General Eligibility Requirements

According to the Web site, applicants must meet the following criteria:

- have a cumulative GPA of 2.80 to 3.60 on a 4.0 scale as an undergraduate
- be currently enrolled in an eligible bachelor- or master's-degree program at an accredited four-year college or university. Eligible degrees include all bachelor degrees, Master of Arts, Master of Science, Master of Public Administration/Policy, Master of Social Work, Master of Education, and Master of Divinity.

- have completed at least one full-time year of study for undergraduate applicants and at least one full-time semester of study for graduate applicants
- reside in the United States

Application Process

Applications must include:

- official university-issued academic transcript(s)
- a letter of recommendation of 200 to 350 words from a university administrator/faculty or community leader demonstrating student leadership and commitment to civic service

Graduate students are required to submit graduate and undergraduate transcripts.

Deadline

Deadline is January 1 or September 1, depending on the start date of the program. Applications are only accepted within a 45-day period prior to the deadline.

For More Information

http://www.lulfoundation.org/

LEADERSHIP ALLIANCE SUMMER RESEARCH-EARLY IDENTIFICATION PROGRAM (SR-EIP)

The Summer Research-Early Identification Program (SR-EIP) is designed to encourage students from traditionally underrepresented groups in the sciences, social sciences, and humanities to consider research careers in the academic, public, or private sectors.

The Leadership Alliance Summer Research-Early Identification Program (SR-EIP) offers undergraduates interested in pursuing a Ph.D. or M.D./Ph.D. the opportunity to work for eight to ten weeks under the guidance of a faculty or research mentor at a participating Alliance institution. Through this one-on-one collaboration, students gain theoretical knowledge and practical training in academic research and scientific experimentation. Students submit a written report and make a presentation at the end of their summer research experience. All participants are expected to make an oral or poster presentation at the Alliance's Annual National Symposium. Alliance members include over thirty highly distinguished institutions, ranging from the Ivy League to HBCUs (Historically Black Colleges and Universities).

General Eligibility Requirements

According to the Web site, applicants must meet the following criteria:

- be in good academic standing with a GPA of 3.0 or better
- have completed at least two semesters and have at least one semester remaining of their undergraduate education by the start of the summer program
- demonstrated interest and potential to pursue graduate study
- be a U.S. citizen or permanent resident
- attend an accredited public or private college or university in the United States or its territories, as recognized by the U.S. Department of Education

Application Process

Applicants are required to provide:

- an online application
- transcripts
- letters of recommendation

Deadline

The deadline is in early February of each year.

For More Information

http://www.theleadershipalliance.org

NATIONAL INSTITUTE OF GENERAL MEDICAL SCIENCES DIVISION OF MINORITY OPPORTUNITIES IN RESEARCH (NIGMS-MORE)

The National Institute of General Medical Sciences (NIGMS), part of the vast complex that comprises the National Institutes of Health, administers several programs that are in fact more famous than the NIGMS itself. The NIH has as alphabet soup of acronyms, but these highly valuable programs are well-worth exploring.

NIGMS-MORE programs are administered at the campus level through multiyear grants. Students interested in these programs need to first discover whether the university they attend has these programs on campus.

- **Minority Access to Research Careers (MARC)**

  The MARC program provides selected undergraduates with mentoring and tutoring in scientific research. MARC scholars are directly involved in original research under the supervision of senior research faculty. MARC scholars are expected to continue their studies at the graduate level, usually pursuing the Ph.D. (MARC is somewhat similar to the McNair Program, which is also described in this chapter.)

- **Minority Biomedical Research Support (MBRS)**

  Similar to MARC, MBRS has three programs to support undergraduate exposure to research careers:

  1. Research Initiative for Scientific Enhancement (RISE) Program
  2. Initiative for Maximizing Student Development (IMSD) Program
  3. Support of Competitive Research (SCORE) Program

- **Annual Biomedical Research Conference for Minority Students (ABRCMS)**

  ABRCMS (pronounced "abbercams") is a program of the American Society for Microbiology (ASM). Scholars in MARC, MBRS, RISE, IMSD, and SCORE are invited to present their research at this conference.

General Eligibility Requirements

MORE "seeks to increase the number of highly-trained underrepresented biomedical and behavioral scientists in leadership positions to significantly impact the health-related research needs of the nation. Nationally, groups found to be underrepresented in biomedical and behavioral research include, but are not limited to, African Americans, Hispanic Americans, Native Americans, Alaska Natives, and natives of the U.S. Pacific Islands."

For More Information

For NIGMS and MORE programs, see http://www.nigms.nih.gov/Minority.

For ABRCMS, see http://www.abrcms.org/index.html.

There are many more NIH programs for minorities, including Minority International Research Training (MIRT), which is administered by the NIH-funded Fogarty International Center. The best way to find more programs is to ask faculty about NIH funding or explore www.nih.gov.

For more NIH programming without a specific minority focus, see http://www.nsfgrfp.org and http://grants.nih.gov/grants/oer.htm.

Cross Pollination

See also the entry for National Institutes of Health Internships in Chapter 5.

THE PHD PROJECT

The PhD Project is committed to increasing the diversity of business school faculty. "The PhD Project has more than tripled the number of minority business school professors" since its inception.

The PhD Project was established in 1994 to increase the number of minority faculty in business schools. The program provides mentoring and support for underrepresented students considering the doctorate in business. The Project is interested in working with students at any stage in their process, from initially considering graduate education in business, to applying to graduate programs, to making the leap from the MBA to doctoral status, to completing the doctorate and getting that first faculty job as a professor of business.

All focus areas are supported, such as management science, leadership, marketing, accounting, finance, technology management, logistics, international business, entrepreneurship, etc. The PhD Project sponsors Minority Doctoral Students Associations (DSAs) in these five major areas of business education: Accounting, Finance, Information Systems, Management, and Marketing.

The PhD Project encourages accomplished businesspeople of color to consider an academic career. They point out that even if a person has had many, many years of experience in industry, the doctorate in business can be an excellent career choice. At the other end of the experience range, for those students interested in a career in research and academe, it is possible to go into a graduate business program straight from an undergraduate program.

Whether you have years of experience or none, if you want to test your interest in the doctorate, the PhD Project recommends the one-year predoctoral intensive program offered by New York University's Stern School of Business.

General Eligibility Requirements

According to the Web site, "[T]he PhD Project is available to anyone of African-American, Hispanic American and Native American descent who is interested in business doctoral studies."

For More Information

http://www.phdproject.org

PROJECT 1000

Project 1000 helps Hispanic and other underrepresented students apply to graduate programs in the STEM disciplines (science, technology, engineering, and math). Project 1000 helps pay for test and application fees and has developed a common application system for STEM applicants.

Project 1000 is a program effort of Arizona State University's (ASU) Hispanic Research Center, ASU's Coalition to Increase Minority Degrees (CIMD), and the Center for Cost-Effective Interactive Learning Excellence (CCILE). It was originally launched to create 1,000 new graduate students of color, especially Hispanic students. It reached that milestone long ago and is now dedicated to generating another 5,000 STEM graduate students.

Benefits

Project 1000 allows a student to apply to seven graduate schools with one common application for free. More than eighty graduate schools and programs participate in Project 1000.

Warning

Some Project 1000 participating institutions require a supplemental essay explaining why the student is interested in that specific program and that specific institution, so the common application feature should not distract students from doing adequate research on the different policies of each institution that he or she applies to.

Eligibility

The focus of Project 1000 is Latino/a students, but eligibility is on a case-by-case basis and starts with a telephone conversation with a Project 1000 counselor. Project 1000 counselors are bilingual, Spanish-English.

For More Information

Call the bilingual Project 1000 academic advisers (toll free) at (800) 327-4893, 9 to 5 Mountain time.

For Project 1000 info, see http://mati.eas.asu.edu/p1000.

For ASU's Coalition to Increase Minority Degrees, see http://mati.eas.asu.edu:8421.

Cross Pollination

Hispanic students interested in Project 1000 should also investigate La Unidad Latina Foundation Scholarship and Hispanic Scholarship Fund Scholarships in this chapter.

CIC FreeApp

CIC is the Committee on Institutional Cooperation, a coalition of Big Ten schools and select affiliated Midwestern universities focused on academic matters of common interest.

CIC FreeApp is a free graduate school application process for students interested in a terminal degree, normally defined as either the Ph.D. or the M.F.A. (Master of Fine Arts). The program is designed to increase the diversity of graduate students and graduate-degree holders at CIC-member institutions. Somewhat similar to the Project1000 program, FreeApp allows a student to apply to a large number of member institutions, all in the same geographical range of the United States, without cost. FreeApp Member Institutions include:

- University of Chicago
- University of Illinois at Chicago
- University of Illinois at Urbana-Champaign
- Indiana University
- Indiana University/Purdue University at Indianapolis
- University of Iowa
- University of Michigan
- Michigan State University
- University of Minnesota
- Northwestern University
- Ohio State University
- Pennsylvania State University
- Purdue University
- University of Wisconsin-Milwaukee

(Note that the list of FreeApp member institutions is not identical to a list of the Big Ten.)

General Eligibility Requirements

All members of underrepresented groups can use FreeApp. "The program seeks to increase graduate school access for students from groups underrepresented in graduate education, including minority students, first-generation college students, and students from low-income families, regardless of race or ethnicity."

You do not need to be *from* a CIC campus to apply *to* a CIC campus using FreeApp.

Application Procedure

Unfortunately, FreeApp members apply criteria for inclusion and participation on an institutional basis, so you should reach out to the FreeApp coordinator at each campus to be sure that you qualify for this valuable service. For a list of coordinators at each campus, go to http://www.cic.net/db/memDisp1.asp?id=270.

For More Information

General information on CIC: http://www.cic.net/Home.aspx.

General information on FreeApp: http://www.cic.net/Home/Students/FreeApp/Introduction.aspx.

RONALD E. McNAIR POSTBACCALAUREATE ACHIEVEMENT PROGRAM (McNAIR SCHOLARS PROGRAM)

Ronald E. McNair was one of thirty-five out of 10,000 applicants selected for NASA's space program in 1977. He was the second African American to fly in space and died tragically in the 1986 Challenger explosion.

The McNair Scholars Program, named in honor of Ronald E. McNair, is designed to assist first-generation, low-income, and minority undergraduate students with effective preparation for doctoral-level education. The goal of the program is to produce terminal-degree holders who will accept faculty positions at institutions of higher education.

The McNair Scholars Program is housed at approximately 200 higher education institutions in the United States. To participate, students must attend one of these institutions, meet the eligibility requirements listed below, and be accepted into the program at the host institution. For information about schools hosting McNair Scholars Programs, contact the Council for Opportunity in Education (COE) at (202) 347-7430.

Benefits

The primary benefit of participating in the McNair Scholars Program is working with a faculty mentor on research. Stipends are paid to students as they engage in research. Students also receive significant coaching and assistance in applying for admission into graduate-level education as well as assistance in preparing for the Graduate Records Examination (GRE).

General Eligibility Requirements

To qualify for the McNair Scholars Program, a student must be either:

- a member of a group underrepresented in his or her field or discipline

or

- a first-generation college student (parents do not hold a bachelor's degree) and have documented economic need

Typically, selected Scholars are motivated students with a strong academic record and a willingness to explore research and teaching as a career option.

Application Process

The application process differs for each host institution's program. Generally, prospective applicants fill out an application form and then go through a selection process that may entail interviews.

Deadline

Enrollment processes and deadlines vary by institution.

For More Information

Find out if your campus has a McNair Scholars Program, or look for information at www.coenet.us.

SOCIETY FOR ADVANCEMENT OF CHICANOS AND NATIVE AMERICANS IN SCIENCE (SACNAS)

SACNAS is both an advocacy group and a service provider, supporting the aspirations of Chicanos and Native Americans in STEM disciplines (Science, Technology, Engineering, and Math). SACNAS has over 23,000 members, affiliates, and partners "from a diversity of disciplines, institutions, ethnic backgrounds, and levels along the educational trajectory."

SACNAS is a unique organization "committed to encouraging minority students and scientists to advance to their utmost capability . . . and to engage in science research and leadership of the highest caliber."

SACNAS programs include the following:

- **Summer Leadership Institute (SLI) and Conference Leadership Workshops**
  SACNAS leadership development is intensive preparation for underrepresented minority (URM) scholars who wish to become leaders in their science communities. Participants learn about a range of career paths, doctoral/postdoctoral education options, leadership styles, the importance of persuasion and influence, professionalism, and networking.

- **Pre-College Teacher Training**
  SACNAS has specialized programs for K–12 instructors to learn the history of the scientific contributions of Chicano, Latino, and Native American scientists, mathematicians, and engineers, as well as techniques to make science come alive in the classroom.

- **Science Policy and Advocacy**
  The organization has the specific goal of influencing national, state, and institutional policy to "inform and advocate for public policies and governmental funding that advance our mission: fostering the success of Hispanic/Chicano and Native American scientists—from college students to professionals."

- **National Conference**
  This conference provides an unparalleled opportunity for scholars to present their research, learn about their disciplines, gain mentoring, and prepare for a career in leadership in science.

General Eligibility Requirements

Anyone who supports the mission of SACNAS can join. Students, faculty, staff, and members of the science community at large are typical members. SACNAS is a diverse community "from all educational and career stages; all fields of science, mathematics, and engineering; and all ethnic backgrounds, genders, and sexual orientations." Students can join for free.

For More Information

http://www.sacnas.org.

SUMMER RESEARCH OPPORTUNITIES PROGRAM (SROP)

"Headquartered in the Midwest, the Committee on Institutional Cooperation (CIC) is a consortium of the Big Ten universities—Universities of Illinois, Indiana, Iowa, Michigan, Minnesota, Wisconsin; Michigan State University; Northwestern University; Ohio State University, Penn State University, and Purdue University—plus the University of Chicago. For half a century, these 12 world-class research institutions have advanced their academic missions, generated unique opportunities for students and faculty, and served the common good by sharing expertise, leveraging campus resources, and collaborating on innovative programs."

The Summer Research Opportunities Program (SROP) is sponsored by the Committee on Institutional Cooperation (CIC). This program is designed to provide undergraduate students from underrepresented backgrounds a rigorous summer research experience. Students are matched with a faculty mentor and provided other enrichment activities in order to prepare them to be successful doctoral program applicants. The program is a gateway to doctoral education at CIC-member universities. Since its inception, the SROP program has provided over 11,000 research experiences for underrepresented students.

Benefits

Participant benefits depend on which CIC institutional member participants apply to for research. Benefits include a living stipend that ranges from $3,000 to $6,000. Institutions may also provide student housing, meals, and travel expenses.

General Eligibility Requirements

Based on the program's requirements, students must:

- have a cumulative GPA of 3.0 or higher (4.0 scale)
- be a citizen or a permanent resident of the United States
- be enrolled in a degree-granting program at a college or university in the United States or Puerto Rico or other U.S. territory
- have completed at least two semesters of undergraduate education
- have at least one semester of undergraduate education remaining after completing the program
- have a strong interest in pursuing a Ph.D.

Application Procedure

Interested applicants must begin the process by filling out an application online. In addition to the online application, applicants must provide:

- academic transcripts
- letters of recommendation

Deadline

Applications open annually in November and close in February.

For More Information

http://www.cic.net/Home/Students/SROP/Home.aspx

UNITED NEGRO COLLEGE FUND (UNCF)

The United Negro College Fund is one of the most highly regarded scholarship funds in the United States. The UNCF coined one of the most effective tag lines in the history of advertising: "A mind is a terrible thing to waste."

The United Negro College Fund (UNCF) does far more than collect funds and administer scholarship programs. The UNCF is, in fact, a broad-ranging advocacy group for the improvement of access to higher education and the paths to success for people of color. Every African American student should approach the UNCF for funding but also to explore some of its other world-class programming.

UNCF is a clearinghouse, or portal, for the following programs:

- over 400 Scholarship and Fellowship Programs, supporting individual students at the undergraduate, graduate, and doctoral levels
- Corporate Scholars Program, supporting students with scholarships and internships at Fortune 500 corporations
- Gates Millennium Scholars Program, supporting high-achieving students from undergraduate through doctoral studies
- UNCF-Merck Science Initiative (UMSI), offering undergraduate, graduate, and postdoctoral students funding, mentoring, and research opportunities in bioscience and biotechnology research
- Institute for Capacity Building, supporting the thirty-nine UNCF-member private historically black colleges and universities in institutional development and advancement

- Frederick D. Patterson Research Institute, an educational research and advocacy group exploring public policy and the African American experience of education

Although much of the work of the UNCF is structural and policy-level, individual students can apply for specific scholarships through the organization's online application service. Additional funding is available for students attending member institutions, a collection of the most elite Historically Black Colleges and Universities (HBCUs) in the United States. A list of member institutions is available on the Fund's Web site.

For More Information

http://www.uncf.org/ForStudents/index.asp

Cross Pollination

If you're Native American, see The American Indian College Fund at www.collegefund.org, The American Indian Graduate Center at http://www.aigc.com (which has scholarships for graduate students *and* undergraduates), and the American Indian Education Foundation at http://www.nrcprograms.org/site/PageServer?pagename=aief_index.

THE WILLIAM RANDOLPH HEARST ENDOWED FELLOWSHIP FOR MINORITY STUDENTS

The Aspen Institute, sponsor of the Hearst Endowed Fellowship for Minority Students, has a two-fold mission: (1) to foster values-based leadership, encouraging individuals to reflect on the ideals and ideas that define a good society, and (2) to provide a neutral and balanced venue for discussing and acting on critical issues.

Three times a year, The Aspen Institute Program on Philanthropy and Social Innovation (PSI) offers the William Randolph Hearst Endowed Fellowship for Minority Students. The fellowship, available to both undergraduate- and graduate-level students of color, provides a valuable internship experience in philanthropy, social enterprise, nonprofit organizations, and other related areas.

Benefits

Hearst Fellows who participate in fall or spring internships receive a $2,000 grant. Hearst Fellows who participate in a summer internship receive a $4,000 grant.

General Eligibility Requirements

According to the Aspen Institute, to be eligible, applicants must meet the following criteria:

- be highly motivated, current, nongraduating graduate or undergraduate students from underrepresented communities of color
- have an excellent academic record
- demonstrate interest or experience in nonprofit organizations, philanthropy, and the social sector
- have excellent research and writing skills
- demonstrate financial need
- be U.S. citizens or U.S. permanent residents

Application Procedure

Interested applicants must mail the following to the Aspen Institute in Washington, DC:

- a letter of interest
- resume
- official transcripts
- documentation from home institution's financial aid office indicating financial need
- two letters of recommendation

Deadline

There are three deadlines each year based on the desired start date of the internship. Please see program Web site for exact deadlines.

For More Information

http://www.aspeninstitute.org/policy-work/nonprofit-philanthropy/leadership-initiatives/hearst

Xerox Technical Minority Scholarship Program

Xerox is a Fortune 500 specialized technology company based in Rochester, New York. In a recent year, it won approval for over 584 U.S. patents.

The Xerox Technical Minority Scholarships are available to graduate or undergraduate students, from freshman through postdoctoral level. Applicants don't have to have career aspirations or prior internships with Xerox in order to be selected for this scholarship.

Benefits

Scholarships range from $1,000 to $10,000.

General Eligibility Requirements

According to the Web site, applicants must meet the following criteria:

- have a GPA of 3.0 or better
- be U.S. citizens or visa-holding permanent residents
- be African American, Asian, Pacific Island, Native American, Native Alaskan, or Hispanic descent
- be enrolled full-time as an undergraduate or a graduate student at any U.S. university in any of the following technical fields: chemistry, information management, computing and software systems, material science, printing management science, laser optics, physics, engineering (chemical, computer, electrical, imaging, manufacturing, mechanical, optical, or software)

Application Procedure

Applicants must provide:

- resume
- cover letter
- application form, which can be downloaded from the Xerox Web site

Deadline

Applications must be postmarked prior to September 30.

For More Information

http://www.xeroxstudentcareers.com/why-xerox/scholarship.aspx

Cross Pollination

Please note that Xerox has other scholarships listed on its main Web site. Also note Xerox's internship program, the Xerox College Experiential Learning Programs (XCEL), in Chapter 5.

CHAPTER 5
A Selection of Top Internships and Experiential Opportunities

Internships and on-campus leadership opportunities used to be called extracurricular opportunities. They have now been elevated to "cocurricular" opportunities and are an important part of your educational planning and educational advancement. Whether you want to be a musician, college professor, scion of business, artist, or politician, you are *expected* to complete internships as part of your undergraduate experience. Your excellent academic record alone may not get you to your goals. If you are interested in an academic or science career, you are *expected* to get involved in research at the undergraduate level or in a postbaccalaureate experience. If you are interested in elite scholarships and fellowships like the ones described in this book, you may be *expected* to have volunteer and service opportunities either during your undergraduate experiences or after college and before graduate school.

IF YOU NEED TO EARN MONEY DURING SUMMERS

If you need to earn money during your summers to afford your college expenses, there are five solutions to this:

1. Find internships and experiential programs that pay. Increasingly, companies are choosing to pay interns rather than risk misclassifying them and owing back wages and taxes.

2. Check with your dean's office and career center to see if your school has income replacement funds for students who pursue unpaid internships.

3. Hold a part-time job in addition to your experiential program.

4. Participate in part-time experiential programs during the school year and work full-time in the summer.

5. Work nights and do your experiential program during the day, and give up some sleep.

The fact that you need to earn money for your educational expenses in no way excuses you from the necessity of getting these types of experiences worked into your undergraduate program.

PLANNING YOUR EXPERIENTIAL OPPORTUNITIES

The following is the preferred formula for integrating experiential opportunities into your academic life:

- First summer: travel, language-intensive program, service/volunteer/leadership experience, any old summer job, or a career-related internship
- Second summer: a career-related internship or a leadership experience
- Third summer: a career-related internship or, if you're going straight to graduate school, you have the option of going to summer school at one of your targeted universities

The Summer Between Freshman and Sophomore Years

Your first summer in college, the one between freshman and sophomore years, can be spent in a wider range of options. You can spend that summer traveling abroad; attending a language-intensive program; pursuing a service, volunteer, or leadership experience; or on a career-related internship. You can even have a meaningless job if that's your preference.

The Summer Between Sophomore and Junior Years

What should you do with the middle summer, the summer between sophomore and junior years? You should spend it in a career-preparatory experiential opportunity. The expectation now is *two* significant internships, rather than just one. Besides, suppose you spend your final summer in a law firm, and discover that you would rather die than become an attorney? If that's your last summer, you've certainly made an important discovery, but it's too late to do anything about it. So by having your first big internship in the middle summer, you can correct a potential mistake in career direction.

If you're highly confident of your career direction, you can spend that middle summer on a significant leadership experience, something that will build maturity, confidence, and leadership skills.

> **Planning Counts**
> Although you can always put together some kind of internship—even at the last moment—you should note that the most competitive opportunities accept resumes beginning in the late fall and over winter break and conduct interviews and select interns as early as February and March.

The Summer Between Junior and Senior Years

The summer before your senior year is an absolutely critical summer for setting up your success after college. Pursuing experiential programs is a fundamental part of preparing for lifelong success and getting the most out of your education. You should have an experience this last summer that supports your career or graduate school goals. The value of your education is endangered if you spend this critical summer goofing off or working in a meaningless job. This summer should be designed by you and your most trusted advisers long before spring of the junior year.

If you're headed for law school, this is a great summer to work for a law firm. If you're headed to graduate school in the sciences, this is a great summer to work in a lab as a research assistant. If you're headed to medical school, you should spend this summer in some type of clinical setting. If you're going to look for a job with a major corporate employer, you need to spend this summer in an internship with that kind of employer. Note that some industries only hire people for permanent jobs who have been interns in the past. Film, television, radio, fashion, engineering, Wall Street, and politics are industries that heavily favor hiring former interns.

For students headed *directly* to graduate school after college, it is all right to pursue summer classes at one of your top-choice universities. Show focus and take classes in the discipline that you plan to pursue upon entering graduate school. By the way, don't overload yourself. Summer classes can be intensive and relentless. Your good grades in the department will be a significant advantage in applying to that graduate school or any similar one.

Postbaccalaureate Internships

If you graduate without the right experiential preparation to go into the field you most want to pursue, there are postbaccalaureate internships you can pursue after graduation. You will find that some of the experiences described in this chapter are for graduates. These programs fit the needs of students headed to law school, to graduate programs in areas such as public policy or international relations, or to careers in government service.

By the way, you can pursue many types of internships and shadowing experiences all year long, not just in the summer. But most of the programs described in this chapter are intense, summer opportunities.

TYPES OF EXPERIENTIAL OPPORTUNITIES

This chapter describes four types of experiential programs: undergraduate research, business, service, and leadership. Each category is not for everyone. You may be attracted to only one, or at most two, but every reader needs to consider these programs as preparation for success with later scholarships, fellowships, graduate programs, and elite jobs.

Research Programs

These programs provide opportunities to learn research methodology and to gain deeper understanding of a specific discipline (whether it is archaeology, biochemistry, historical preservation, or whatever interests you). Undergraduate research experiences used to be the narrow province of those headed to laboratory-science careers. Now any serious student can find an undergraduate research opportunity, no matter the discipline. Incidentally, the National Science Foundation (NSF) recently changed the rules for Research Experiences for Undergraduates (REUs), and they are now available to students in all disciplines. You might ask any faculty member to sponsor you. Your campus undergraduate research program director (URPD) can support you and your faculty member in applying for these programs. Many faculty and departments outside the sciences do not yet know that there is significant new funding available to support undergraduate research assistants.

Business Programs

The right corporate internship can change your life forever. If you want to work on Wall Street, get on the management track in a technology company, or learn whether you have what it takes for international sales, a summer internship with a major corporate employer is the first step. Recruiters who hire college graduates for full-time, permanent jobs upon graduation will expect you to have had summer internships prior to graduating. If no one in your family has ever worked in a professional position for a major corporation, one internship can set you up for a very different future.

Service Programs

Service programs are great for students who are seeking a structured experience during summers or after graduation. Habitat for Humanity, Alternative Spring Break (ASB) service programs, and similar opportunities are available to students during their academic programs. If you want a meaningful experience to bridge the time between college and either graduate school or entry into the so-called "real world," a service opportunity can be a great choice. Besides, there is no better time in a person's life to give back than just after college, after one acquires useful skills, but before a mortgage, marriage, and children enter the picture. Many of these postbaccalaureate programs have excellent reentry programs to smooth your return from the program to graduate school or a career. You'll be more mature, and, in some cases, you'll have a significant lump-sum payout to pay for grad school or to lighten your existing student loans.

Leadership Programs

Developing your leadership and organizational skills is great preparation for certain types of careers, such as government service, law, diplomacy, public administration, city planning, and international development. The programs in this section are foundational experiences for students interested in these areas and are a great experience for those wanting to understand how our government and world systems work and to improve their ability to effect change.

GETTING THE MOST OUT OF YOUR EXPERIENCE

There are some bad internships out there; they exploit young people and offer them no benefit in return. When you're looking at experiential opportunities like the ones in this chapter, ask yourself and the program representatives, "What are the learning objectives of this opportunity?" You should have the chance to learn new skills and to apply existing ones to real projects. If you don't see a learning opportunity, then don't go into the program.

A very attractive aspect of some internships is the opportunity to rotate through different departments. This is not as common as it used to be, but a rotational program allows a young person the opportunity to gain exposure to different departments and functions and to identify where he or she would be most happy, challenged, and engaged. So, ask if the program has a rotation feature.

Also, it's a benefit to a young person to have a work product at the end of the experience, some accomplishment or completed project, study, report, or plan that can be talked about with or presented to the next employer.

For career-preparatory internships, you will want to leave the internship with a job offer. Even if you decline it, you want to get the offer because for the rest of your career, hiring managers will ask you whether you did or did not get a permanent job offer.

Finally, no matter what kind of experience you have, you ask your immediate supervisor for a letter of recommendation—before the experience is over. Never leave an experiential program without at least asking, firmly, for a letter of recommendation that you can show to future employers. This is different from a letter of recommendation for a graduate program, scholarship, or fellowship, but it can serve as a model if you need that type of letter later.

TOP INTERNSHIP AND EXPERIENTIAL OPPORTUNITIES

The internships and experiential opportunities presented in this section are not a comprehensive list but rather a sampling of some of the more popular, prestigious, and lucrative opportunities available. The information presented is adapted from the program Web sites and summarized in a form that allows for quick reference and comparison between programs. For more information, it is important that you visit and thoroughly examine the official Web site of each program that you are considering.

Again, as we mentioned in the Author's Note in the beginning of this book, *The Best Scholarships for the Best Students* is an *idea book*, not a complete listing of opportunities in any given category. Peterson's has a companion guide to this book, *Scholarships, Grants & Prizes*, which is the definitive listing of thousands of options.

We hope you find several programs of interest in the following pages!

RESEARCH PROGRAMS

Undergraduate research programs and similar postbaccalaureate programs provide an opportunity for students to work closely with faculty on research. These programs are designed to provide students with training in research methods and to give them exposure to research in practice. Note that some programs are structured to provide students with an experience supporting faculty in their ongoing research, and other programs are designed to have faculty coach students through their own independently designed and conducted research projects. That's an important difference.

Prior research experience is the secret key to getting into elite graduate research programs. No matter how good you are at passing tests, research itself is totally different. So these programs are a foundation to getting into highly competitive graduate programs, as well as preparation for scientific and technical jobs in industry. Plus, they're fun!

- Amgen Scholars Program
- AT&T Labs Summer Internships
- Morris Arboretum
- NASA Ames Research Programs
- National Institutes of Health Internships
- National Science Foundation REU Program (Research Experiences for Undergraduates)
- National Science Foundation Science and Technology Centers Summer Internship Program
- Smithsonian Environmental Research Center (SERC) Internship Program
- Smithsonian Museum(s) Internship Programs
- Xerox College Experiential Learning Programs (XCEL)

AMGEN SCHOLARS PROGRAM

"The Amgen Foundation seeks to advance science education; improve patient access to quality care; and strengthen the communities where Amgen staff members live and work. Since 1991, the Foundation has made more than $140 million in grants to nonprofit organizations across the United States, Puerto Rico and Europe that impact society in inspiring and innovative ways, and has also supported disaster relief efforts both domestically and internationally."

The Amgen Scholars Program is designed to provide an intensive summer research experience for undergraduate students in science- and biotechnology-related fields. Students are placed at one of ten top-tier universities and paired with a research mentor. The host institutions are California Institute of Technology, Columbia University/Barnard College, Howard University, Massachusetts Institute of Technology, Stanford University, University of California Berkley, University of California Los Angeles, University of California San Diego, University of California San Francisco, and the University of Washington. Students participate in hands-on research. They also attend a three-day symposium with other Amgen Scholars, which features leading scientists working in both universities and industry.

Benefits

Students receive financial support from their host institution. Amounts vary by institution. In addition to financial support, scholars receive hands-on lab experience, faculty mentors, and other professional experiences such as attendance at the three-day symposium.

General Eligibility Requirements

Based on the foundation's requirements, students must:

- be U.S. citizens or U.S. permanent residents
- be undergraduate students enrolled in accredited four-year colleges or universities in the United States, Puerto Rico, or other U.S. territories
- be sophomores (with four quarters or three semesters of college experience), juniors, or nongraduating seniors (who are returning in the fall to continue undergraduate studies)
- have a cumulative grade point average of 3.2 or above
- have an interest in pursuing a Ph.D. or M.D./Ph.D.

Application Process

Each of the ten host institutions has its own application process. Students may choose to apply to more than one host institution. They begin the application process on the Amgen Scholars Web site by clicking on the host institution to which they are interested in applying.

Deadline

The deadline for applications is February.

For More Information

http://www.amgenscholars.eu/web/guest/home

AT&T LABS SUMMER INTERNSHIPS

"AT&T Labs Research is one of the world's premier research institutions, dedicated to advancing the science and technology of communications and information and to creating innovative services founded on these advancements."

AT&T Labs offer summer research internships for students currently enrolled in Ph.D. programs. Students planning to enroll in Ph.D. programs are also welcome to apply. Interns work closely with AT&T personnel on various research projects. Internships are awarded to students in science, technology, engineering, and math-related fields. The research internship lasts for ten weeks over the summer.

Benefits

The AT&T Summer Internship is a ten-week unpaid summer internship. Help with travel costs to and from the research site is provided.

General Eligibility Requirements

According to the program Web site, applicants must meet the following criteria:

- be currently enrolled, or planning to enroll, in a PhD. program in computer science, math, statistics, electrical engineering, operations research, systems engineering, industrial engineering, or a related field
- have a U.S. social security number; U.S. citizenship or residency is NOT a requirement

Application Procedure

Interested students begin the process by filling out an application online. In addition to the online application, applicants must provide supplemental materials through regular mail. Completed applications include:

- an application form
- a resume
- one letter of recommendation required, but up to three acceptable
- personal statement
- official transcripts
- selected standardized test scores

Deadline

Applications open in September and are due in January.

For More Information

http://www.research.att.com/internships

Cross Pollination

See also AT&T Labs Fellowship Program in Chapter 4.

MORRIS ARBORETUM

"The Morris Arboretum of the University of Pennsylvania is an interdisciplinary center that integrates art, science and the humanities. Thousands of rare and lovely woody plants, including some of Philadelphia's oldest, rarest, and largest trees, are set in a romantic, 92-acre, Victorian landscape garden of winding paths, streams, flowers and special garden areas."

The Morris Arboretum of the University of Pennsylvania has a variety of internship opportunities for undergraduate and graduate-level students. Opportunities include possible placement in the following areas: Arboriculture, Education, Horticulture, Plant Protection, Urban Forestry, Bloomfield Farm, Flora of Pennsylvania, Plant Propagation, and Rose and Flower Garden. Internships begin annually in June and last for one year. The program focuses on providing practical training and developing management skills.

Benefits

Interns work a 40-hour week and are paid approximately $9.18 per hour. Additional benefits include health, vision, and dental insurance. Interns also earn graduate-level academic credit through the University of Pennsylvania.

General Eligibility Requirements

Please check the Morris Arboretum Web site for complete eligibility details.

Application Process

A completed application consists of the following:

- a cover letter indicating how this internship program can help you attain your goals and specify which position(s) you are applying fora resume
- an academic transcript
- three letters of recommendation

In addition, intern applicants must also complete the application process requested by the University of Pennsylvania.

Deadline

The deadline for these internships is mid-February.

For More Information

http://www.business-services.upenn.edu/arboretum/ed_internships.shtml

NASA AMES RESEARCH PROGRAMS

"NASA Ames Research Center, located at Moffett Field, California, was founded December 20, 1939 as an aircraft research laboratory by the National Advisory Committee for Aeronautics (NACA) and in 1958 it became part of the National Aeronautics and Space Administration (NASA)."

The NASA Ames Research Center offers a variety of internship opportunities for students at various levels. A short summary of select opportunities are listed below. For a more complete list, as well as eligibility and application instructions, see the Ames Research Center Web site.

Programs for High School Students

- NASA Student Involvement Program (NSIP) is a nationwide competition that encourages high school students to participate in NASA research topics. Students compete in the areas of engineering, computation, journalism, and art.
- Summer High School Apprenticeship Research Program (SHARP) is designed to provide research work experience for underrepresented high school juniors. Applicants must be U.S. citizens residing within commuting distance of NASA Ames Research Center. This is an eight-week summer program. The application deadline is March 1 of each year.
- Student Temporary Experience Program (STEP) provides training and work opportunities. To be eligible for hire, applicants must be over 16 years old, U.S. citizens, and at least half-time students (high school or college).

Community College and Undergraduate Programs

- Ames Associate Program allows researchers with unique scientific backgrounds to utilize their services for the mutual benefit of themselves and the Ames Research Center.
- Education Associates Program (EdAP) is a cooperative space grant program that provides work/study opportunities for university students enrolled in B.S., M.S., or Ph.D. programs. The program's main objective is to link students and faculty with projects at the NASA Ames Research Center.
- NASA Scholars are students from Historically Black Colleges and Other Minority Institutions throughout the United States who spend the summer at the Ames Research Center. NASA Scholars are exceptional undergraduate students whose fields of study range from engineering to computer sciences.
- Student Temporary Experience Program (STEP) provides training and work opportunities. To be eligible for hire, applicants must be over 16 years old, U.S. citizens, and at least half-time students (high school or college).

Undergraduate Student Research Program (USRP) is an onsite mentored research experience. Open to full-time rising undergraduate juniors or seniors, USRP provides challenging ten- to fifteen-week internships at all NASA Centers. Only individuals enrolled in U.S. colleges or universities, who are majoring in engineering, physical/life sciences, mathematics, or computer science, with at least a 3.0 grade point average may apply. Stipends and travel expenses are provided.

Graduate Programs

- Education Associates Program (EdAP) is a cooperative space grant program that provides work/study opportunities for university students enrolled in B.S., M.S., or Ph.D. programs. The program's main objective is to link students and faculty with projects at the NASA Ames Research Center.
- Graduate Student Researchers Program offers competitive fellowships to U.S. citizens who are pursuing gradate degrees at the master's and doctoral levels at U.S.-accredited colleges and universities in areas of science and engineering that support the NASA research and development mission.

For More Information

http://education.arc.nasa.gov/pages/students.html#Undergrad

NATIONAL INSTITUTES OF HEALTH INTERNSHIPS

The National Institutes of Health, an agency of the U.S. Department of Health and Human Services, consists of twenty-seven separate institutes and centers conducting biomedical research. It is believed to be the largest health-related research network in the world.

The National Institutes of Health is not one entity, but a collection of institutes and centers with a networked organizational structure under the Office of the Director. The NIH has many facilities and programs such as the National Cancer Institute, National Human Genome Research Institute, National Institute on Aging, and National Institute on Environmental and Health Sciences. A student might choose to apply for acceptance into several programs at the same time. The following are some of the main ones:

For High School Students

Note that the NIH Summer Internship Program is one of the only programs in the nation to allow high school students to work on "real" science teams.

- **NIH Summer Internship Program (SIP)**
  This program allows eligible high school, college, graduate, and professional students to spend eight to ten weeks conducting biomedical research with NIH investigators.
- **Undergraduate Scholarship Program (UGSP)**
  The UGSP is not an internship but a $20,000 per year scholarship for eligible undergraduates pursuing degrees in fields related to biomedical research. (For more information on this program see Chapter 3.)

- **Postbaccalaureate Intramural Research Training Award (IRTA)**

  With the Postbaccalaureate Intramural Research Training Award (IRTA) Program, grantees can spend one or two years working with investigators at the NIH before going on with their graduate-school plans.

- **NIH Academy**

  The NIH Academy is a yearlong biomedical research program (renewable for a second year) for eligible recent college graduates who (1) are planning to apply to graduate or professional school and (2) wish to pursue an interest in domestic health disparities.

- **Technical IRTA Program**

  The Technical IRTA Program is a unique program for college graduates who want to develop their skills as research support personnel, that is, those who might eventually want to become science program administrators or research program administrators. No particular academic background is required, but obviously some proven interest in and facility with science would be preferred.

The NIH also has a range of programs for graduate students, medical students, dental students, and postdocs. For example, there are programs for doctoral students to complete all or part of their dissertation phase in an NIH research setting. See the NIH Web site for more information.

Warning

The NIH is so large and complex that students should expect to spend some time familiarizing themselves with the NIH Web site, programs, and requirements.

For More Information

https://www.training.nih.gov/student/sip

> **Cross Pollination**
>
> See also the National Institute of General Medical Sciences Division of Minority Opportunities in Research (NIGMS-MORE) in Chapter 4.

NATIONAL SCIENCE FOUNDATION REU PROGRAM (RESEARCH EXPERIENCES FOR UNDERGRADUATES)

The Research Experiences for Undergraduates (REU) Program supports active research participation by undergraduate students in any of the areas of research funded by the National Science Foundation (NSF). REU projects involve students in meaningful ways in ongoing research programs or in research projects specifically designed for the REU Program.

The National Science Foundation Research Experiences for Undergraduates Program has two mechanisms for support of student research: REU Sites and REU Supplements. REU Sites are based on independent proposals to initiate and conduct projects that engage a number of students in research. REU Sites may be based in a single discipline or academic department or on interdisciplinary or multidepartment research opportunities with a coherent intellectual theme. Proposals with an international dimension are welcome. A partnership with the Department of Defense supports REU Sites in DoD-relevant research areas.

REU Supplements may be requested for ongoing NSF-funded research projects or may be included as a component of proposals for new or renewed NSF grants or cooperative agreements.

This program provides educational opportunities for undergraduate students, but indirect funding for undergraduate students to participate in research. To inquire about possible funding opportunities, contact the organizations that have received awards.

Benefits

Students have the opportunity to work directly with renowned scientists who have been funded by the NSF to pursue their own research. Research stipends vary depending on the grant proposal submitted by the faculty member and/or lead scientist.

General Eligibility Requirements

Eligibility varies with each opportunity, but students who participate in an REU must be citizens of the United States or its possessions. They should also be prepared to indicate their experience with the research subject and maintain a strong GPA.

Application Process

Students *may not* apply to NSF to participate in REU activities. Students apply directly to REU Sites and should consult the directory of active REU Sites on the Web at http://www.nsf.gov/crssprgm/reu/reu_search.cfm.

Deadline

Deadlines vary by location. Consult the relevant Web site for further details.

For More Information

http://www.nsf.gov/funding/pgm_summ.jsp?pims_id=5517&from=fund

NATIONAL SCIENCE FOUNDATION SCIENCE AND TECHNOLOGY CENTERS SUMMER INTERNSHIP PROGRAM

The National Science Foundation Science and Technology Centers (STCs) offer summer internships at each of seventeen centers located at prestigious universities around the United States. These summer internships provide undergraduates an opportunity to conduct research in a "graduate school" setting in the following fields: biological sciences, computer and information sciences, engineering, geosciences, and mathematical and physical sciences.

The NSF Science & Technology Centers (STCs) each have a specific research focus. Interns will be part of a unique national scientific community consisting of undergraduates, faculty, and graduate students and be exposed to professional development, technical, and academic seminars. Depending upon the nature of the research, the internship will culminate in the development of a scientific paper, poster, and/or presentation.

Benefits

The summer research experience lasts eight to ten weeks, and the award covers the cost of transportation to the STC, stipend, room and board, and participation in STC-planned events.

Benefits also include the opportunity to engage in hands-on research, gain a competitive advantage while having fun, conduct research in a cutting-edge field, and be mentored by top research faculty. Students are given the opportunity to make a difference scientifically and socially, interact with a national community of peers, and discover pathways to graduate school.

General Eligibility Requirements

According to the Web site, eligibility requirements vary with each opportunity. However, in general, applicants:

- must be enrolled as full-time students at a two- or four-year college or university
- must have a 2.7 GPA or better
- should be studying subjects relevant to the topic of each STC opportunity

Application Process

The application process varies with each internship, but most require the following:

- an online application form
- an official copy of applicant's most recent transcript
- a resume
- two letters of recommendation

Deadline

Applications are generally released in mid-October with the deadline in January.

For More Information

General information: http://www.nsfstc.org/undergraduate_internships.htm

Specific information about each STC option: http://www.nsfstc.org/centers.htm

SMITHSONIAN ENVIRONMENTAL RESEARCH CENTER (SERC) INTERNSHIP PROGRAM

"The Smithsonian Environmental Research Center (SERC) leads the Nation in research on linkages of land and water ecosystems in the coastal zone and provides society with knowledge to meet critical environmental challenges in the 21st century."

The Smithsonian Environmental Research Center (SERC) offers paid internships for advanced undergraduates and beginning graduate students in the areas of environmental research and environmental education. Interns work with SERC personnel on designated research as well as independent projects. The SERC Internship program Web site indicates that, "Students will have the opportunity to expand their knowledge in a selected field of study and to learn a variety of research techniques through firsthand experience. At the conclusion of the internship, student participants will be expected to present the findings of their independent projects in a formal seminar to the SERC community." For each year of the program, the Web site lists research areas for that particular year and desirable characteristics in potential applicants for the respective research areas. A wide variety of science backgrounds is acceptable.

Benefits

Interns are paid $425 per week and may be eligible for housing in a residence hall for $75 per week. Academic credit may be possible if arranged through the intern's home institution.

General Eligibility Requirements

According to the SERC Web site, applicants must meet the following criteria:

- be currently enrolled as an undergraduate or beginning graduate student or have recently graduated from an undergraduate or master's program
- be in a position to commit fully to the completion of a project

U.S. citizenship is NOT a requirement to participate in this program.

Application Procedure

Applicants may register at the Smithsonian Online Academic Appointment System to submit an online application system or submit an application by mail. Applications include:

- a completed application form
- an essay
- academic records
- two letters of recommendation

Deadline

Interns may apply for one of three internship terms. For winter/spring appointments, the deadline is in November. For summer appointments, the deadline is in February. For fall appointments, the deadline is in June. Check the Web site for exact deadline dates.

For More Information

http://www.serc.si.edu/pro_training/internships/internships.aspx

SMITHSONIAN MUSEUM(S) INTERNSHIP PROGRAMS

The Smithsonian Institution is the world's largest museum complex with nineteen museums, 168 affiliate museums, and nine research centers. The Smithsonian hosts 30 million visitors a year.

The Smithsonian offers a staggering number of internships from Smithsonian Garden interns to National Sciences Resources Center interns to ZooGoer interns—too many to list in this text. But each is clearly described on the Smithsonian's Web site and falls into one of the following five categories: art; history and culture; libraries, archives, and preservation; professional services; and science and research.

As part of its mandate for "the increase and diffusion of knowledge," including the diverse ideas, skills, and cultures of the nation, the Smithsonian Institution pursues policies of equal opportunity and cultural diversity. Smithsonian fellowships and internships are awarded on the basis of these policies. Applicants are evaluated on their academic standing, scholarly qualifications, experience, the quality of the research project or study proposed, and its suitability to Smithsonian collections, facilities, and programs.

Scholars and students with outside sources of funding are also encouraged to utilize the Institution's resources and facilities. The Office of Fellowships can facilitate visiting appointments in such cases provided that the investigator obtains approval from the staff member with whom he/she would consult.

Benefits

An internship at the Smithsonian Institution is a prearranged, structured learning experience scheduled within a specific time frame. The experience must be relevant to the intern's academic and professional goals and to research and museum activities of the Institution. An internship is performed under the direct supervision of Smithsonian staff.

Some internships carry a stipend.

General Eligibility Requirements

Internships, for the most part, are arranged individually. Information and applications may be obtained by contacting the appropriate internship coordinator or by contacting the Smithsonian Center for Education and Museum Studies, the central referral service for internships. Refer to the Smithsonian's Web site for deadlines, addresses, and other specific information regarding various internship programs. Please note: All Smithsonian interns must be at least 16 years old.

Application Process

The applications processes vary slightly according to each internship, but most require:

- a proposal
- a CV
- an online application form
- references

Deadline

Deadlines vary, but many are in early February.

For More Information

http://www.si.edu/ofg/intern.htm

For High School Students

Note that high school students are eligible for Smithsonian internships.

Xerox College Experiential Learning Programs (XCEL)

Xerox practically invented the office imaging business, and its name is synonym *photocopies of office documents. Today, it is a specialized technology company.*

Hundreds of interns gain real experience every year with the Xerox College Experiential Learning Programs (XCEL). XCEL has summer and year-round internship and co-op programs. Interns work on imaging systems (mechanical/electrical engineering, materials science, industrial design, and even chemistry and physics), software innovation, finance, marketing, and more.

Xerox's main internship assignments are in Rochester, New York (research and engineering); Wilsonville, Oregon (color printing systems and solid ink technology); and El Segundo, California (software development, engineering, research and development).

Benefits

Xerox internships and co-ops are paid. Xerox provides travel, housing, and local transportation assistance to interns. As in most internship and co-op programs, once accepted for an internship or co-op, a person is considered for additional opportunities, including permanent hiring. Those who are accepted into XCEL participate in social networking events and senior leadership roundtables, panels, and presentations.

General Eligibility Requirements

General eligibility requirements include:

- be pursuing a bachelor's or master's degree
- have a cumulative 3.0 GPA on a 4.0 scale or equivalent
- demonstrate leadership and communication skills
- commit to working for a minimum of ten weeks
- have authorization to work in the United States

Co-op work blocks are available throughout the year for full-time matriculated students enrolled in their institution's co-op programs.

Application Process

Xerox concentrates its on-campus recruiting on twenty core universities, which it declines to specify. Contact your career center to see if Xerox holds information sessions or interviews at your school.

Xerox also actively seeks recruits through student chapters of the Society of Hispanic Professional Engineers and the National Society of Black Engineers and applicants to its own Xerox Technical Minority Scholarship Program in Chapter 4.

The company also supports INROADS, Inc., the national nonprofit that identifies and places ethnically diverse students in internships at leading companies. The current president of Xerox Global Services serves as chairman of the national INROADS board. For more on INROADS see Chapter 4.

You can send your resume to the Xerox career site (http://www.xeroxcareers.com), but it seems that your best bet is to go through one of the above channels.

For More Information

See http://www.xeroxstudentcareers.com and http://www.xerox.com/about-xerox/citizenship/news/college-internships/enus.html.

BUSINESS PROGRAMS

Working for major corporations is a career path that many students choose. Large, multinational organizations can provide career challenges and opportunities for decades. The skills set that these organizations are seeking includes more than just technical competency. They are looking for people who can work effectively on teams, who may be willing to relocate for periods of time to achieve career advancement, and who have the self-discipline to learn new skills needed for the next assignment even as they perform the demanding assignments they already have.

The requirements for success in most of these organizations are stringent. They are looking for people who look the part, act the part, work ethically, and constantly improve. Although some employers in this category, for example, some technology companies, are tolerant of individual quirkiness, by and large these organizations favor hires with the "total package" of performance and professionalism. The companies are looking for people who can meet with clients and represent the company to the public, whether the clients and the public are in Chicago, Dallas, London, or Mumbai.

Major corporate employers like to hire their interns, and many actually make *all* their permanent hire offers only to former interns. So gaining access to these employers in experiential programs like the following can open the door to a career path.

- Alcatel-Lucent Technology Internships
- Apple Internships
- The Chronicle of Higher Education Editorial Internships

- Echoing Green Fellowships
- Getty Museum Internship Programs: Multicultural Undergraduate Internships
- Getty Museum Internship Programs: Graduate Interns
- Goldman Sachs Internship Programs
- Google Internships
- Los Angeles County Museum of Art (LACMA) Internship Program
- Merck Internships
- Metropolitan Museum of Art Internships Program
- Microsoft Internships
- National Football League (NFL) Summer Internship Program
- National Gallery of Art Internship Program (Summer Internships)
- National Parks Business Plan Internship
- The New York Times Summer Internship
- PricewaterhouseCoopers (PwC) Internships

ALCATEL-LUCENT TECHNOLOGY INTERNSHIPS

Alcatel-Lucent is the contemporary iteration of the legendary Bell Labs, once one of the world's largest research, technology, and innovation organizations focused on communications.

Launched by Alexander Graham Bell with a gift from the French government, Bell Labs has a long history of revolutionary innovation. Bell Labs is the birthplace of the transistor, the laser, and the C and C++ programming languages! Numerous Bell Labs alumni have won Nobel prizes for work done at the research center. Once part of AT&T, it's now part of Alcatel-Lucent, a global technology company with headquarters in Paris. Befitting the company's global reach, internships are available in many functions, not just technology development.

Lucent Technology internships are available in the United States and dozens of other countries. The company is fostering a decidedly internationalist culture, and teams may include people from all over the world.

Benefits

Interns are given project-focused summer assignments and have the benefit of a cultural integration program and educational programming. According to Alcatel-Lucent's Web site, "On arrival, interns are orientated in the Alcatel-Lucent family and the individual work group to which they will contribute. Development opportunities may include meetings with corporate executives, educational workshops, business-unit information exchanges and networking events."

General Eligibility Requirements

Applicants for internships must be enrolled in an undergraduate program—and intend to return to that program upon completing any Alcatel-Lucent program. Preference goes to students in engineering, business, and finance.

Deadline

Although the company's own Web site lists no deadline, other sources cite a January deadline for summer intern applications.

For More Information

http://www.alcatel-lucent.com/careers/startyourjourneywithus.html

---

Cross Pollination

There are other Alcatel-Lucent programs that may be of interest to you: Cooperative Education Program, Apprenticeship Program, Research Partner Program, and Alcatel-Lucent AIESEC Global Exchange in Chapter 5.

APPLE INTERNSHIPS

Apple is a leading-edge technology company best known for its i-products—iPod, iPad, iPhone—as well as its laptops and PCs known for their highly reliable OS.

Apple has regular internships during the summer, co-op opportunities during the semester, and special postbaccalaureate internships as well. Apple prides itself on throwing interns into work teams to work alongside regular employees on actual projects. According to its Web site, "You might help engineer the next iPhone, develop the next generation of Mac OS X, create the in-store posters for a top-secret product launch, or travel internationally to help open a new store."

Apple also has two unique opportunities to become involved in the Apple family while still on campus: Apple Campus Reps and Student Developers. Campus representatives demonstrate Apple products to students, faculty, and administrative staff. Student developers work remotely on OS software development, earn scholarships for developing effective code, and are invited to attend the Worldwide Developers Conference.

Benefits

The main benefits of Apple internships are the opportunity to work on real projects, instead of the make-work that some other companies assign to interns. Interns also have the chance to be considered for permanent hire by Apple, a company with cult-like devotion among employees and consumers alike. Also, you'll have bragging rights forever.

General Eligibility Requirements

Apple likes people who use its products. It helps to be a fan, although Apple explicitly says this is not a prerequisite. Like any global technology company, Apple seeks interns with a range of backgrounds and skills, from marketing and merchandising to engineering and design.

Application Process

Apple uses a dual-application process: an online application and a network of Apple university relations officers (campus recruiters). The Web site is confusing and unclear about upcoming internship opportunities, so we strongly recommend you try to discover if Apple recruiters come to your university. First step: contact your career center. The best online technique is to go to the "corporate jobs" section and type the word "intern" into the search window (don't enter anything else), and some options will appear.

For More Information

http://www.apple.com/jobs/us/students.html

iTunes Your Way to an Internship

You can sign in to Apple's Human Resources Web site using your iTunes Apple ID.

THE CHRONICLE OF HIGHER EDUCATION EDITORIAL INTERNSHIPS

The Chronicle of Higher Education, based in Washington, DC, is the premier newspaper for university faculty members and administrators.

The Chronicle of Higher Education offers internships for undergraduates and recent graduates pursuing careers in journalism. Interns work full-time gaining valuable experience reporting and writing on higher education–related news. Interns may be asked to write features that will appear in the online version of *The Chronicle of Higher Education.* Internships are offered throughout the year, during the fall, winter-spring, and summer terms.

Benefits

Interns are paid $500 a week. They may arrange to receive credit at their home institution.

General Eligibility Requirements

According to the Web site, applicants must meet the following criteria:

- be current sophomores, juniors, seniors, or recent graduates
- must attend or have graduated from an accredited, four-year college or university
- have experience writing for publication, either at a student newspaper or a professional publication

Candidates with previous internships and deadline-reporting experience are preferred.

Application Procedure

Applicants prepare an application packet that includes:

- a cover letter
- a resume with contact information
- a maximum of five varied writing clips

Deadline

Interns may apply to work during any of the three terms during the year: fall, winter-spring, and summer. Deadlines vary per term. Check program Web site for exact deadlines.

For More Information

http://chronicle.com/section/Editorial-Internships/158/

ECHOING GREEN FELLOWSHIPS

Echoing Green is an innovative organization whose mission is to accelerate social change by supporting ". . . outstanding emerging social entrepreneurs to launch new organizations that deliver bold, high-impact solutions."

Echoing Green was founded in 1987 by a group of investors desiring to bring venture capital strategies to the social sector. Each year, the organization funds two-year fellowships to enable entrepreneurs to create organizations that tackle some of the world's most difficult social problems. Past recipients have proposed ideas ranging from an educational training program in India designed to systemically impact the Indian education system to a disaster accountability project designed to provide accountability to government agencies and a voice to those impacted by natural disasters.

Benefits

Echoing Green provides outstanding resources for budding entrepreneurs who are selected for the fellowship. Each year, twelve to fifteen two-year fellowships are awarded to the applicants with the most outstanding ideas. These fellowships provide seed money to launch an organization ($60,000 for individuals and $90,000 for partnerships). In addition, entrepreneurs are provided resources that include technical support, consultation with the Echoing Green staff of experts, and professional and organizational development opportunities. Winners are also connected to a growing network of social entrepreneurs.

General Eligibility Requirements

Echoing Green has few restrictions for fellowship applicants:

- Applicants must be at least 18 years of age.
- The organization is open to individual as well as partnership applications.
- Citizens from any country or nationality may apply, and the ideas proposed by applicants may be located in any country.
- Ideas submitted must be original ideas for social change–based organizations not currently part of another umbrella organization.
- It is recommended that applicants have a strong working knowledge of the English language.

The Echoing Green Web site provides a useful preapplication questionnaire for potential applicants.

Application Process

The application process entails three phases, with each phase narrowing the number of applicants.

- Phase 1: Applicants fill out an online application form, which requires a resume and short essay about the proposed organization. Usually between 800 and 1,400 applications are reviewed.
- Phase 2: Applicants are asked to submit more material, including longer, more detailed essays about the organization, a sector analysis, a proposed budget, and references. This narrows the pool of applicants to between 150 and 300.
- Phase 3: About 30 of the original applicants are flown to New York City to present a 90- second idea pitch and participate in two interviews.

For More Information

http://www.echoinggreen.org/fellowship

Getty Museum Internship Programs: Multicultural Undergraduate Internships

The Getty offers multicultural undergraduate internships at the Getty Center. In addition, the Getty supports multicultural internships at Los Angeles area museums and visual arts organizations.

Since 1993, the Foundation's Multicultural Undergraduate Internship program has provided substantive, full-time work opportunities to more than 2,100 multicultural undergraduates, exposing them to potential careers in the arts. The Foundation's support enables Los Angeles-area museums and visual arts organizations to host students in full-time, paid internships for ten weeks during the summer. The Getty Foundation supports more than 100 internship positions at organizations throughout Los Angeles County. Fifteen to twenty internships are also funded at the Getty Center in Los Angeles and the Getty Villa in Malibu.

The internships are intended specifically for outstanding students who are members of groups currently underrepresented in careers related to museums and the visual arts. Students gain experience in key areas such as curatorship, conservation, education, publications, and related programmatic activities. Candidates are sought from all areas of undergraduate study and are not required to have demonstrated a previous commitment to the visual arts.

Benefits

The internships are full-time (40 hours/week) positions, each with a salary of $3,500, for a consecutive ten-week work period between June and August.

General Eligibility Requirements

According to the Web site, applicants must meet the following criteria:

- be of African American, Asian, Latino/Hispanic, Native American, or Pacific Islander descent
- be currently enrolled as an undergraduate
- have completed at least one semester of college by the time the internship begins or will complete their degree by the following September. Students who are enrolled in a second B.A. or B.S. program are not eligible.

- reside or attend college in Los Angeles County
- be a U.S. citizen or permanent resident

Application Process

Students apply directly to the participating organizations for the internships at the Los Angeles-area museums and visual arts organizations and to the Getty Foundation for internships at the Getty Center and Getty Villa. Each has its own application process.

Deadline

Most deadlines are in mid-March.

For More Information

http://www.getty.edu/foundation/funding/leaders/current/mui_students.html

GETTY MUSEUM INTERNSHIP PROGRAMS: GRADUATE INTERNS

The Getty Museum publishes the Getty Research Journal, highlighting work by scholars and staff associated with the museum's Research Institute and other programs supported by the J. Paul Getty Trust.

Getty Graduate Internships are offered in the four programs of the J. Paul Getty Trust: the J. Paul Getty Museum, the Getty Research Institute, the Getty Conservation Institute, and the Getty Foundation. The internships are open to students of all nationalities who intend to pursue careers in fields related to the visual arts. Training and work experience are available in areas such as curatorial, education, conservation, research, information management, public programs, and grant-making. Approximately twenty graduate internship positions are funded each year, and the internships are located at the Getty Center in Los Angeles or the Getty Villa in Malibu.

Benefits

All positions are full-time. Most begin in September and run until the following May. However, conservation internships are twelve months, ending the following September. Grant amounts are $17,400 for eight months and $26,000 for twelve months. The grant includes health benefits, but housing and relocation funds are not provided.

General Eligibility Requirements

According to the Web site, applicants must meet the following criteria:

- be currently enrolled in a graduate program leading to an advanced degree in a field relevant to the internship(s) for which they are applying

or

- have completed a relevant graduate degree on or after January 1, 2007, with postgraduate activities in their field, paid or unpaid

Internships are open to students of all nationalities.

Application Process

Students must complete and submit:

- an online application, including a Personal Statement and Supplemental Applicant Information form

and, by mail:

- copies of academic records or transcripts
- two letters of recommendation

The process varies significantly with each program, and the number of awards changes each year depending on the endowment.

Deadline

The deadline is December 15 prior to the year an intern would like to begin work with the Getty.

For More Information

http://www.getty.edu/foundation/funding/leaders/current/grad_internships.html

GOLDMAN SACHS INTERNSHIP PROGRAMS

Goldman Sachs is arguably the most prestigious Wall Street investment bank and securities firm. In recent years, it has been at the cutting edge of both Wall Street's successes and excesses.

Goldman Sachs has a wide range of internship programs, including programs at financial centers abroad where language skills in Japanese, for example, may come into play. There is a plethora of opportunities for undergraduates and MBA students alike. Goldman, like most large financial services companies, favors recruiting from the most elite colleges and universities, but it is a myth that successful candidates have to come from the Ivy League or that simple attendance at an Ivy League institution will garner Goldman's attention. One way Goldman recruiters tend to think of it is: If you did not attend an elite university, you could have.

It is also important to note that you do not have to major in business or have any particular academic preparation to be accepted as an intern. "A financial background is not necessary," states the Web site, but it does have a caveat. "Whatever your discipline or major, we encourage you to apply, provided you share an interest in the financial markets and have demonstrated strong academic performance and professional drive."

Benefits

A Goldman Sachs internship is an entry key to a career at Goldman Sachs in particular and Wall Street in general. Some of the highest salaries in the world come from Goldman and its fellow financial services companies with global operations headquartered in New York. Goldman Sachs is an innovative and wide-ranging financial services firm, with many divisions and locations in financial centers around the world. A bright, motivated student can find an area of interest. Goldman is known to provide top pay to its interns, and other firms are glad to hire Goldman alumni later in their careers.

General Eligibility Requirements

Applicants must meet the following criteria:

- knowledge of and interest in the financial markets
- enrollment in a bachelor's degree program in any major, or an MBA program, with a record of top performance
- a keen interest in Goldman Sachs itself

Students who advance with Goldman tend to spend a great deal of time learning about the firm, its lines of business, history, and culture.

Application Process

You can apply online for Goldman internships, but, realistically, you have to get the attention of one of the Goldman recruiters to be selected. Contact your college or university career center to discover whether Goldman recruits on your campus. If it doesn't, you will need to enlist the career center's help in identifying the Goldman college relations manager or MBA recruiter. If you personally know anyone at Goldman, that person can easily find out this information for you. You will need the standard application materials of a resume and cover letter.

Success in the interviews is critical. You should work with your career center to prepare for a rigorous interview that may include case questions.

For More Information

http://www2.goldmansachs.com/careers/your-career/positions/intern/index.html

> **Cross Pollination**
>
> If Goldman Sachs is of interest to you, all the larger investment banks and financial services companies should also be of interest. Wikipedia keeps an up-to-date list. Also, private equity, hedge funds, the largest accounting firms, and large consulting organizations seek a similar skills set and mind-set and might be of interest. For a very different banking option, see the listing for World Bank internships in Chapter 5. Also, check out www.inroads.org, described in Chapter 4, for additional business internships.

GOOGLE INTERNSHIPS

Google is one of the most powerful media and technology companies in the world. It has a wide range of products and services and robust research and development efforts in myriad directions.

Google expressly seeks applications from all types of majors from engineering to psychology, art to finance. As Google says on the first page of its internship Web site, "Don't let that arts degree keep you from applying to Google." Google has many internship programs for new grads (postbaccalaureate internships) as well as more traditional student opportunities. Google also highlights that it seeks interns for all seasons of the year and for locations in North America, Europe, and China (mostly Hong Kong).

Google looks for brilliant applicants who already have interesting accomplishments. As a U.S.-headquartered, leading-edge technology company, Google is more tolerant of quirkiness than most companies. As the Web site says, "Googlers range from former neurosurgeons and puzzle champions to alligator wrestlers and Lego maniacs. Tell us what makes you unique!"

Benefits

If you want to be hired by Google after college, the best way in is to serve as a Google intern before you graduate. Google prides itself on its flat organizational structure; even if you don't pursue a career with the company, you will have experience in a dynamic company where ideas flow in all directions. Dress is decidedly casual.

Intern Early and Often

Google likes serial interns, that is, people who come back for more than one internship opportunity. So, the earlier you can try to crack this egg, the better. Google has a very strong company culture, so get ready for a little indoctrination as a Noogler (New Googler).

General Eligibility Requirements

Applicants must meet the usual criteria:

- resume or CV featuring accomplishments, honors, and awards
- three references

Deadline

Applications are accepted continuously.

For More Information

www.google.com/jobs/students/intern

If you want to know what it's like to work for Google, check out what current interns have to say at http://www.youtube.com/googlestudents.

Cross Pollination

If Google is attractive to you, also consider internships at one of the other leading-edge tech companies such as YouTube, Facebook, or Apple in Chapter 5. Of course, you may also want to consider internships at some of the more traditional technology companies such as IBM or Microsoft in Chapter 5.

LOS ANGELES COUNTY MUSEUM OF ART (LACMA) INTERNSHIP PROGRAM

"With 100,000 objects dating from ancient times to the present, the Los Angeles County Museum of Art (LACMA) is the largest art museum in the western United States. A museum of international stature as well as a vital part of Southern California, LACMA shares its vast collections through exhibitions, public programs, and research facilities that attract nearly a million visitors annually."

The Los Angeles County Museum of Art has a variety of internship opportunities for undergraduate and graduate-level students. Opportunities include:

- Rights and Reproductions Internship
- Corporate Development Internship
- Human Resources Internship
- Collections Management Internships
- Government and Foundation Relations Internship
- Registrar's Office Internships

Internships are open to a wide variety of majors; these include, but are not limited to, museum studies, art history, anthropology, archaeology, history, library science, general law, and human resource management. Internships are available during the academic year as well as in the summer.

Benefits

Internships with LACMA offer professional experience in a variety of areas. It is possible to arrange academic credit for internships in select areas.

General Eligibility Requirements

Eligibility requirements vary depending on the internship. Please check the LACMA Web site for complete details.

Application Process

To apply, interested applicants must send a resume and cover letter to the appropriate area within LACMA. The process varies with each internship and involves sending applications to named staff, which changes, so be sure to check the Web site.

Deadline

Deadlines vary depending on the internship. Please check the LACMA Web site for complete details.

For More Information

http://www.lacma.org/info/Interns.aspx

MERCK INTERNSHIPS

Merck and Co., Inc., is one of the largest pharmaceutical companies in the world. It supports research and development in a number of areas and is considered by a number of measures a great place to work. Among the workplace awards that it has garnered are "Best Company" and "Blue Ribbon Company," according to Fortune Magazine; "Top 50 Companies for Diversity," "Top 10 Companies for People With Disabilities," and "Top 10 Companies for GLBT Employees," according to Diversity, Inc.; "Top 100 Companies for Latinos," according to Hispanic Magazine; and "Top 30 Companies for Executive Women," according to National Association for Female Executives (NAFE).

Merck develops new medicines in over twenty therapeutic categories and manufactures and markets medicines and vaccines globally. Merck also has an innovative program to publish health-education information as a not-for-profit service, including extensive patient and doctor education materials and the *Merck Manual of Diagnosis and Therapy,* the world's bestselling medical textbook.

Merck seeks undergraduate and graduate student interns and co-ops with almost any academic background, including finance, biological sciences, chemistry, physics, immunology, physiology, pharmacology, pharmaceutical sciences, materials science and engineering, chemical engineering, mechanical engineering, electrical engineering, industrial engineering, mathematics, statistics, computer science, computer engineering, information systems, marketing, market research, sales, health care, liberal arts, business, organizational development, psychology, veterinary anatomy, veterinary pathology, veterinary medicine, and medicine.

Benefits

Interns receive salary, housing assistance, transportation to and from work, structured acculturation program (also known as social activities), exposure to senior management, and on-site gym.

General Eligibility Requirements

According to its Web site, applicants must meet the following criteria:

- be currently enrolled in a degree program (undergraduate or graduate)
- be in their junior or senior year if an undergraduate
- be planning to enter graduate school right after graduation if a senior
- have a GPA of 3.3 or higher for those students seeking to work at the Merck Research Laboratory (MRL); no GPA requirements for other assignments

For More Information

http://www.merck.com/careers/explore-careers/students-and-graduates/home.html.

For a list of campuses around the world where Merck actively recruits and for a schedule of information sessions, see http://www.merck.com/careers/campus-calendar.html.

> **Cross Pollination**
>
> If you like Merck, you might also consider other "big pharma" companies, the largest pharmaceutical companies active in the U.S. health-care market, although many of the companies are in fact headquartered abroad. To find a list, see Wikipedia at http://en.wikipedia.org/wiki/List_of_pharmaceutical_companies. Also, look at Merck's joint program with the United Negro College Fund, UNCF/Merck Science Initiative (UMSI), which provides undergraduate, graduate, and postdoctoral support to outstanding African American students who are pursuing studies and research careers in biological and chemical sciences in Chapter 4.

METROPOLITAN MUSEUM OF ART INTERNSHIPS PROGRAM

"The Metropolitan Museum of Art [in New York City] is one of the world's largest and finest art museums. Its collections include more than two million works of art spanning five thousand years of world culture, from prehistory to the present and from every part of the globe. . . . Nearly five million people visit the Museum each year."

The Metropolitan Museum of Art (the Met) has three primary types of internships:

- Paid Internships for College and Graduate Students at the Main Building, which include a summer internship program, a mentoring program for college juniors, six-month internships, Web development/video internship, and others
- The Cloisters Summer Internship for College Students, which is a nine-week internship for students interested in art and museum careers
- Unpaid Internships for College and Graduate Students at the Main Building, which may be full- or part-time and may result in academic credit

According to the program Web site, ". . . interns work in one of the Metropolitan's departments—curatorial, education, conservation, administration, or library. Most projects require a strong knowledge of art history."

Benefits

The compensation provided by the Paid Internships for College and Graduate Students at the Main Building varies by opportunity. The amounts range from $3,250 to $25,000. The Cloisters Summer Internship for College Students pays $2,750.

General Eligibility Requirements

Eligibility requirements vary depending on the internship. Please check the MET Web site for complete details.

Application Process

For all types of internships, applicants must:

- fill out an online application
- provide academic transcripts
- letters of recommendations

Interviews may be required.

Deadline

The application deadline varies with the opportunity; however, most internship opportunities have a January due date.

For More Information

http://www.metmuseum.org/education/er_internship.asp#junior

For High School Students

The Metropolitan Museum of Art also has paid internships for high school seniors. Interns work behind the scenes and meet members of the Museum staff. They also participate in gallery, studio, and museum learning projects.

MICROSOFT INTERNSHIPS

Microsoft is the world's leading provider of PC software, with market penetration reaching monopoly proportions and global reach into every corner of the planet.

Microsoft involves interns in all phases of the product development and placement life cycle. Its Web site provides a map of the process to help you see where you might fit in. Areas include software and hardware development, information technology, user experience, finance, legal, human resources, marketing, and sales.

Many of the internships are in technical product development and business units with narrow tasks, so you'll see a bit less of the "we take anybody" rhetoric and more listings for specific educational backgrounds. Families of development include software, desktop, Web, phone, and cloud computing.

Microsoft is known as an intense place to work, where fun is sometimes a thin veneer over high expectations for both hours and productivity. For a contrasting opinion, check out their Web site for intern videos: http://www.msstudentlounge.com/tabid/60/default.aspx?id=334.

Benefits

Microsoft gets interns involved in projects that tend to have a defined work product for the term of the internship, so you should get a chance to finish a plan, design, or module that you can brag about in the future. Microsoft pays interns a competitive salary that varies with assignment, provides a free health club membership, and assists with travel to and from your assignment. The Web site promises that "You'll learn more in 12 weeks here than you would in a whole school year. It's the kind of work that gets noticed by millions of people all over the world."

Like many companies, Microsoft favors interns when it's hiring for permanent jobs.

Application Process

Call your career center and see if Microsoft is going to have any information sessions during the school year. Ask if yours is a campus that Microsoft sends college relations managers to visit. Or you can just apply online.

For More Information

https://careers.microsoft.com/careers/en/us/collegeinternships.aspx

NATIONAL FOOTBALL LEAGUE (NFL) SUMMER INTERNSHIP PROGRAM

The internship program is an "opportunity to catch a rare glimpse into the NFL's playbook of business strategies." Interns get to see how the organization "integrates its rich tradition with innovative approaches to entertain over 120 million fans each week during the season."

The National Football League consists of the thirty-two local teams attached to major media markets throughout the United States. The NFL headquarters internship program allows interns "to contribute to the organization's success while receiving an unmatched, behind-the-scenes learning experience. Though interns work within specific departments, they are able to explore all aspects of the business of professional football through speaker presentations, mentoring relationships and networking opportunities."

Assignments are typically available in these departments:

- Media
- Marketing and Sales
- Communications and Public Affairs
- Community Affairs
- Consumer Products
- Promotional Events
- Finance and Accounting
- Football Operations
- Human Resources
- Information Technology
- Internal Audit
- International
- Labor and Legal

Also note that the NFL has a Junior Rotational Program, which, in spite of its name, is not a classic rotational management training program but an assignment to departments in the NFL that need interns who can dedicate themselves to six- to twelve-month, project-based assignments. Initial information is available on the same Web site as the NFL Summer Internship Program.

General Eligibility Requirements

According to the Web site, applicants must meet the following criteria:

- be currently enrolled as undergraduates entering their senior year in the fall of the coming year
- be legally permitted to work in the United States (international students must have all visas and employment authorizations prior to the beginning of the internship)
- be available within the United States during the interview period
- an overall GPA of at least 3.0 is preferred

Legal interns must be law students currently enrolled at and returning to law school in the fall of the year of the internship. First consideration is given to law students in the top half of their class.

Application Procedure

The process begins by applying online. Those who pass the first cut are invited to interview. The interview period lasts from January to March.

Deadline

The window for applications begins in October and ends in mid-December.

For More Information

www.nfl.com/careers/internships

Cross Pollination

If you like the idea of interning in a professional sports organization, consider the national headquarters of Major League Baseball, the National Hockey League, and the National Basketball Association as well as the quadrennial Olympics, all of which have internship programs.

Also, contact your local team! If you don't find success at a sport's national headquarters, the local team, including minor leagues, may have a spot for you. In addition to the "official" application process for local sports teams, these organizations are known to be responsive to personal introductions from current and former executives and players.

NATIONAL GALLERY OF ART INTERNSHIP PROGRAM (SUMMER INTERNSHIPS)

"The National Gallery of Art was created in 1937 for the people of the United States of America by a joint resolution of Congress, accepting the gift of financier and art collector Andrew W. Mellon. During the 1920s, Mr. Mellon began collecting with the intention of forming a gallery of art for the nation in Washington. In 1937, the year of his death, he promised his collection to the United States."

The National Gallery of Art has internship opportunities for undergraduate and graduate students. Applications for all academic backgrounds are acceptable. Possible placements include Archives, Conservation: Photographs, Curatorial: American and British Paintings, Curatorial: Photographs—19th-Century French Photography, Development: Fundraising and Stewardship, Education: Art Information for the Public, Exhibition Design: Design and

Architectural Practices, Exhibition Design: Silkscreen Shop, Exhibition Programs: Documentary Films and Other Materials, Facilities Management: Life-Cycle Analysis of Physical Plant Assets Horticultural Services, Personnel: Labor and Employment Law, Publishing Office: Production Processes, Special Events: Event Management, and many others. Summer internships last nine weeks.

Benefits

Summer interns work full-time at the Gallery from mid-June to mid-August and receive a stipend of approximately $4,500.

General Eligibility Requirements

According to the program Web site, eligibility varies according to internship, and applicants from all backgrounds are encouraged to apply. The majority of slots are for currently enrolled graduate students of all levels and those graduating in spring of the year of application with a relevant degree (such as M.A., M.B.A., M.F.A., M.Arch., M.Ed, J.D., or M.L.S.). Please check prerequisites carefully. This is an international program.

For International Students

The National Gallery of Art Summer Internship Program is open to international students.

Application Process

A complete application packet must include six copies each of the following:

- the completed application form
- a full resume or CV
- a writing sample
- academic transcripts (copies are acceptable)

Deadline

The deadline is mid-January for the internship commencing that summer.

For More Information

http://www.nga.gov/education/internsumm.shtm

NATIONAL PARKS BUSINESS PLAN INTERNSHIP

"National Park Business Plan and Consulting Interns (summer consultants) promote the long-term health of our national parks by developing and improving financial planning and management tools at the park or program level."

The National Parks seek highly qualified graduate students in the areas of business, public policy, environmental management, public administration, and related fields to intern at various national parks. Interns work on team-based projects that focus on improving park planning and management over an eleven-week period during the summer. Fifteen "summer consultants" are chosen annually.

Benefits

Summer consultants are paid a living stipend of $725 a month. Other benefits include housing, limited insurance, and transportation to and from the assigned post.

General Eligibility Requirements

According to the program Web site, students must:

- be U.S. citizens or permanent residents
- have at least two years of professional work experience
- have excellent time-management/project-management and analytical skills
- possess superb oral and written communication skills, including presentation skills
- have a flexible work style and the ability to work in a team
- demonstrate an understanding of and commitment to the mission of the National Park Service
- have a valid U.S. driver's license

Consulting, government, or nonprofit experience is preferred.

Application Procedure

Interested applicants must send:

- a cover letter
- a resume
- a writing sample
- names and contact information of two references

A select number of applicants will be chosen for interviews.

Deadline

Applications are due in January. Early application is highly recommended.

For More Information

http://www.nps.gov/aboutus/consultinginternship.htm

THE NEW YORK TIMES SUMMER INTERNSHIP

"The Times began the [internship] program in 1984. In its first 17 years, it was aimed at members of minority groups who, because of race or ethnicity, had been historically excluded from opportunities in America's newspaper industry. While the internships are now open to all applicants, the program remains as an integral part of The Times's commitment to recruit and hire as diverse and as highly qualified a staff as possible."

The New York Times provides four different summer internship experiences for college seniors and graduate students seeking careers in journalism. Internship possibilities include the:

- James Reston Reporting Fellowships
- David E. Rosenbaum Reporting Internship in Washington, DC
- Thomas Morgan Internships in Visual Journalism
- Dow Jones Newspaper Fund Editing Internship

All are paid and last for ten weeks during the summer. Experiences vary by internship.

Benefits

Interns receive a salary of approximately $900 a week for ten weeks. The Dow Jones Newspaper Fund Editing Internship offers an additional $1,000 scholarship upon successful completion of the internship.

General Eligibility Requirements

According to the Web site, applicants must:

- be seniors or graduate students at the time of application
- be seeking a career in journalism

Application Procedure

The application procedure and requirements differ for each fellowship/internship program. Generally, all applicants must submit:

- a cover letter
- a resume
- writing samples

Deadline

Applications are due in November.

For More Information

http://www.nytco.com/careers/internships/summer.html#jamesReston

PricewaterhouseCoopers (PwC) Internships

PricewaterhouseCoopers (PwC) is one of the "big four" accounting/consulting firms with a global reach. PwC is made up of member firms that operate locally in 151 countries and employ more than 163,000 people. In the United States, it is the eighth-largest privately owned organization.

PricewaterhouseCoopers (PwC), like most financial and consulting firms, likes to make permanent hires from its pool of interns. So if this career direction is attractive to you, it's vitally important to become an intern at one of these companies. Although the PwC Internship program focuses on accounting opportunities, PwC has lines of business in the following categories: audit and assurance, consulting, deals (mergers and acquisitions), human resources, legal services, and tax services. In all, PwC has twenty-two industry-specialized practices.

For More Information

http://www.pwc.com/us/en/careers/pwctv/pwc-internships.jhtml

Cross Pollination

If you're interested in PricewaterhouseCoopers, you should take a look at the other major accounting and consulting organizations: Deloitte Touche Tohmatsu, Ernst and Young, KPMG. There are also other accounting and consulting firms of note such as Accenture and McKinsey and Company, as well as major consulting organizations inside other types of companies, such as IBM and HP.

These types of organizations are vigorous recruiters at major universities, typically hosting information sessions in the fall, collecting resumes in late fall to early winter, and interviewing prospective interns late fall to early spring, and sometimes throughout the year. If your campus does not host these recruiters, it can be harder than you might think to get their attention. An introduction from a current employee is one route. Dressing the part and walking into a branch and asking for the manager to sponsor you is another. Or, in some cases your college or university will have a reciprocal agreement between your university's career center and the career center at a university where recruiters do visit. If so, ask to be allowed to approach company representatives at that campus. Although everyone will tell you "just apply online," our discussions with students and consultants indicate that this has a modest rate of success. You need to try to get face-to-face with a recruiter or a sponsor, if you can.

A Career Thought

Accountants and consultants are expected to put in long hours, travel frequently—often with little or no notice—look and act professional at all times in spite of the wear and tear of travel and long days, and never complain. If this doesn't sound like you, don't head in this direction.

SERVICE PROGRAMS

Serving others can be a great break before you go to graduate school or launch a career, or it can be a career in itself. The opportunities in this section are experiences that will mold you in ways you cannot even anticipate. You will gain real-life and career skills, but you will also have an opportunity to challenge yourself and learn about people, places, and things you would not experience in your "normal" life.

Some of these programs provide an excellent structured gap year or two before a young person returns to studies or more traditional employment. Also, some of these programs have outstanding returnee and alumni programming to help you make that transition back to graduate school or a job.

One warning, though: Some of these opportunities are *highly competitive.* It might be easier to get a coveted, career-track job, or be admitted to an Ivy League graduate program than to be selected for some of these programs. Keep that in mind as you consider your goals and plan your options.

- AmeriCorps
- City Year Program
- Doctors Without Borders Office Internships
- FBI Honors Internship Program
- Humanity in Action (HIA) Summer Fellowships
- Mercy Corps Internships
- Oxfam America Internship Program
- Peace Corps Volunteer
- Teach For America
- Teaching Assistantship Program in France
- United Nations Internship Program
- World Health Organization (WHO) Internships
- WorldTeach

AMERICORPS

AmeriCorps is a federal program that was created as part of the National and Community Service Trust Act of 1993. More than 70,000 individuals join AmeriCorps each year.

AmeriCorps is a domestic program with a vast array of service opportunities available throughout the United States. Opportunities include, among others, tutoring and mentoring disadvantaged youth, fighting illiteracy, helping improve health services, and building affordable housing. AmeriCorps has three primary programs, each with a slightly different focus. According to the Web site:

- AmeriCorps State and National supports a broad range of local service programs that engage thousands of Americans in intensive service to meet critical community needs.
- AmeriCorps VISTA provides full-time members to community organizations and public agencies to create and expand programs that build capacity and ultimately bring low-income individuals and communities out of poverty.
- The AmeriCorps National Civilian Community Corps (NCCC) is a full-time residential program for men and women, ages 18-24, that strengthens communities

while developing leaders through direct, team-based national and community service.

Benefits

AmeriCorps members receive a living allowance during their term of service as well as help with college costs and student loans through the Segal AmeriCorps Education Award. This award can be used to pay educational expenses at qualified institutions, for educational training, or to repay qualified student loans. Several universities match the award.

General Eligibility Requirements

AmeriCorps members must:

- be U.S. citizens or permanent residents
- be at least 17 years old

Certain positions have additional requirements that can be found on the AmeriCorps Web site.

Application Process

To apply, visit the "I am ready to serve" area of the AmeriCorps Web site. Select an area of service interest and then select a state. A list of openings and eligibility requirements will be displayed.

Deadline

Applications are accepted year-round.

For More Information

http://www.americorps.gov/

CITY YEAR PROGRAM

City Year's vision is that one day the most commonly asked question of a young person will be, "Where are you going to do your service year?"

City Year is a program established with the belief that young people can influence and change the world in positive ways. City Year is a 10-month program with service opportunities available in cities throughout the United States and South Africa. City Year participants, called "corps members," primarily work in and around academic settings, helping children stay in school while working to positively affect the local community.

Benefits

City Year corps members receive a living allowance as well as help with college costs and student loans through the Segal AmeriCorps Education Award. This award can be used to pay educational expenses at qualified institutions of higher education, or for educational training, or to repay qualified student loans. Several universities will match the award. (Check this link to see if your university participates: http://www.americorps.gov/for_individuals/benefits/ed_award_match.asp.)

General Eligibility Requirements

Based on City Year's list of requirements, applicants must:

- be between the ages of 17 and 24
- be a U.S. citizen or legal permanent resident
- be ready to dedicate 10 months to full-time service
- be a high school graduate, GED recipient, or agree to work toward the GED while serving at City Year
- have served no more than two terms in another AmeriCorps, National Civilian Community Corps (NCCC), or VISTA program
- agree to and pass a background or security check

Application Process

To apply for City Year, register on the City Year Web site. Once registered, the online application is available. The selection process usually takes between two and four weeks. Typically, 1 out of 6 applicants is selected for City Year.

Deadline

The City Year program has four application cycles each year beginning in November. The last cycle is in May.

For More Information

http://www.cityyear.org/

DOCTORS WITHOUT BORDERS OFFICE INTERNSHIPS

"Doctors Without Borders/Médecins Sans Frontières (MSF) is an international medical humanitarian organization working in more than 60 countries to assist people whose survival is threatened by violence, neglect, or catastrophe."

Doctors Without Borders was established in 1971 in France by doctors and journalists who wanted to provide medical care in areas of the world with critical needs. Currently, the New York office offers paid internships that last approximately ten to twelve weeks. Applicants may apply for a fall, spring, or summer term. Interns gain experience with the operational side of the organization and an introduction to international medical humanitarian aid.

Benefits

Interns are paid $10 an hour. They must arrange their own travel and housing.

General Eligibility Requirements

No specific eligibility requirements are stated. This internship is a competitive program, and candidates are selected on a merit basis. International candidates are responsible for securing a U.S. work permit.

Application Procedure

Interested applicants should e-mail a resume and cover letter to internships@newyork.msf.org. Due to the high volume of applications, only finalists will be contacted *after* the application deadline. Candidates may apply for more than one term but will only be contacted regarding the most current term.

Deadline

Interns may apply to work during one of three terms in the New York office. Applications for the spring term are due in January, applications for the summer term in April, and applications for the fall term in August.

For More Information

http://www.doctorswithoutborders.org/work/office/internships.cfm?ref=main-menu

FBI Honors Internship Program

The Federal Bureau of Investigation (FBI) is part of the U.S. Department of Justice. The FBI serves as a federal criminal investigation unit as well as an intelligence-gathering entity. The FBI has offices across the United States and also operates inside U.S. embassies around the world as "legal attaches."

The FBI Honors Internship Program is available to both undergraduate and graduate students. The purpose of the FBI Honors Internship is to provide selected interns ". . . an exciting insider's view of FBI operations and . . . an opportunity to explore the many career opportunities within the Bureau." The Honors Internship lasts approximately nine weeks during the summer. Interns may be placed at FBI headquarters in Washington, DC, or in a Regional Computer Forensics Laboratory.

Benefits

The FBI Honors Internship is unpaid. It does, however, provide some travel costs to and from the placement site.

General Eligibility Requirements

According to the program Web site, students must meet the following criteria:

- be attending an accredited college or university
- be in their junior or senior year, though graduating seniors may also apply
- have a minimum cumulative GPA of 3.0 or above on a 4.0 scale
- be in good standing
- be U.S. citizens
- meet all FBI employment requirements, including passing an FBI background investigation and receipt of a Top Secret Security Clearance

Application Procedure

The application is online. Selected applicants will be invited to interview at a regional FBI Field Office. Final candidates will be interviewed at FBI Headquarters in Washington, DC, and a selection committee at FBI Headquarters will make final decisions. Conditional offers will be made dependent on receiving clearance after an extensive FBI background investigation.

Deadline

Visit the program Web site for deadline information.

For More Information

http://www.fbijobs.gov/231.asp#3

HUMANITY IN ACTION (HIA) SUMMER FELLOWSHIPS

"HIA is an international educational organization that engages, inspires, and continuously develops a network of students, young professionals, and established leaders committed to protecting minorities and promoting human rights—in their own communities and around the world."

The Humanity in Action Summer Fellowship program is a five-week intensive experience designed to explore minority and human rights issues in one of five host countries: Denmark, France, Germany, The Netherlands, Poland, and the United States. The summer program has two parts:

> During the first phase, recognized leaders of human rights organizations, politicians, diplomats, philanthropists, journalists, scholars, artists, and authors meet with the Fellows during three-and-a-half weeks of intensive seminars, site visits, and focus-group activities. [The second part] culminates in a period of research and writing. International teams of Fellows focus on past and current minority issues in their host country, producing a written report.

Benefits

During the five-week fellowship, participants receive housing and a modest food stipend. Fellows are responsible for their own travel expenses.

General Eligibility Requirements

According to the Web site, applicants must meet the following criteria:

- be current sophomores, juniors, seniors, or recent graduates at accredited four-year colleges or universities in the United States
- are mature, proactive, self-reliant, and comfortable in intensive group activity and interaction

All majors and academic disciplines are encouraged to apply.

Application Procedure

Interested applicants fill out an online application. Completed applications include:

- an application form

- a resume
- official transcripts
- a response essay
- a personal statement
- two letters of recommendation

Applicants may apply to the American Program and/or the European Programs but can only participate in one. Applicants to the European Programs may not apply to a program in a specific country and cannot choose their city of participation.

Deadline

Applications are due in January.

For More Information

http://www.humanityinaction.org/programs/summerfellowship

Mercy Corps Internships

"Mercy Corps helps people in the world's toughest places turn the crises of natural disaster, poverty and conflict into opportunities for progress. Driven by local needs and market conditions, our programs provide communities with the tools and support they need to transform their own lives. Our worldwide team of 3,700 professionals is improving the lives of 16.7 million people in more than 40 countries."

According to the Mercy Corps Web site:

Every year, some of the most talented students from around the world set out on internships with Mercy Corps with particularly demanding terms of reference—to change the world. Internships are challenging opportunities for aspiring international relief and development practitioners. They are a chance to apply your education to hands-on projects that contribute to Mercy Corps' efforts to end world poverty.

Mercy Corps offers two types of internships: domestic internships and field internships. Internships vary in duration.

- **Domestic Internships**
  Domestic internships are for students interested in careers in international development and nonprofit management and are located in the following Mercy Corps office locations: Portland, Oregon; Manhattan, New York; Washington, DC; Cambridge, Massachusetts; and Edinburgh, Scotland.

- **Field Internships**

  Field internships are for more advanced students. Field internship placements are made in various locations throughout the world.

Benefits

Interns receive valuable experience in the areas of global relief and global development. Interns may arrange academic credit. Most internships are unpaid.

General Eligibility Requirements

Eligibility requirements vary depending on the internship. Please check the Mercy Corps Web site for complete details. Minimally, students must be receiving academic credit or formal academic sponsorship throughout the duration of the internship.

Application Process

To apply, interested applicants must search for available internships on the Mercy Corps Web site. Listings will describe expectations, qualifications, and responsibilities. Interested applicants must create a profile and submit for review materials that are very specific to each opportunity.

Deadline

The application deadline varies with the opportunity.

For More Information

http://www.mercycorps.org/internships

OXFAM AMERICA INTERNSHIP PROGRAM

"Oxfam was the original postal abbreviation for the Oxford Committee for Famine Relief, which was started in England during World War II to provide relief to war victims in Europe. Since then, Oxfams have been established in 13 countries. Oxfam America is an international relief and development organization that creates lasting solutions to poverty, hunger, and injustice. Together with individuals and local groups in more than 100 countries, Oxfam saves lives, helps people overcome poverty, and fights for social justice. [Oxfam America is] an affiliate of Oxfam International."

The Oxfam America Internship Program offers internships annually at the Oxfam offices in Boston and Washington, DC. Interns work for a set number of hours each week. Participants gain valuable experience in the areas of international development and nonprofit management. Interns are welcomed from a wide variety of academic backgrounds.

Benefits

Students may arrange academic credit for their internship experience. This is an unpaid internship.

General Eligibility Requirements

According to the Oxfam Web site, applicants must be students in an accredited educational program or have visas for their year of training after graduation.

For International Students

This program is open to international applicants as long as they have valid visas or work papers that allow them to legally work in the United States.

Application Process

Interested applicants should start the process by reviewing the list of current internship opportunities. To apply, applicants must e-mail a cover letter and resume to internsandvolunteers@ oxfamamerica.org.

Deadline

Deadlines vary based on current internship opportunities.

For More Information

http://www.oxfamamerica.org

PEACE CORPS VOLUNTEER

The idea for the Peace Corps was born out of a campaign speech made by John F. Kennedy in 1960 at the University of Michigan. Kennedy challenged students to serve the United States by using their skills and training to help people in developing nations. As President, Kennedy signed an Executive Order creating the Peace Corps.

The mission of the Peace Corps is to ". . . promote world peace and friendship." Currently the Peace Corps is active in seventy-seven countries. Peace Corps Volunteers commit to twenty-seven months of service. Volunteers' skills and training are taken into consideration, and placement is made in one of the following areas: education, youth and community development, health, business and information and communication technology, agriculture, environment; HIV/AIDS, food security, and Earth Day.

Two Peace Corp programs, Master's International and Fellows/USA, provide Peace Corp Volunteers graduate-level educational opportunities.

- **Master's International**

  This program combines Peace Corps service with a master's degree program. Candidates apply both to the Peace Corps and to the participating graduate school. Once accepted, students study on campus, usually for a year, and then spend the next two years earning academic credit while working overseas in a related Peace Corps project. Tuition may be waived by the school for the period spent serving in the Peace Corps, or the institution may provide research or teaching assistantships or scholarships.

- **Fellows/USA**

  This program offers scholarships or reduced tuition for advanced-degree programs for returning Peace Corps volunteers. There may also be housing allowances, paid employment, or health benefits as part of the program. In return, Fellows commit to working in underserved U.S. communities as they pursue their degrees.

Benefits

Peace Corps Volunteers receive a monthly living allowance and medical insurance while on assignment. Upon completion of the twenty-seven-month service period, Volunteers receive a $6,000 transition stipend.

General Eligibility Requirements

Peace Corps Volunteers must meet the following guidelines:

- commit to twenty-seven months of work in a foreign country
- be U.S. citizens
- be at least 18 years old; there is no upper age limit

An earned bachelor's degree is not necessarily required for selection.

Application Process

To apply for Peace Corps service, applicants must first fill out an application located on the Peace Corps Web site. Applicants are then interviewed by a Peace Corps representative. After the interview stage, applicants seek medical and legal clearance. An acceptance decision is made based on an applicant's skills, training, and suitability. Applications are accepted anytime throughout the year. The entire application process can take up to nine months.

For applications to the Master's International and Fellows/USA programs, check the Peace Corps Web site under "Educational Benefits."

For More Information

http://www.peacecorps.gov/

Cross Pollination

If the Peace Corps appeals to you, you should know that it is not the only option. Check out Save the Children (www.savethechildren.org), Catholic Relief Services (http://crs.org), and the Bridge Span Group (http://bridgespan.org), all of which have global operations run by site volunteers.

TEACH FOR AMERICA

Wendy Kopp founded Teach For America in 1990. Its foundational ideas were formed during her senior year at Princeton University in 1989 to fulfill the requirements for her senior thesis.

Teach For America is an organization whose ultimate aim is to end educational inequality in the United States. The program enlists graduating college students and recent graduates to help meet this goal by committing to teaching at least two years in low-income communities. Applicants accepted into the Teach For America corps begin with a required five-week summer training session designed to prepare them for the classroom.

Teach For America corps members come from a variety of academic and professional backgrounds. The organization seeks individuals "who have what it takes to excel as teachers and to ultimately exert broader societal influence in our nation." The program has grown significantly in popularity, according to its Web site. In a recent year, 35,000 individuals applied. "At more than 130 colleges and universities, over 5 percent of the senior class applied. At Ivy League universities, 11 percent of all seniors applied, including nearly 20 percent of African-American and Latino/Hispanic seniors. Teach For America is the No. 1 employer of graduating seniors at more than 20 schools, including Georgetown University, Spelman College, and the University of Chicago." Keep in mind that it is about as easy to get into an Ivy League university, statistically, as it is to be selected for Teach For America.

Benefits

Corps members are paid a full teacher's salary—usually between $27,000 and $47,000 depending upon their placement region. They also receive full health benefits for the duration of their tenure in the program.

Participants may be eligible to receive an AmeriCorps grant to pay past loans or future educational expenses. Scholarships are available for graduate school from Teach For America graduate school partners. "Transitional expenses" are available to help students move and settle into the community in which they will work.

General Eligibility Requirements

Teach For America is open to recent college graduates with any academic background. Students must have completed their baccalaureate degree from an accredited institution of higher education by the beginning of the summer training session. Students may apply as graduate students or working professionals. There is no maximum age limit.

Application Process

Applicants may apply at any one of four times throughout the year. The process begins by filling out an online application that requires:

- a one-page resume
- a letter of intent
- a personal essay

The online application is reviewed by Teach For America personnel. Applicants may check the Web site concerning the status of their application.

Selected applicants will then be asked to participate in a 30-minute phone interview. At this point, students must submit letters of recommendation. If applicants are selected to go on after the phone interview, they are invited for a daylong final interview.

For More Information

http://www.teachforamerica.org/

TEACHING ASSISTANTSHIP PROGRAM IN FRANCE

The Teaching Assistantship Program in France is administered by the French Ministry of Education and the Cultural Services at the French Embassy.

Each year, approximately 1,500 Americans explore French culture and society by serving as English teaching assistants in French public schools. This seven-to-nine week program is designed so that French students can hear a native speaker while studying English. Teaching assistants also work to promote cultural understanding between France and the United States.

Benefits

Teaching assistants are provided a monthly stipend of about $1,000. Limited health insurance is provided after being in the country for several weeks.

General Eligibility Requirements

According to the Web site, applicants must meet the following criteria:

- be U.S. citizens or foreign nationals with a U.S. green card. French permanent residents of the United States are not eligible to apply.
- be between 20 and 29 years of age
- have completed at least two years of higher education before beginning the program
- have completed the majority of their elementary, secondary, and university studies in the United States
- be proficient in French

Applicants who do not have a major or minor in French may apply if they have developed at least a basic proficiency in French, equivalent to three semesters, and/or lived abroad in a French-speaking country.

Application Procedure

Interested applicants must complete an online application and show proficiency in French.

Deadline

Applications are due in January.

For More Information

http://www.frenchculture.org/spip.php?rubrique424andtout=ok

UNITED NATIONS INTERNSHIP PROGRAM

"The United Nations is an international organization founded in 1945 after the Second World War by 51 countries committed to maintaining international peace and security, developing friendly relations among nations and promoting social progress, better living standards and human rights."

The United Nations (UN) provides opportunities for students enrolled in a graduate program to undertake an internship at its headquarters in New York or in Geneva, Vienna, Nairobi, Addis Ababa, Bangkok, Beirut, Santiago, Arusha, and The Hague. According to the program Web site:

> The objective of the internship is to give you a first-hand impression of the day-to-day working environment of the United Nations. You will be given a real chance to work with our people. As part of our team, working directly with outstanding and inspiring career professionals and senior management within the Organization, you will be exposed to high-profile conferences, participate in meetings, and contribute to analytical work as well as organizational policy. Initially you will take on the amount of responsibility you can shoulder; the potential for growth, however, is yours to develop.

Benefits

Funding varies according to the internship, but working for the UN provides the obvious benefit of exposure to the world of international affairs, law, culture, and diplomacy.

General Eligibility Requirements

To qualify for the United Nations Headquarters Internship Program, applicants must:

- be enrolled in a degree program in a graduate school (second university degree or higher) at the time of application and during the internship
- be able to secure the necessary visas and arrange travel to the relevant UN site
- be able to secure the funds necessary to cover the costs of travel, accommodations, and living expenses
- be 30 years old or younger
- be fluent in English and/or French (many opportunities require both languages)
- carry medical insurance

Application Process

Eligible candidates interested in participating in an internship at the United Nations Headquarters in New York can apply by visiting the United Nations Human Resources Web site: http://careers.un.org.

All applicants are strongly encouraged to apply online well before the deadline stated in the Vacancy Announcement.

Deadline

Generally, deadlines will be four months before the start of the Internship Session.

- End of January: Deadline for the Summer Session, running from early June to early August
- Mid-May: Deadline for the Fall Session, running from mid-September to mid-November
- Mid-September: Deadline for the Spring Session, running from mid-January to mid-March

For More Information

http://careers.un.org/UNCareers/tabid/65/viewtype/IP/language/en-US/Default.aspx

WORLD HEALTH ORGANIZATION (WHO) INTERNSHIPS

"WHO is the directing and coordinating authority for health within the United Nations system. It is responsible for providing leadership on global health matters, shaping the health research agenda, setting norms and standards, articulating evidence-based policy options, providing technical support to countries and monitoring and assessing health trends."

The World Health Organization (WHO) offers internships for graduate-level students at its headquarters in Geneva, Switzerland. Applicants may select placement in one of a variety of WHO departments, including Family and Community Health; Global Polio Eradication Initiative; Health Action in Crisis; Health Security and Environment; Health Systems and Services; HIV/AIDS; TB, Malaria and Neglected Tropical Diseases; Information, Evidence and Research; and Noncommunicable Diseases and Mental Health. Interns are expected to work full-time for six to twelve weeks.

Benefits

The World Health Organization Internship is unpaid.

General Eligibility Requirements

According to the WHO Web site, applicants must meet the following criteria:

- be enrolled in graduate school at the time of application and during the internship

- be pursuing studies in countries where higher education is not divided into undergraduate and graduate stages
- have completed at least three years of full-time study at a university or equivalent institution toward the completion of a degree
- be at least 20 years old
- possess a first degree in a public health, medical, or social field related to the technical work of WHO
- be fluent in the language of the assigned office

Application Procedure

Interested applicants fill out an application online through the WHO e-Recruitment system.

Deadline

Interns may apply to work either during the summer term (May to October) or winter term (November to April). Applications are accepted for the summer term from December 1 to January 31 each year and for the winter term from August 1 to September 30.

For More Information

http://www.who.int/employment/internship/en/

WORLD TEACH

"WorldTeach partners with governments and other organizations in developing countries to provide volunteer teachers to meet local needs and promote responsible global citizenship. WorldTeach is a non-profit, non-governmental organization founded by a group of Harvard students in 1986 in response to the need for educational assistance in developing countries."

The WorldTeach program sends volunteers into schools and educational agencies in sixteen countries around the world. According to the WorldTeach Web site:

> You will share the skills and knowledge gained through your education and life experience with students who have not had the same advantages, and you will make a concrete and lasting difference in their lives. You will gain cultural understanding and the ability to work independently in a new environment. You will have a role in the community, and an opportunity to learn about the local culture and contribute to community life and development. And you will develop key skills—including teaching, language, cross-cultural communication, and leadership—that will be useful in any career.

To help fund the volunteer experience, participants are asked to make a financial "volunteer commitment" to help offset expenses of traveling and living abroad. The WorldTeach program does provide participants the tools to help them raise funds to cover the "volunteer commitment."

Benefits

WorldTeach participants receive valuable life and career experience.

General Eligibility Requirements

According to the WorldTeach program Web site, participants must meet the following criteria:

- For yearlong programs, volunteers must have a bachelor's degree. Summer program volunteers do not need to have a college degree but must be at least 18 years of age. WorldTeach programs are open to native speakers of English; volunteers do NOT have to be U.S. citizens.
- The program is seeking individuals who show a commitment to teaching, volunteer service, international development, and intercultural understanding.

WorldTeach volunteers range in age from college students (summer programs) and recent college graduates to mid-career professionals and retirees. People of all ages and backgrounds are encouraged to apply.

Application Process

A completed application consists of an online two-part application. Part two of the application requires the following materials:

- three essays
- a resume
- references
- academic transcripts (only for semester and yearlong programs)

An interview may be required.

Deadline

Deadlines vary significantly depending on which program is of interest.

For More Information

http://www.worldteach.org/

Cross Pollination

Note the other teaching opportunities, such as Knowles Science Teaching Foundation (KSTF) Teaching Fellowship in Chapter 3 and Teach For America in Chapter 5.

LEADERSHIP PROGRAMS

Leadership programs are designed to prepare young people for careers in government, the law, activism, public service, and politics. In programs such as the following, you may learn how power works, how public opinion is formed and shaped, and how communities work from the local level on up to the global sphere. You may gain skills in media relations, program design and development, and public administration.

In addition to gaining an understanding of these structures, these programs are designed to challenge and develop a young person's skills set. Components of these programs may focus on persuasive public speaking, team leadership, effective writing, proposal development, and similar tasks that people in public service do. We have only a few programs featured here, but if this type of opportunity is of interest to you, your career center can guide you to others.

- AIESEC
- Capital City Fellows Programs
- CIA Undergraduate Internship Program
- CIA Undergraduate Scholarship Program
- Coro Fellows Program in Public Affairs
- Global Engineering Education Exchange
- Institute of International Education Internship Program
- The Japanese Exchange Programme (JET)
- Library of Congress Internship and Fellowship Programs
- The Merage Foundation American Dream Fellowship
- Next Step Connections
- Robert Bosch Foundation Fellowship Program
- U.S. Agency for International Development Student Intern Program (USAID)
- U.S. Department of State Student Internships
- U.S. International Trade Commission Internships
- Washington Center for Internships and Academic Seminars
- White House Internship Program
- World Bank Internship Program

AIESEC

AIESEC stands for "Association Internationale des Etudiants en Sciences Economiques et Commerciales," but it long ago expanded beyond these two areas. These days as a global organization, it mostly goes by its acronym, like KFC, which is also global, but without the food.

The Association Internationale des Etudiants en Sciences Economiques et Commerciales (AIESEC) is the largest student-run organization in the world, with 45,000 members active in over 107 countries. By providing leadership opportunities before and after students pursue global internship experiences, "AIESEC offers young people the opportunity to be global citizens, to change the world, and to get experience and skills that matter today."

AIESEC's Web site states, "Society needs leaders who are entrepreneurial, culturally sensitive, socially responsible and take an active part in their own learning. To gain a holistic experience AIESEC offers you the opportunity to take on a leadership role before or after your internship. Learn how to lead a team, manage large projects and run a local or national organization along with people all over the world!"

AIESEC offers the following programs:

- **Professional International Exchange**
  With a vigorous network of global partners (major corporations and governmental entities) that recruit transnational interns, AIESEC is a leading placement service for transnational internships. Specific language skills are not required.
- **Global Theme Programme (GTP)**
  GTP is an education/outreach/think-tank-type training and development program focusing on sustainable development, globalism, and public/private enterprise.
- **Issue-Based Experiences (IBXPs)**
  IBXPs are similar to other organizations' leadership development programs but with more emphasis on skills development to create effective leaders to face the world's future challenges.

Benefits

A lifetime benefit of AIESEC is access to program alumni in positions of leadership and power all over the world through the Global Alumni Network.

AIESEC in Numbers

- 107 countries and territories
- 1,700 universities
- 45,000 members
- 8,500 international internships

- 9,000 leadership roles
- 4,000 partners/sponsors
- 470 conferences annually
- 60 years of experience

For More Information

See http://www.AIESEC.org and http://www.AiesecUs.org.

Capital City Fellows Programs

The City of Washington, DC, created the Capital City Fellows program to provide public service opportunities to recent master's-level graduates in public service–related fields and to attract talented students to work for the Washington, DC, city government.

The Capital City Fellows Program is designed to give recent graduates of master's degree programs experience working for the city of Washington, DC. Fellows are appointed for a two-year term and rotate through four city agencies. Possible agencies include the Office of the City Administrator, Department of Human Resources, Office of the Chief Financial Officer, Department of Transportation, Department of Corrections, Department of Real Estate Services, and the Metropolitan Police Department. Fellows receive numerous professional development opportunities during their two-year term.

Benefits

Capital City Fellows receive a salary of $50,000 a year and are eligible for a benefits package that includes healthcare.

General Eligibility Requirements

According to the program Web site, applicants must meet the following criteria:

- have earned their graduate degree (with a GPA of 3.5 or higher) within two years prior to the start of the Fellowship. Waivers to this requirement may be granted in exceptional cases
- be U.S. citizens or have legal noncitizen residence status

Capital City Fellows are required to live in the District of Columbia.

Application Procedure

Interested applicants must fill out an online application that includes submission of:

- a resume
- official academic transcripts
- three letters of reference

Selected applicants are invited to an interview.

Deadline

Applications are due at the beginning of April.

For More Information

http://dchr.dc.gov/dcop/cwp/view,a,1222,q,530470.asp

CIA UNDERGRADUATE INTERNSHIP PROGRAM

"This is an opportunity to learn from highly skilled professionals who support U.S. officials that make our country's foreign policy. You'll assist with substantive and meaningful work assignments, while earning a competitive income and gaining invaluable practical experience. There's no better place to learn than at the center of intelligence."

The Central Intelligence Agency (CIA) offers a competitive internship program for high-achieving college students. The program is designed for undergraduates interested in careers in either the CIA or foreign affairs. The CIA seeks undergraduates for this program who are majoring in the following disciplines: engineering, computer science, mathematics, economics, physical sciences, foreign languages, area studies, business administration, accounting, international relations, finance, logistics, human resources, geography, national security studies, military and foreign affairs, political science, and graphic design. Those selected as interns must complete two 90-day summer internships or a combination of one semester and one summer internship.

Benefits

The CIA Undergraduate Internship Program is a paid internship program. In addition to competitive salaries, the CIA offers a full range of employee benefits, including health insurance.

General Eligibility Requirements

According to the program Web site, applicants must meet the following criteria:

- be U.S. citizens
- be in at least their second year of college

- have a minimum 3.0 GPA
- demonstrate outstanding interpersonal skills, the ability to write clearly and accurately, and a strong interest in foreign affairs
- successfully complete medical and polygraph examinations, as well as pass a background investigation

Foreign-language skills, previous international residency, and/or military experience are pluses.

Application Procedure

Create an account to log in to the online application system. The application must be completed within three days after establishing the account. The application is comprehensive and candidates must provide:

- significant background information
- CIA job preferences
- resume
- transcripts
- writing samples
- a Personnel Evaluation Form

Deadline

Check the official program Web site for deadline information.

For More Information

https://www.cia.gov/careers/student-opportunities/

CIA UNDERGRADUATE SCHOLARSHIP PROGRAM

The Central Intelligence Agency (CIA) is an independent federal government agency that is responsible for providing national security intelligence to senior government policymakers.

The Central Intelligence Agency (CIA) Undergraduate Scholarship program is available to high school seniors planning to enroll in four-year higher education degree programs as well as to college sophomores currently enrolled in such programs. The CIA Scholarship Program is designed to provide high-achieving students with meaningful professional experience related to their college major. Selected CIA Scholars work for the agency during their summer breaks and commit to working full-time after graduation.

For High School Students

Note that the CIA Undergraduate Scholarship Program is another one of the few experiential programs open to high school seniors.

Benefits

CIA Scholars are provided an annual salary, optional health benefits, life insurance, and retirement. Scholars also receive educational funding up to $18,000 a year for tuition, fees, books, and supplies. Travel costs to and from the Washington, DC, area for summer work are also covered.

General Eligibility Requirements

According to the program Web site, applicants must meet the following criteria:

- be U.S. citizens
- be at least18 years of age
- score 1000 SAT (Math and Verbal) or 21 ACT for high school students
- have a minimum 3.0 on a 4.0 scale in high school or a college minimum GPA of 3.0 on a 4.0 scale
- demonstrate financial need (income of $70,000 for a family of 4, or $80,000 for a family of 5 or more)
- successfully complete both a security and a medical screening
- be available to work in the Washington, DC, area during employment

Application Procedure

Create an account to log in to online application system. The application must be completed within three days of establishing the account. The application is comprehensive and candidates must provide:

- significant background information
- CIA job preferences
- resume
- transcripts
- writing samples
- a Personnel Evaluation Form

Deadline

Applications open in August and are due in October.

For More Information

https://www.cia.gov/careers/student-opportunities/

CORO FELLOWS PROGRAM IN PUBLIC AFFAIRS

"Coro trains ethical, diverse civic leaders nationwide. Coro leaders develop skills; master tools needed to engage and empower communities; gain experience in government, business, labor and not-for-profit community organizations; and participate in special community and political problem-solving processes."

The Coro Fellows Program in Public Affairs is a graduate-level, experienced-based leadership development program. Fellows participate in a nine-month program based at one of five national Coro Centers located in Los Angeles, New York, Pittsburgh, San Francisco, and St. Louis. Through a variety of rigorous educational experiences, such as field placements, group interviews, seminars, focus weeks, and individual and group projects, Fellows are prepared for high-level leadership positions in public affairs. Sixty-eight Coro Fellows are chosen annually.

Benefits

Coro Fellows may arrange for graduate-level academic credit for their participation in the nine-month program. Partnerships with several graduate programs have been established. Graduates also benefit from a strong network of Coro alumni and community partners.

General Eligibility Requirements

According to the program Web site:

> Coro is looking for people who have demonstrated some leadership either academically, or within a community and have an interest in public affairs. In addition, Coro is looking for the following qualities: ability to work within a diverse group, commitment to public service, flexibility and intellectual curiosity.

Application Process

Students must first submit an online interest form. This gives access to the full application. The online portion consists of:

- the application form
- three essays
- a resume

Applicants mail in the second portion of the application that consists of:

- a signed declaration of application
- three letters of recommendation
- official academic transcripts

There is a $75 application fee.

Deadline

The application is due in January.

For More Information

http://www.coro.org/site/c.geJNIUOzErH/b.4667963/k.725D/Coro_Fellows_Program.htm

GLOBAL ENGINEERING EDUCATION EXCHANGE

Global E3 Consortium is made up currently of forty-five universities worldwide—about thirty-five in the United States and ten in the United Kingdom, Central and Eastern Europe, Asia, Latin America, and the Middle East. Students from universities in this consortium may apply to attend any participating university outside their own country.

The Global Engineering Education Exchange Program is administered by the Institute for International Education (IIE). The program is designed to allow engineering students at member universities to participate in study-abroad experiences at other international partner institutions. After completing course work at the partner institution, students are eligible to participate in paid internship opportunities in their host country. Check the Global E[3] Web site for participating institutions.

Benefits

Students participating in the Global Engineering Education Exchange are eligible for a tuition swap, which means they pay the tuition rate at their home institution while taking courses and receiving academic credit at a foreign institution. Housing, meals, health insurance, and airfare costs are the responsibility of the student. Paid internships are usually available after the academic course work is completed.

General Eligibility Requirements

To be eligible, students must meet the following requirements:

- be currently enrolled at one of the participating U.S. universities
- be currently studying engineering or show demonstrated commitment to the field
- be approved to submit an application by the home campus's Global E3 adviser
- qualify to attend one of the participating international universities

Application Process

Applications are online. Students should work closely with their institutional advisor to ensure their applications are complete.

Deadline

The deadline for fall semester applications is in March. The deadline for spring semester applications is in October. Campus deadlines will be earlier; check with the campus Global E^3 adviser.

For More Information

http://www.iie.org/programs/GlobalE3/

INSTITUTE OF INTERNATIONAL EDUCATION INTERNSHIP PROGRAM

"In 2009, IIE celebrated its 90th anniversary and lasting commitment to developing leaders, educating global citizens, and advancing social justice."

Founded in 1919, the Institute of International Education (IIE) is a private, nonprofit leader in the international exchange of people and ideas. In collaboration with governments, foundations, and other sponsors, IIE creates programs of study and training for students, educators, and professionals from all sectors. These programs include the flagship Fulbright Program, administered for the U.S. Department of State. IIE also conducts policy research, provides resources on international exchange opportunities, and offers support to scholars in danger.

Benefits

All internships are unpaid, but they provide the opportunity to work with one of the most established organizations focused on study abroad.

General Eligibility Requirements

According to the Web site, applicants must:

- be currently enrolled in an accredited institution
- be able to receive credit for the internship

or

- complete an internship as a requirement of the academic program

Application Process

If you are interested in interning at the Institute of International Education, please contact the appropriate office below. Please note that internships at IIE are posted as divisions request them.

- New York: HR-NY@iie.org
- Washington, DC: HR-DC@iie.org
- CIES, Washington, DC: CIES-HR@iie.org
- Houston: HRhouston@iie.org

Deadline

IIE internships have different deadlines depending on each program.

For More Information

http://www.iie.org/en/Careers/Jobs-and-Internships

THE JAPANESE EXCHANGE PROGRAMME (JET)

The Japanese Exchange Programme was begun in 1986 and since then has grown into one of the world's largest educational exchange programs.

The purpose of the Japanese Exchange Programme is to increase ". . . mutual understanding between the people of Japan and the people of other nations. It aims to promote internationalization in Japan's local communities by helping to improve foreign language education and developing international exchange at the community level." The program is administered by local Japanese authorities in cooperation with several Japanese federal agencies.

The applicants apply for one of three job types and must commit to work in Japan for one year. Jobs types are:

- Assistant Language Teacher
- Coordinator for International Relations
- Sports Exchange Advisor

Each job type has a separate set of eligibility criteria based on the functions and duties of each position.

Benefits

Once selected, JET participants sign a one-year contract that begins the day after they arrive in Japan. Participants are compensated 3,600,000 yen a year (approximately $35,000 to $37,000 USD). Participants are also provided transportation to and from Japan and health insurance for the duration of their stay in Japan.

General Eligibility Requirements

As previously mentioned, eligibility requirements vary depending on job type. Generally, the following requirements apply to all applicants:

- be interested in engaging the Japanese people and culture for the duration of their time in Japan
- be mentally and physically healthy
- have the ability to successfully adapt to life and work in the Japanese culture
- be less than 40 years of age
- be fluent in either English or Japanese

Applicants must not have lived in Japan for more than a total of three years since 2001.

Application Process

Applicants for the JET Programme must request an application at the Japanese Embassy or one of the Japanese Consulates located in various cities throughout the United States. Applications are reviewed, and candidates who pass the review stage are invited for interviews at the various Consulates. Successful applicants are notified and begin the placement process.

For More Information

http://www.jetprogramme.org

LIBRARY OF CONGRESS INTERNSHIP AND FELLOWSHIP PROGRAMS

"The Library of Congress is the nation's oldest federal cultural institution and serves as the research arm of Congress. It is also the largest library in the world, with millions of books, recordings, photographs, maps and manuscripts in its collections," including a print copy of the book in your hands. "The Library's mission is to make its resources available and useful to the Congress and the American people and to sustain and preserve a universal collection of knowledge and creativity for future generations."

The Library of Congress offers a wide variety of internships, fellowships, and volunteer program opportunities for undergraduate and graduate students. Search the Library of Congress Web site for opportunities that interest you. Opportunities exist in collections, conservation and preservation, geography and maps, government and business administration, humanities, art and culture, information technology, law, library sciences, policy analysis, and public relations. In addition, the Library of Congress has created strong partnerships with various outside organizations to offer experiences for students.

Benefits

Benefits depend on the specific opportunity. Some opportunities offer pay, whereas others do not.

General Eligibility Requirements

Requirements will vary depending on the specific opportunity.

Application Procedure

Applicants must first conduct a search for available opportunities. The search allows the user to narrow opportunities by stipend availability, qualifications required, work areas within the Library, and availability (time frame the opportunity is available). Once an applicant finds an internship, fellowship, or volunteer opportunity he or she is interested in applying for, specific application instructions are provided.

Deadline

Deadlines vary by opportunity.

For More Information

http://www.loc.gov/hr/employment/index.php?action=cMain.showFellowships

THE MERAGE FOUNDATION AMERICAN DREAM FELLOWSHIP

"The Merage Foundation for the American Dream was established in 2004 by Paul and Lilly Merage, both immigrants to the United States. In establishing the Foundation, they hope to help immigrants join mainstream America."

The Merage Foundation for the American Dream awards fellowships to graduating seniors from twenty-two participating universities. (For a list of these institutions, see the program Web site.) Applicants must be immigrants to the United States who demonstrate outstanding potential. Applicants are selected based on a variety of factors that include, "their academic record, their leadership, their consistent ethical behavior, the clarity of their American Dream, and their potential to make an important contribution to America."

Benefits

American Dream Fellows receive a $20,000 stipend over a two-year period to pursue their American dream. Fellows are provided mentors in their chosen career field and are able to network with alumni. Fellows may use their stipends for a variety of educational/professional development purposes.

General Eligibility Requirements

According to the Foundation, applicants must meet the following criteria:

- be immigrants to the Unites States
- be citizens or permanent residents of the United States (or be seeking citizenship)
- be full-time students with senior class status
- graduate between December of the year they apply and August of the following year

Application Procedure

Students must be nominated by a participating university. For a complete list of "nominating" institutions, see the official list on the program Web site. Students must submit several documents as part of their application packet, including:

- an application form
- a summary of their proposal
- transcripts
- three letters of recommendation
- immigration status
- resume

Students must submit a completed application to the appropriate office at their universities by the deadline established by the university.

Deadline

Participating institutions must have their nomination into the Foundation by December 4. Institutional deadlines for material will be earlier. Check with your campus representative for the program.

For More Information

http://www.meragefoundations.com/mfad_fellows.html

NEXT STEP CONNECTIONS

Next Step Connections is a leading global professional education organization offering internships and experiential study programs. Next Step Connections believes in opening doors around the world for students who have a passion and commitment to developing their global careers. This involves adaptability and flexibility, interest and appreciation for new cultures, and desire for new adventures.

Next Step Connections builds customized global internships and experiential learning programs that give students opportunities to experience the world in a low-risk environment. All student majors are welcome, and there are no foreign language requirements. Programs through Next Step Connections are offered all year-round and for flexible lengths of time. This enables students to build the experience that they seek and that will add the most to their resume.

Next Step Connections has built a significant global network to create high-quality experiential learning programs that are meaningful to the students involved and the greater communities with which they interact. Global career development in Next Step Connection's view is about being immersed in the world around us and gaining confidence in one's abilities to excel in any company in any country.

General Eligibility Requirements

Applicants must meet the following criteria:

- be fluent in English
- be highly motivated and ambitious
- want to enhance professional skills in an internationally competitive setting

For More Information

www.nextstepconnections.com

To gain insight from interns with broad experience, take a look at http://www.youtube.com/user/NextStepConnections.

Cross Pollination

For more work-abroad and internship-abroad programming, see your internships office or specialists such as International Cooperative Education of Menlo Park, California, for assistance.

ROBERT BOSCH FOUNDATION FELLOWSHIP PROGRAM

The Robert Bosch Foundation is one of the largest charitable organizations in Germany. The Foundation works in the areas of science, health, international relations, education, and culture to find solutions to the problems facing today's society.

Tangible Benefit to a Global Internship

Statistics show that having an internship increases a student's employability upon graduation by over 10 percent and increases a student's salary upon graduation by over 30 percent. A global internship experience compounds these figures as employers realize the leaders of tomorrow are those who truly understand globalization.

The goal of the Bosch Foundation Fellowship Program is to create ". . . a new generation of American leaders who have firsthand experience in the political, economic and cultural environment of Germany and the E.U. [European Union]." Each year, the 20 individuals who are named Bosch Fellows spend nine months in Germany working at selected host institutions and attend several seminars throughout Europe. Traditionally, Bosch Fellows come from business administration, journalism, law, public policy, and closely related fields.

Benefits

Bosch Fellows receive approximately 2,000 euros a month as a living stipend, which is equivalent to about $2,440 USD. In addition, Fellows are provided health, accident, and liability insurance and travel to and from Germany. Support for dependents is also available.

General Eligibility Requirements

To be eligible, students must meet the following requirements:

- be U.S. citizens
- be 23 to 34 years old

- have at least two years of relevant work experience
- hold a graduate degree, or equivalent training, in business administration, journalism, law, public policy, international relations, or a closely related field
- demonstrate evidence of outstanding professional performance and community involvement

No German language skills are required at time of application; however, the commitment to participate in language training is essential. Most Bosch Fellows are required to complete four months of private tutoring in the United States (up to 8 hours a week) and three months of intensive language training in Berlin prior to the start of the program. All language training is funded by the Fellowship.

Application Process

Applicants first fill out an online interest form, which is followed by an online application. In addition to the application form, candidates must submit:

- a personal statement of no more than 850 words
- a resume
- official university transcripts
- two letters of recommendation

Deadline

The deadline for applications is in October.

For More Information

http://www.cdsintl.org/fellowshipsabroad/bosch.php

U.S. Agency for International Development Student Intern Program (USAID)

President John F. Kennedy created the United States Agency for International Development (USAID) in 1961. The primary purpose of the agency is the administration and oversight of nonmilitary foreign aid. The mission of USAID is ". . . the twofold purpose of furthering America's foreign policy interests in expanding democracy and free markets while improving the lives of the citizens of the developing world."

USAID offers paid internship programs for both U.S. undergraduate and graduate students. These programs are the Student Career Experience Program (SCEP) and the Student Temporary

Experience Program (STEP). The SCEP offers the possibility of conversion into full-time employment; the STEP does not offer this option. To fill these positions, USAID seeks ". . . students studying in a wide variety of fields, including engineering, computer science, mathematics, economics, foreign languages, area studies, business administration, accounting, international relations, finance, logistics, human resources, geography, public health, national security studies, military and foreign affairs, political science and public administration."

Benefits

Students receive valuable work experience in a federal agency. Internship pay depends on the position.

General Eligibility Requirements

According to the program Web site, applicants must meet the following criteria:

- be U.S. citizens
- be currently enrolled in an accredited college or university
- be in good academic standing
- have a minimum grade point average (GPA) of 2.0
- submit a transcript indicating a student's major and GPA

Application Procedure

According to the Web site, application processes and deadlines vary depending on the particular student internship or fellowship available at the U.S. Agency for International Development. Some positions require you to be nominated for application; others you can initiate on your own. We suggest you review the various opportunities to determine which one is the best match for you. At the end of each description is information, or a link to information, that provides details about the position's specific requirements, application process, vacancy announcements, and deadlines.

Deadline

Applications are due in January.

For More Information

http://www.usaid.gov/careers/paid_interns.html

U.S. DEPARTMENT OF STATE STUDENT INTERNSHIPS

"The U.S. Department of State is focused on accomplishing America's mission of diplomacy at home and around the world." Through these internships, recipients learn about how and where this important work is performed, as well as the influential history of the State Department.

U.S. Department of State internships are designed to give advanced undergraduates a look at the Foreign Service as a possible career. Interns have an opportunity to gain a professional experience in a foreign affairs–related position. They may be placed in Washington, DC, or a foreign setting. Internships are available during the fall, spring, and summer.

Benefits

The U.S. Department of State offers a variety of paid and unpaid internships. Paid internships are usually awarded based on demonstration of financial need. For interns working abroad, housing is usually provided.

General Eligibility Requirements

According to the U.S. State Department Web site, applicants must meet the following criteria:

- be a U.S. citizen
- be in good academic standing
- successfully complete a background investigation
- be able to receive either a Secret or Top Secret clearance
- be a sophomore, junior, or senior in an accredited college or university

Graduate students are also eligible.

Application Procedure

Interested applicants need to fill out an online application to begin the process.

Deadline

Applications for summer internships are due at the beginning of November, applications for fall internships at the beginning of March, and applications for spring internships at the beginning of July.

For More Information

http://www.careers.state.gov/students/ug_students.html#SIP

U.S. INTERNATIONAL TRADE COMMISSION INTERNSHIPS

The U.S. International Trade Commission (USITC) is charged with representing the United States both internally and externally in matters to do with global trade. It is "an independent, quasi-judicial federal agency with broad investigative responsibilities on matters of trade. . . . Through [its] proceedings, the agency facilitates a rules-based international trading system."

The U.S. International Trade Commission (USITC) provides advice and counsel to both the legislative and executive branches of government. With heavy emphasis on both economics and international law and diplomacy concerning trade issues, the USITC has a major role to play in the continuing globalization of the U.S. economy. The emergence of the World Trade Organization (WTO) has made its work all the more critical. The USITC assesses the impact of imports on U.S. business sectors, protects U.S. producers from illegal dumping (the exporting and selling of products below cost of production in order to destroy competitors), and represents U.S. interests on international patent and intellectual-property issues.

For High School Students

Note that the Student Temporary Employment Program is one of the rare experiential programs open to high school students.

- **Student Temporary Employment Program (STEP)**
  This is the USITC program that most people would call an "internship" program. "STEP provides paid work experience for high school, undergraduate, or graduate students. STEP allows students to work year-round while they are in school in part-time or full-time positions. To be eligible, students must be enrolled in an accredited educational institution at least half-time. Most STEP students at USITC work during the summer months."

- **Presidential Management Fellow (PMF) Program**
  The PMF is a paid, structured, two-year fellowship. To be selected for the PMF program, a student must be enrolled in a graduate program (master's, law, or doctoral-level degree program), with emphasis on subjects most pertinent to the work of the USITC, such as law or economics. "Students interested in becoming a (PMF) must first apply with their college or university. Application packets are initially received, screened, and nominated by the educational institution and then forwarded to the PMF board for a preliminary review."

- **Student Career Experience Program (SCEP)**
  Also known as the co-op program, SCEP interns gain paid work experience related to their academic areas of interest and are then eligible for permanent hire by the USITC. Again, you need to start with a nomination from your undergraduate institution. Students must be enrolled in an official co-op program to be eligible, and the program

must be completed prior to graduation. "A written agreement between the school, student, and USITC is required."

For More Information

To see all the student-focused programs at USITC, go to http://www.usitc.gov/employment/positions.htm. Also see https://www.opm.gov/careerintern.

Cross Pollination

If you are interested in USITC, check out the next opportunity, a clearinghouse for similar opportunities with the U.S. government and its many branches.

WASHINGTON CENTER FOR INTERNSHIPS AND ACADEMIC SEMINARS

The Washington Center is the entrée for thousands of domestic and international students to find Washington, DC-based experiential programs in the federal government and public service and nongovernmental organizations.

The largest program of its kind, the Washington Center provides internships for domestic and international students in a wide range of assignments in Washington, DC, and in the surrounding metro area, as well as some select government and political assignments outside the DC area. The Center has 70 full-time staff and over 40,000 alumni.

The Washington Center places students in the White House, the U.S. Department of State, U.S. Department of Justice, U.S. Department of Education, U.S. Department of Health and Human Services, U.S. Marshals Service, U.S. Department of the Interior, U.S. Department of Housing and Urban Development, National Defense University, Federal Trade Commission, U.S. Department of Homeland Security, Small Business Administration, U.S. Congressional Offices, as well as public service nonprofit and nongovernmental (NGO) organizations based in the Washington, DC, area, and many other programs and sites as well. Some programs are limited to U.S. citizens, but many others are available to students from all over the world.

The Washington Center itself has modest fees, and the majority of the internships are unpaid, but financial assistance is available for fees, housing, and, in some cases, income replacement. No student should fail to explore this option just because of financial need.

Each internship includes three components: the internship itself, a related academic course, and the Leadership Forum. "The Leadership Forum is a structured set of activities that enriches your experience by helping you to understand leadership and the opportunities you have to contribute to your community locally, nationally and internationally. You hear and engage with speakers, are introduced to public policy debates and the people who shape them and attend activities related to your professional field."

The Center has more programs than this brief introduction could begin to cover, but here are some examples. Watch for early deadlines!

- **Federal Internship Programs in Washington, DC**
  This program covers a complete range of federal service, nonprofit, and NGO activities centered in the Washington, DC, metro area. The Washington Center can arrange all local issues, including guaranteed housing and transportation. Application policies can be complicated, with a two-stage acceptance process; you must be accepted by TWC *and* the destination internship opportunity.

- **Sophomore Exploration Program**
  The SEP program is for students who are not yet juniors. "SEP participants take a course in which most of the time is spent outside the classroom, visiting organizations and embassies and taking part in career exploration activities. Students also have the opportunity to participate in several career inventories to help them determine which academic and career choices may be the best match for their abilities and interests."

- **American Indian and Alaska Native Initiative**
  This program prepares Native students from colleges and universities across the United States to assume leadership positions in the public sector. Selected students have an internship assignment, as well as exposure to senior government representatives and a structured leadership development program. Applicants must be an enrolled tribal member. The program provides a scholarship, housing fees, and a stipend.

For More Information

See http://www.twc.edu.

To learn what students say about their TWC experiences, go to http://www.twc.edu/students/blogs.shtml.

WHITE HOUSE INTERNSHIP PROGRAM

"This program will mentor and cultivate young leaders of today and tomorrow and I'm proud that they will have this opportunity to serve. I look forward to working with those that are selected to participate and I want to commend all who apply for their desire to help through public service to forge a brighter future for our country."

—President Barack Obama, May 22, 2009

The mission of the White House Internship Program is "to make the 'People's House' accessible to future leaders all around the nation and cultivate and prepare those devoted to public service for future leadership opportunities." This competitive internship locates students near the center of political power in Washington, DC. Participants are placed in one of the Presidential departments, including the White House Department of Scheduling and Advance, the Office of Cabinet Affairs, the White House Communications Department, the Office of the First Lady, and the Office of the Chief of Staff.

Benefits

The White House Internship Program is an unpaid internship. However, it is expected that interns will gain valuable experience and network with other future leaders in public service.

General Eligibility Requirements

According to the Web site, applicants must meet the following criteria:

- be U.S. citizens
- be at least 18 years of age
- be currently enrolled in an undergraduate or a graduate program at a college, community college, or university

or

- graduated in the past two years from an undergraduate or a graduate program at a college, community college, or university

or

- be a veteran of the U.S. armed forces who possesses a high school diploma or its equivalent and has served on active duty at any time over the past two years

Application Process

The application is online and includes:

- two essay questions
- three letters of recommendation
- a resume

Deadline

Applications are accepted for three internship periods, spring, summer, and fall. See program Web site for exact deadlines.

For More Information

http://www.whitehouse.gov/about/Internships

WORLD BANK INTERNSHIP PROGRAM

The World Bank was formed in 1944 to provide loans to countries in crisis and is charged with the goal of reducing poverty worldwide by influencing the financial practices of its 187 member countries.

The World Bank Group is made up of two development institutions owned by its member countries: the International Bank for Reconstruction and Development (IBRD) and the International Development Association (IDA). The World Bank is based in Washington, DC, and has more than 10,000 employees in more than 100 offices worldwide. Internships are available for Americans and for nationals of the bank's other member countries.

The bank seeks candidates with a wide range of academic backgrounds, including economics, finance, human development (public health, education, nutrition, population studies), social science (such as anthropology, sociology), agriculture, environmental studies, private-sector development, and more. An international outlook is a plus (extensive travel, language skills, area studies background, periods of living abroad). Most opportunities are postbaccalaureate, and successful candidates generally have completed one year of graduate studies.

Benefits

The bank pays a salary to all interns and covers travel expenses to some locations (although most positions are in Washington, DC). The real benefits are learning how the global financial system works and being involved in international development. The bank explicitly uses the internship program to find and develop individuals who would like to pursue a career there.

General Eligibility Requirements

According to the Web site, applicants must meet the following criteria:

- English is required and knowledge of languages such as French, Spanish, Russian, Arabic, Portuguese, and Chinese is advantageous

- enrollment in a graduate studies program, preferably completion of one year before acceptance into the intern program
- plans to return to school in a full-time capacity after the internship

Application Process

The World Bank Group Internship is highly structured, with specific application and service periods. Applications must be submitted online.

Deadline

The Summer Program, June to September, accepts applications only during the period December 1 to January 31 of each year. The Winter Program, December to March, accepts applications only during the period September 1 to October 31 of each year.

For More Information

http://web.worldbank.org/WBSITE/EXTERNAL/EXTHRJOBS/0,,contentMDK:205252 01~pagePK:64262408~piPK:64262191~theSitePK:1058433,00.html

CHAPTER 6
Scholarship and Fellowship Resources for International Students

As authors, we recognize the challenges that international students face in finding funding for opportunities outside their home countries. This chapter represents our attempt to provide international readers a starting point for academic and experiential opportunities located primarily in the United States. (Some opportunities in the United Kingdom have also been included.) The benefits of an international experience for the individual, as we argue in other places in this book, are numerous. But, you as the individual are not the only beneficiary. As many of these organizations articulate, an international presence in our country is vital to the open exchange of ideas, diverse perspectives, and cultural talent that institutions, organizations, and corporations in the United States seek.

We believe the advice presented in other chapters in this book such as how to write a personal statement and how to interview well will also be helpful in navigating the application process. However, please be mindful that English proficiency is very important for these awards.

THE BEST RESOURCES

Albright Institute Fellowships

Scholarships for archaeological research.

http://www.aiar.org/fellowships.html

Amelia Earhart Fellowships (Zonta International Foundation)

Funding for women pursuing Ph.D./doctoral degrees in aerospace-related sciences and aerospace-related engineering.

http://www.zonta.org/WhatWeDo/InternationalPrograms/AmeliaEarhartFellowship.aspx

American Association for University Women (AAUW) International Fellowships

Scholarships for graduate-level studies. Applicants must demonstrate commitment to the enhancement of women and girls.

http://www.aauw.org/fga/fellowships_grants/international.cfm

American Institute of the History of Pharmacy Grant

Support grant related to the history of pharmacy.

http://pharmacy.wisc.edu/aihp/programs-services/thesis-support

American Nuclear Society (ANS) Scholarships

Undergraduate and graduate scholarships to help students prepare for careers in nuclear science and technology.

http://ans.org/honors/scholarships/

American Scandinavian Foundation

Funding opportunities for Scandinavians desiring to study or conduct research in the United States.

http://www.amscan.org/fellowships_grants.html

A. Patrick Charnon Memorial Scholarship

Scholarships for undergraduate students attending accredited institutions in the United States.

http://www.cesresources.org/charnon.html

Asian Cultural Council

Grants for Asian individuals to study and perform in the United States.

http://www.asianculturalcouncil.org/

Asian Development Bank (ADB): Japan Scholarship Program

Graduate-level funding for citizens of ADB's developing member countries (see program Web site for a complete list of developing member countries).

http://www.adb.org/JSP/default.asp

BMI Student Composer Awards

A competition for young composers of classical music. (BMI is a music company.)

http://bmi.com/foundation/

Caldwell Fellowships at North Carolina State University

A leadership development program for undergraduate students attending North Carolina State University.

http://www.ncsu.edu/fellows/

Canon Collins Educational Trust

Scholarship funds for African students who want to do graduate work in the United Kingdom.

http://www.canoncollins.org.uk/

Carnegie Endowment for International Peace Junior Fellows Program

A one-year paid fellowship at the Carnegie Endowment for International Peace.

http://www.carnegieendowment.org/about/index.cfm?fa=jrFellows

Center for Neuroscience at the University of Pittsburgh (CNUP) Summer Fellowship

A funded undergraduate research experience.

http://cnup.neurobio.pitt.edu/training/summer/index.aspx

Center for Strategic and International Studies (CSIS) Internships

Internship in a Washington, DC, bipartisan political organization.

http://csis.org/about/jobs_interns/

Charles G. Koch Summer Fellow Program

A summer public policy internship in Washington, DC, or at a state agency.

http://www.theihs.org/internship_programs/id.329/default.asp

Chevening Scholarship Program

For graduate-level study in the United Kingdom.

http://www.chevening.com

Christine Mirzayan Science and Technology Policy Graduate Fellowship Program

Graduate and postgraduate funding designed to engage fellows in the analytical process that informs U.S. science and technology policy.

http://www7.nationalacademies.org/policyfellows/

Cosmos Scholars Grant Program

Research funding for graduate students attending schools near Washington, DC.

http://www.cosmosclubfoundation.org/scholars/

DAAD Annual Grants (German Academic Exchange Service)

Provides a variety of funding opportunities for study, research, and professional experiences in Germany.

http://www.daad.org/?p=50407

Davis-Putter Scholarships

Provides funding for students actively seeking peace and justice.

http://www.davisputter.org/

Echoing Green Foundation Fellowships

Provides funding and support for emerging social entrepreneurs.

http://www.echoinggreen.org/index.cfm?fuseaction=Page.viewPageandpageId=411

Edmund S. Muskie Ph.D. Fellowship

Grants for master's-level study and professional development in the U.S. for citizens from Eurasian countries.

http://www.muskiefoundation.org/fellowships.html

Elie Wiesel Prize in Ethics

An essay contest designed to encourage students to consider important ethical issues.

http://www.eliewieselfoundation.org/prizeinethics.aspx

Elizabeth Greenshields Foundation Grant for Artists

Grants for early-career artists.

http://www.elizabethgreenshieldsfoundation.org/main.html

Explorers Club Student Grants

Grants for scientific and exploration research projects conducted in conjunction with an institution of higher education.

http://www.explorers.org/index.php/expeditions/funding/expedition_grants

Fulbright Foreign Student Program

Grants for graduate-level study and research in the United States.

http://foreign.fulbrightonline.org/

Gates Cambridge Scholarships

Fully funded scholarship for study at Cambridge University.

http://www.gatesscholar.org/

Hellenic Times Scholarship Fund

Undergraduate and graduate level scholarship for students of Greek descent.

http://www.htsfund.org/guidelines.html

Herbert Scoville Jr. Peace Fellowships

A Washington, DC, academic internship in the area of peace and security.

http://www.scoville.org/

Humane Studies Fellowships

Scholarships for undergraduate and graduate students planning academic careers with liberty-advancing research interests.

http://www.theihs.org/programs/humane-studies-fellowships

Inter American Press Association (IAPA) Scholarship

Scholarship and grant funding for Latin American, Caribbean, and Canadian scholars who are planning careers in journalism.

http://www.sipiapa.org/otheractivities/scholarships.cfm

International Dissertation Research Fellowship

Funding for humanities and social science students enrolled in doctoral programs in the United States who are planning dissertation research outside of the United States.

http://www.ssrc.org/programs/idrf/

Jennings Randolph Peace Scholarship Dissertation Program

Awards nonresidential Peace Scholar Dissertation Scholarships to students at U.S. universities who are writing doctoral dissertations on topics related to peace, conflict, and international security.

http://www.usip.org/fellows/scholars.html

John Bayliss Radio Scholarship

Scholarship for undergraduates who are majoring in broadcast communication.

http://www.baylissfoundation.org/radio.html

Josephine de Kármán Fellowships

Fellowships for undergraduates entering their senior year and doctoral students set to defend their dissertations. Applicants must be attending U.S. institutions.

http://www.dekarman.org

MacDowell Colony Residencies

Artists-in-residence program for individuals in the following fields: architecture, music composition, film and video, interdisciplinary art, theater, visual art, and literature.

http://www.macdowellcolony.org/index.html

Margaret McNamara Memorial Fund (MMMF) Grants

Scholarships for female students from developing countries to study in the United States.

http://web.worldbank.org/WBSITE/EXTERNAL/EXTSTAFF/WBFN/0,,contentMDK:21
084882~isCURL:Y~pagePK:64156201~piPK:64156133~theSitePK:444098,00.html

Mayo Summer Undergraduate Research Fellowship (SURF) Program

Summer research experience for undergraduates at the Mayo Graduate School.

http://www.mayo.edu/mgs/surf.html

Microsoft Scholarships

Undergraduate scholarships for students majoring in computer science, computer engineering, or a related technical discipline such as electrical engineering, math, or physics.

http://www.microsoft.com/college/scholarships

Organization of American States (OAS) Scholarships for Academic Studies

Undergraduate- and graduate-level scholarships for citizens of OAS member states.

http://www.educoas.org/portal/en/oasbecas/announcement11-12.aspx?culture=en&navid=44

Phi Kappa Phi Fellowships

Fellowships for Phi Kappa Phi members entering the first year of graduate or professional study.

http://www.phikappaphi.org/Web/Awards/Fellowship.html

Rhodes Scholarships for Non-U.S. Citizens

Fully funded scholarship for study at Oxford University.

http://www.rhodesscholar.org

The Roothbert Fund Scholarship Program

Grants for undergraduate or graduate study at accredited colleges or universities in the United States.

http://www.roothbertfund.org/scholarships.php

Samuel Huntington Public Service Award

Funding for one year of public service anywhere in the world for graduating college seniors.

http://www.nationalgridus.com/masselectric/about_us/award.asp

Sir John M. Templeton Fellowships Essay Contest

An essay contest that asks essayists to consider the meaning and significance of economic and personal liberty.

http://www.independent.org/students/essay/

Smithsonian Fellowships

A variety of scholarship and fellowship opportunities offered through the Smithsonian Institution.

http://www.si.edu/ofg/fell.htm

Society of Women Engineers

Funding for women admitted to accredited baccalaureate or graduate programs in preparation for careers in engineering, engineering technology, and computer science.

http://www.societyofwomenengineers.org/scholarships/brochure.aspx

Spencer Foundation Dissertation Fellowship

Funding for doctoral students from a wide range of academic disciplines and professional fields to undertake research relevant to the improvement of education.

http://www.spencer.org/content.cfm/dissertation-fellowships-in-education-program

Student Academy Awards

An annual competition for collegiate filmmakers.

http://www.oscars.org/saa/

Swiss Benevolent Society of New York Scholarships

Scholarships for students of Swiss descent.

http://www.swissbenevolentny.com/scholarshipprograms.htm

United States—South Pacific Scholarship Program

Scholarship for study in the United States for citizens from the following: Cook Islands, Fiji, Kiribati, Nauru, Niue, Papua New Guinea, Samoa, Solomon Islands, Tonga, Tuvalu, and Vanuatu.

http://www.eastwestcenter.org/?id=872

U.S. Golf Association (USGA) Fellowship in Leadership and Service

A two-year professional development experience for recent college graduates.

http://www.usga.org/about_usga/philanthropy/fellowship/Fellowship/

Villers Fellowship for Health Care Justice

A year-long fellowship working to promote healthcare justice.

http://www.familiesusa.org/about/the-villers-fellowship.html

How to Write About Yourself

Writing what is most often called a personal statement is, arguably, one of the most difficult parts to any application process, but it can also be the most rewarding. This chapter focuses on providing you both an understanding of how these documents are used and several tools to help you craft a strong personal statement. We also hope that you'll realize the personal benefits from the process as you work through it.

Once you have a strong statement, it can often be used repeatedly with minor adjustments, depending on the type of program you are applying to. Therefore, it is well worth the effort and time you will need to put into it.

WHAT A PERSONAL STATEMENT IS NOT

Let's start by describing what a personal statement is *not*. A personal statement is not meant to be a complete narrative account of your entire curriculum vitae (CV). Apart from the limits of the word count, there is little need to rehash a document already in front of the review committee. And, honestly, a personal statement that only fleshed out your CV would be a very boring document to read.

WHAT A PERSONAL STATEMENT IS

Your personal statement is meant to give the review committee a brief but specific indication of *who you are, why you are who you are, and why you are intending to move forward in the direction you are proposing* in your application. A personal statement is meant to give a narrative picture of your personal and academic development so far. It's one of the primary documents requested for most scholarship and fellowship applications. In fact, it is at the heart of your application. It tells your "story," though that word is used in a cautionary manner here given that a personal statement is a very *brief* description of your story. Most personal statements are between 1,000 and 2,000 words, so every word counts.

It is impossible for you to describe your entire life in a document of this length and, in fact, that isn't what a review committee expects. What committee members do want to see is the writing of a student who has taken the time to reflect on key moments in his or her personal, professional, and academic careers that have guided the student in making the decisions clearly laid out in great detail in the CV. The personal statement is also a window into the potential of an applicant. The question every reviewer asks at some point is, "Will this candidate be the very best reflection of the mission of our organization and have the potential to carry on with serving in the global community because they have received funding?"

DEVELOPING YOUR PERSONAL STATEMENT

Writing your personal statement gives you the opportunity to tease out those key moments that have shaped your interests and pursuits and then provides you with a chance to weave those moments into an interesting, compelling story. Generally, the personal statement describes your personal and professional experiences since the beginning of your undergraduate experience. There are always exceptions, however. How far back you reach into your memory is often entirely up to you, but it's useful to bear in mind that you will need to build a strong case for what you intend to do beyond your undergraduate career—and you have a word count to keep in mind as you choose what to include.

For example, if you are interested in studying English literature at an advanced level, harkening back to the days when your mother read Beatrix Potter to you at age 4 may not be especially compelling. However, if your parents survived the terrorist attacks in Beirut and now you are interested in questions about global terrorism at an advanced level, there would be reason to include this fact about your parents in your personal statement. This is why it is so important to devote time to reflecting, drafting, writing, and revising your statement. At each stage, you will need to determine what is important to include and what needs to be cut.

While your personal statement is not a narrative version of your CV, it is helpful to draft your CV before embarking on your personal statement. In reviewing your CV, you may find that certain patterns emerge that may guide the writing of your personal statement.

Stating Your Ambitions

Your personal statement will give you the chance to communicate to the review committee your ambitions and what you expect to do beyond the term of your financial award. It's also an appropriate place for you to comment on how you might contribute to your own discipline or profession and how you expect to serve the larger community in which you live. It's also an opportunity for you to express precisely why you must study within a certain department, with a particular faculty member, at a specific institution, in a certain country, and consult certain relevant resources. Or, if you are applying for an internship or other experiential learning opportunity, your personal statement will address similar concerns specific to that particular opportunity and why it is so important that you have the chance to participate.

Explaining Gaps

If you have a particular gap in your transcript or if you have had to work to support your studies and, therefore, your CV is on the slimmer side, your personal statement can serve as platform for explaining such circumstances. Keep in mind that anything you put in your personal statement, like any other part of your application, is fair game for an interview committee. If you wouldn't be comfortable discussing a particular life circumstance, leave it out of the statement!

Piquing the Review Committee's Interest

Your personal statement can also be viewed as your "request" for an interview. Along with your CV and other parts of your application, the personal statement is meant to wet the review committee's appetite. Crafted carefully and creatively, it should make the committee wish to speak with you in person and at further length about what you have included in your statement. While it's important that you avoid the overuse of florid language, your "voice" has a place in a personal statement. Remember, committees are reading hundreds of statements, possibly more, and if they come across a statement that is especially well-written, creative, and interesting, they are more likely to pay further attention to your entire application.

A PERSONAL STATEMENT AS AN ACT OF SELF-REFLECTION

The reason a personal statement takes a significant amount of time beyond the writing and editing is that it requires self-reflection. Writing a personal statement means going back and starting from the moment you were cognizant of your dreams, ideals, and ambitions, and then moving forward to select those pivotal moments leading up to the present and pressing you forward into the future. This isn't as easy as it may sound, but it is a terrific practice to incorporate into your life because it provides a kind of vision statement for your life.

Writing a personal statement is a serious examination of your experiences; even if you are not nominated or do not win, you will find it useful as you move ahead with other professional opportunities. In our own experiences and in hearing from student advisees, we find that a well-thought-out personal statement often remains a fluid, but generally constant, reflection of one's course of life.

FINDING YOUR "VOICE"

Voice is the tone of your presentation, how formal or informal you are with your reader, how much you reveal or hold back, what point of view you write from, and what level of language you choose, from the universally accessible to the type of vocabulary only an academic in your field might understand. Perhaps one of the most challenging parts about a personal statement is that it requires you to bring together both your academic or intellectual voice, the one you are likely most comfortable with at this stage of your life, *and* your more personal voice, the voice narrating the story. It can be a delicate balancing act!

THE DIFFERENCE BETWEEN A PERSONAL STATEMENT AND A RESEARCH PROPOSAL

A personal statement is a unique document; it asks you to address a variety of aspects about your life and ambitions. As you write, you should constantly ask yourself the questions suggested earlier: *who* are you, *why* are you, and *how* do these two questions address the third about the intent outlined in your application. As a result, a portion of your personal statement, often included toward the end, should address your research interests, specific details about the program for which you are applying, relevant faculty, and resources. However, a personal statement is *not* a "research proposal" that one might include for a program like the Fulbright or for a graduate program.

A research proposal is focused solely on your research interests and, often more explicitly, your research plan with anticipated outcomes. For some applications, you may be asked for both a personal statement and a research proposal. Remember that they are very different types of documents in style and in purpose.

It is worth noting that if you are applying to a British institution of higher education for graduate studies, you will most likely be asked for a research proposal, not a personal statement. In general, British institutions have less interest in your personal life and are highly focused on your academic experience. The exceptions to this are scholarships and fellowships like the Rhodes, the British Marshall, and the Mitchell, all of which require a personal statement.

Fifteen Do's for Writing a Personal Statement

1. Determine early on in your application process what is required for your personal statement in terms of word-count, etc.

2. Make sure that you tailor your statement to the purpose of the opportunity and to the application. Spend time reviewing the mission of the organization to determine what parts of your "story" should be included.

3. Identify the main points of your CV. Bear in mind that even your letters of recommendation are going to cover certain parts of your experiences and can be used to fill in things not covered in your personal statement.

4. This is your time to shine! Many students who approach competitive scholarship and fellowship applications are surprisingly humble and reticent about sharing their experiences. While it's important to avoid coming across as arrogant, your personal statement is a chance for you to be confident and proud of your achievements.

5. Give yourself plenty of time to craft your personal statement. This may mean beginning months in advance of your deadline, which will allow you to draft, revise, and edit—more than once if necessary. Check grammar, proper citation, and consistent use of style, diction, and tone. The professional presentation of your statement, as with your entire application, speaks for your commitment and interest in the opportunity.

6. Ask others whose judgment you trust to read your statement. Outside readers will bring a fresh perspective to it.

7. Plan on using your personal statement as part of the materials you give to your letter writers; again, plan ahead!

8. Your first paragraph is critical. It sets the direction of the entire essay and serves as the portal for your readers. It needs to grab their attention and build a sense of anticipation for the rest of the statement.

9. The conclusion draws the statement together but, because of the brevity of the statement, it should also give the reader a sense of your future ambitions, the link between the statement and your proposed course of study, and how the particular opportunity will influence your future.

10. Use specific examples and life-changing moments from your experience to illustrate your enthusiasm for a particular subject. It makes for a much more interesting read.

11. Be authentic and honest. These qualities are critical.

12. Your personal statement will be one of the documents referred to in your interview, so you should be prepared to discuss at further length anything you include in the statement. So don't include anything you wouldn't want to discuss in an interview situation.

13. Keep in mind the way in which the statement fits into your overall application.

14. Use the personal statement to explain any shortcomings evident in your transcripts, CV, etc.

15. Write about what you are passionate about but in a temperate manner. Omit loaded words and unsubstantiated opinions. The personal statement—along with any interview you may have—is your opportunity to share with others what you care most about.

Ten Don'ts for Writing a Personal Statement

1. Avoid overly florid language.

2. Avoid using the first person too often.

3. Don't recount every item in your CV in narrative form. Focus on those experiences most relevant to the purpose of your statement.

4. Avoid references to any past family or personal trauma relating to drug abuse, death, etc. It can be difficult to write about such subjects with the distance and objectivity necessary for a personal statement. Also, if it's in your personal statement, it could resurface as the basis of questioning in your interview.

5. Avoid subjects that are either overly personal or political. You want to avoid making your reader uncomfortable. You especially want to avoid having the reader's memory of your application tied to an unpleasant topic in your statement.

6. Avoid an overly academic tone and word choices. Try not to be totally dispassionate and detached. Keep in mind the necessary balance between your academic and personal voice.

7. Avoid journalistic writing. Don't explain the discipline or basic facts in a pedantic manner.

8. Don't share your journal writing in your essay. While you may have started thinking about your personal statement by writing in a journal, avoid copying that overly private and personal tone in your essay.

9. Don't waste words trying to convince the review committee of your need for a particular source of funding or opportunity. You have made that perfectly clear simply by submitting an application.

10. Unless advised otherwise, it is also not necessary for you to include closing statements like "thank you very much for your consideration."

WHY YOU SHOULD AVOID READING OTHER PERSONAL STATEMENTS BEFORE YOU WRITE

You will not find any examples of personal statements in this book. There is an intentional reason behind this decision.

A personal statement is exactly that, *personal*. Each and every personal statement is—or should be—unique to its author and his or her ambitions. Using others' statements as examples means risking that you will write a formulaic and possibly unconvincing statement. Once you have completed your first draft from your heart, without mimicking others, your advisers will help make sure that you're on the right track. You may get extensive help from others in *editing* your essay, but no one but you should be *writing* your essay.

Only after you have worked hard on your statement should you look at others' work. Your scholarships office or your academic departments usually keep essays from students from prior years. If you want more help after you've done your first draft, see Donald Asher's best-selling guide *Graduate Admissions Essays: Write Your Way into the Graduate School of Your Choice,* which includes advice for scholarship and fellowship applicants.

Finally, we have looked carefully at the Web sites and services offering "editing" assistance, and we want to warn you about two things. First, most of these services seem to be thinly disguised writing services, providing wholesale composition for a fee. We strongly discourage you from allowing anyone else to write portions of your essay. It is unethical in the first place and foolish as well. You never know how much of your essay was recycled from other sources. Second, we found the advice on many of these sites to be flat-out wrong and misguided. How useful could their editing be if their basic advice is bad? The only time you should use a site is when a faculty member or a scholarships adviser specifically recommends it. Otherwise, stay away!

SOME TIPS AND REFLECTION QUESTIONS TO GET YOUR IDEAS ROLLING

Your thinking and writing process will be as unique as your personal statement. But, here are some suggestions gleaned from our personal experience and from talking with students and advisers about how to get started.

Six Tips to Help the Flow of Ideas

1. Keep a journal with you and use it during the day to jot down ideas that may be helpful in developing your statement.

2. List all the papers, labs, research projects, etc., that you have done.

3. List all of your publications and conference presentations.

4. Use the reflection questions below to help you jog your memory.

5. Intentionally change your environment. Take a walk, go for a run, engage in some type of nonacademic activity in order to allow for your more personal voice to come through as you sort through the reflection questions and journal notes.

6. Once you begin writing, approach it from a variety of angles. Free-write, brainstorm, use an idea board if you think better visually, and/or draft a timeline of your life in addition to your CV to help guide your thinking.

Twenty Questions to Reflect On

We have also provided you with the following set of questions to aid in your reflection and eventually in your writing. To warm up, you might write one- or two-paragraph responses to each of these prompts. Ask yourself what other questions may be relevant to your own background and interests. Consider writing responses of greater length addressing those questions that are most relevant to your efforts.

1. What first interested you in this particular field of study?

2. How has this interest grown and changed over time? List the events, people, research, books, etc., that have influenced, and continue to influence, you.

3. Write about what you will be doing between when you apply and when you actually might begin the experience for which you are writing. What will you be doing that will add to your academic record, skills set, or service experiences?

4. What obstacles have you had to overcome to reach this time and place?

5. How have you overcome these obstacles?

6. Why are you unique or unusual? List several reasons.

7. What sports do you play? How long have you played them? Have you earned any distinctions in these sports? What do you like about these sports?

8. What are your hobbies and leisure pursuits? How long have these been hobbies? Have you earned any distinctions in these pursuits? What do you like about these hobbies?

9. How will your participation in this scholarship, fellowship, or opportunity contribute to others in the program—other participants or the recipients of services?

10. List five reasons why you want this particular scholarship, fellowship, or opportunity?

11. Once the program is over, what will you do with what you have learned and/or the degree you have earned?

12. What does being "you" mean? When do you feel the most "you" and the least "you"?

13. What kinds of books do you read when you're not reading for courses? Why do you like these kinds of books? What are you currently reading?

14. Where is "home"? Is it a place or a feeling? Describe "home" for you.

15. What global issue is of most concern to you? Is your interest in a scholarship, fellowship, or experiential opportunity connected to this issue? How?

16. What famous person do you most identify with? Why?

17. Have you traveled much, either nationally or internationally? Has travel changed you? How? Do you have any compelling stories from these travels?

18. What's the biggest change you have seen in yourself since you began your undergraduate or graduate studies? Why do you think this change has occurred? How do you feel about it?

19. What mistakes in life have you made? What have you learned from them? How did you resolve or address them?

20. Where do you expect to be in five years? In ten years? Why?

CHAPTER 8
Preparing a Strong Curriculum Vitae/Resume

You will find that a resume or a curriculum vitae (CV) is often required as part of the application process for elite academic and experiential opportunities. In a packet with so much other information, a resume or CV may seem like a trivial and redundant document, but a resume or CV is often used as a tie-breaker when everything else about a portfolio leaves a candidate sitting on the bubble of selection. When the committee cannot decide whether to advance a candidate to the next stage—or reject the person—the committee will often turn to the CV or resume. A professional presentation full of relevant content can tip the decision in favor of advancing the candidate, and a perfunctory presentation may tip it the other way.

Remember, there are many opportunities to fail to advance, and you have to maximize every chance that you will be considered favorably. You can be knocked out at any stage, for failing to appear more compelling than the competition and even for seemingly small errors and omissions. So, no part of your application is trivial or redundant, especially your resume/CV.

A resume or CV is an opportunity to shine in two distinct areas, professionalism and who you are. A good resume or CV is a marriage of style and content. It's a chance to show that you understand how to present yourself in a professional manner, and it's a chance to present meaningful information about your background, your accomplishments, your character, and your skills. A resume is also a useful tool for organizing your thoughts about your candidacy. What do you have to offer? Have you considered *all* your relevant experience? Have you practiced the art of thinking like a selection committee so that you have the right emphasis on your various experiences? Or have you given too much attention to the wrong items?

In this chapter, we will walk you through preparing your resume or CV for your applications.

RESUME OR CV?

A resume is a document used to describe your prior experience relevant to a future opportunity, usually a job. The word resume comes to us from the French *résumer,* which means to summarize. So by its very name, a resume is a summary of one's background and not a full explication of it.

A CV, on the other hand, is a particular type of resume, most commonly used in academic settings. CV stands for *curriculum vitae,* which is Latin meaning, literally, "race course of life," more commonly interpreted as "the course of one's life." So a CV is a document reporting on accomplishments in "the course of one's life."

Differences Between Resumes and CVs

CVs and resumes differ in both content and style, and it is important for you to know which you need to present. This task is complicated because people use the terms interchangeably, in particular in Europe and Asia, but even in the United States and Canada. Programs may request a resume when they mean a CV or vice versa. Read and follow the instructions carefully! To provide the document that is requested, you will need to look beyond the instructions. But first, you will need to know the differences yourself.

All CVs are technically resumes, but not all resumes are CVs.

- Resumes tend to focus on jobs and internships, and CVs tend to focus on academic experiences that may not be related to any employment.
- Resumes often have an objective statement, but CVs never do.
- Resumes may be rather self-promotional in tone, with enthusiastic claims of skills and accomplishments, whereas CVs are rather muted in tone, focusing more on bare listings of experiences without a lot of trumpeting of one's awesome contributions.
- CVs always have the education listings ahead of the experience listings, even for a 60-year-old scientist who obtained a terminal degree decades ago. Resumes can have either section first, "experience" ahead of "education," or the other way around.
- CVs feature academic honors and awards, such as summa cum laude, forever, but job resumes tend to drop academic awards after one has been in the job market for a number of years.
- CVs tend to have many more headings than resumes; for example, breaking "experience" into subsets of "teaching experience," "research experience," "service appointments," and so on. (One can also do this with resumes, but it is not as common.)
- Resumes, for college students, are expected to be one-page long or, in rare circumstances, two pages. CVs can be any length, and, indeed, a graduate student may have a CV that is ten or more pages in length; long CVs are perfectly acceptable as long as all the information conforms to the standard CV topics.

- On a resume, you usually don't mention your bosses by name, although it is common enough to mention them by title, as in, for example, "reported to the district sales manager." On a CV, you normally mention your bosses by name and title, in particular for any academic experiences. For example, this would be a typical citation: "research assistant in the biophysics laboratory under the supervision of Prof. L. Wilson, the William J. Danforth Professor of Biomedical Sciences." If the professor is famous, you list the whole name; if he or she is not famous, you usually list just first initial and last name, as in "Dr. L. Wilson" or "Prof. R. Johnson."

Here is a table to help you sort it out:

Resumes	CVs
objective statement okay	never has an objective statement
list either education *or* experience first	always list education ahead of experience
limited to one page, maybe two	no length limit
focuses on relevant jobs and internships	focuses on relevant academic experiences
features accomplishments and contributions at each assignment	generally lists just the assignment
limited number of headings, principally "experience" and "education"	many more heading options, e.g., "publications," "presentations," "teaching," "research," etc.
may mention boss by title, but not by name	if it's an academic experience, usually cite supervisors by name
usually used to get a job	usually used in a science or academic setting

Anyone's experience can be presented in either style, as a CV or as a resume. Depending on your goals and the specific requirements of the programs you are applying to, you may need to prepare both types of document. You might use a CV approach to get into graduate school, to get a job in a lab, or for an academic fellowship or award, and you might use a resume to get a job in pharmaceutical sales or for a management-track position in industry. What follows are job listings for the same research experience, presented in typical CV and resume formats.

For a CV:

School of Life Sciences, Stanton University
Research Assistant, Biomedical Engineering Lab, Fall 2011

Assisted in the design, prototyping, and testing of biomedical engineering devices, under the supervision of Prof. R. Simmons. Contributed to preparation of three journal articles. For more information, see first three articles under "Publications."

Or, a CV might just list the job citation alone, with no descriptive information at all:

School of Life Sciences, Stanton University
Research Assistant, Biomedical Engineering Lab, Prof. R. Simmons, Fall 2011

A resume will have more information on individual contributions, more description of the work itself, and more self promotion, as in this version:

School of Life Sciences, Stanton University
Research Assistant, Biomedical Engineering Lab, Fall 2011

Assisted in the design, specification, prototyping, and testing of biomedical engineering devices, mainly innovative electromechanical "helper" modules to improve coordination of large-muscle movements in patients with advanced Parkinson's disease. Collaborated with engineers and technicians to fabricate the devices. Used bench lab skills to calibrate and test devices. Collaborated with animal lab technicians for animal trials phase. Designed data capture protocols for testing. Provided first-level data analysis for review by the principal investigator. Contributions earned recognition as coauthor on three peer-reviewed journal articles (see "Publications"), the only undergraduate so honored.

Please note that the detailed and self-promoting style of a resume, when applying to some of the elite scholarships and fellowships, would grate on the ears of some readers. Can you imagine a reader from England, steeped in the tradition of self-deprecation and understatement, reading a U.S. undergraduate's self-congratulatory resume listings like the one above? On the other hand, a manager in a technology company looking for aggressive, ambitious, smart, young people might be delighted to read such a listing. Just remember to be sensitive to your reader, and be sure to provide a document that complies with all specified requirements. For example, many fellowships in business will specifically request a one-page business resume. Any other document you may submit will count against you.

With some practice you should be able to develop either style, or convert resume listings into CV listings, or vice versa, with some facility and confidence. We will use the terms somewhat interchangeably for the rest of this chapter, except when we are warning you about subtle differences that you should note.

EXPERIENCE MEANS MORE THAN EMPLOYMENT

For a person with ten or more years of experience, the word "experience" in a resume usually refers to full-time, paid employment. For most young people, however, the word "experience" can mean full- or part-time experiences, paid or unpaid, from any form of internship, co-op, or paying job, or even from a volunteer assignment, and may at times even refer to work done in a graded class. So before you prepare your resume or CV, your prewriting task is to prepare a catalog of all the experiences that might be pertinent. What follows is a list of prompts to help you be through in this process.

Paid Employment, Co-op, and Internship Experiences

One of the first things you will want to do is to make a list of all your paid employment and your co-op and internship experiences, full- or part-time, summer or during the school year. Include even casual employment such as editing for someone as a favor. Make a complete list, including experiences that aren't obviously relevant. For example, you may want to forget your history in fast-food employment during high school, but if your resume ends up having a heading "Management and Supervisory Experiences," the fact that you were a shift supervisor in an ice cream shop may suddenly be more germane than you thought. For the purposes of preparing to write your resume, make a complete list. We'll address later in this chapter how to sort and rank experiences, and when to omit irrelevant and distracting items.

Volunteer, Leadership, and Service Experiences

Most students have unpaid volunteer and service experiences of one kind or another, from tutoring at the local high school to food drives sponsored by your fraternity or sorority to working as a peer counselor for the career center. List all your experiences, even if some were just short-term. Some important leadership experiences may be related to a special event, such as being the speaker coordinator for a Drug and Alcohol Awareness Weekend or the student representative to the Alumni Engagement Steering Committee, and so on.

For many students, their volunteer experiences are more impressive and more relevant for their future than their paid employment. The fact that you worked 20 hours a week as a cashier in a convenience store is not as important as the fact that you started a new student club or served as the media manager for a student body election campaign. Think hard and remember all your volunteer, leadership, and service experiences.

Elected or Appointed Positions

Serving as student body president is, obviously, an item that should find its way onto a resume. There are many similar assignments that students may overlook, however. If you were selected by the assistant residence-life director to be the hall safety monitor in your dorm, that's an appointment. Being selected for any elected or appointed position shows that others hold a high opinion of your character, judgment, work ethic, maturity, and sense of responsibility. If you were elected student senator or appointed by the Dean to a term on the Student Academic Integrity Committee, be sure to catalog it for possible inclusion in your resume or CV. List all such appointments, no matter how trivial.

Academic Honors, Awards, and Merit Scholarships

Make a complete list of all recognitions that you have received for your academic performance, whether monetary (merit scholarships) or ceremonial. Include campuswide acknowledgments such as honor role or dean's list; departmental awards such as "Most Improved Junior in Biochemistry;" and awards you may have won for an assignment within a single class, such as "Most Outstanding Business Plan 2011" for your work in a class called "Business Modeling 456." You may have forgotten some of your awards or scholarships, so check with your dean's office and the office of financial aid, which often keep records of such awards on an ongoing basis. Finally, be sure to include national, extra-institutional honors, such as Golden Key or Phi Beta Kappa or election to some of the myriad iterations of the *Who's Who* concept. (We will have a warning about citing some of these national honors later, but for now make a complete list.)

Major Academic Projects, Field Studies, Interdisciplinary Projects, Undergraduate Research Programs, and Independent Study

Have you conducted any major studies, larger or more profound than the typical undergraduate paper? If so, it's important to include them in your catalog of resume ideas. If you'll write a thesis or deliver some kind of senior capstone project, this fact should appear on your resume.

Other types of academic projects can be prestigious, as well. Have you had the opportunity to get involved in undergraduate research, whether designed and conducted by you or as part of a faculty member's ongoing research? List any field studies that you have conducted. Think if you have any labs or research projects that are particularly impressive and list them. Have you ever designed and structured an independent-study project working under the tutelage of a professor? That can be impressive. These types of projects indicate that students are engaged, enthusiastic, capable of enlisting faculty support for their ideas, and unusually ambitious.

TA, RA, Study Group Leader, Lab Instructor, Tutor, or Test Proctor Assignments

Being a teaching assistant, a research assistant, a study group leader, a lab instructor, or a tutor is a very positive sign for any student. It shows above-average enterprise, academic acuity, and familiarity with the discipline. Even serving as a test proctor, the police officer of the academic world, shows faculty trust in a student's maturity, judgment, and responsibility. Make a list of any experiences that you might have that fit under this rubric.

Presentations

Of course, if you have presented a paper or a poster topic at an academic meeting, that should be noted on your resume. Your presentations don't have to be this formal, however, to be included. Your department may offer opportunities to present papers at departmental meetings. Undergraduate research programs often have symposia or fairs where student research can be presented. Many undergraduate (and graduate) classes now feature opportunities for students to present their work to the class as a whole. Even if the presentation was only to the members of a class, include it in your list for now. Try to remember and log all the presentations you've made as a student.

Publications

Whether you are the primary author or deep in the coauthor list, what publications do you have, if any? Articles in peer-reviewed journals are the pinnacle of academic publishing, but consider also other forms of publication. There are many journals of undergraduate research now, and perhaps your work has been featured there. Your abstract that appears in the proceedings of an academic meeting is a publication. Frankly, even a letter to the editor is a publication. A poem in the student newspaper is a publication. It would be at times unwise to include irrelevant publications in an academic CV; for example, a biologist might think twice before mentioning the story in the *Journal of Midwestern Erotica,* but as part of your preparation for writing your CV, include *everything* you have published. (Just as a trivia item, we know of a professor who got tenure with a collection of book reviews, but that was truly an extraordinary case.)

Academic Meetings, Conferences, and Symposia

If you present at an academic meeting, that experience may appear in a CV under presentations, but even meetings that you simply attend can be listed on a CV. List all the academic meetings, conferences, and symposia that you have attended relative to your academic discipline, and any that are not related specifically to your academic discipline, but may be of interest for other reasons, such as leadership development. So, for example, even if you're an anthropologist, your attendance at the Post-Oil Energy Future Summit in Washington, DC, should be noted.

Certifications

Do you have any professional or academic certifications? Certified public accountant? Chartered financial analyst? Member of the state bar? If you have any certifications, list them, whether they are obviously related to your current goals or not.

Laboratory Skills and Other Special or Technical Skills

Can you do DNA sequencing? Operate the latest and greatest fMRI equipment? Any background in a machine shop or in prototyping of scientific devices or apparatus? Do you have experience using specific equipment that would be of interest to readers of your CV? Do you have experience in laboratory animal husbandry? Make a list of all your applied skills that fall into the categories of laboratory, special, or technical skills.

Computer Skills

It is passé to list basic computer skills on most resumes, but sometimes they will be pertinent, especially if you're proficient in the use of common academic applications, such as the SPSS statistical application. Make a list of computer skills, platforms, programs, and applications that may be of importance to readers of your resume or CV. We'll decide later what to include.

Study-Abroad, Travel, Languages, Inter- and Crosscultural Experiences

List all languages you know, and consider describing your skills according to this taxonomy: bilingual/bicultural, fully fluent, proficient, conversational, basic. Some academics who follow research in a language may designate their skills this way: "read, write, translate, but do not speak." Also, make a list of your study-abroad and travel experiences, and any other exposure to other cultures.

Sports

List all the organized and informal sports that you have participated in, from varsity table tennis to intramural flag football. Note that physical prowess and participation in sports is actually a requirement for some of the most prestigious global academic honors programs, such as the Rhodes.

Anything else?

Can you think of other parts of your background that might add important content to your resume? If so, list them as well. Some examples might be patents; speeches, keynotes, and workshops; hobbies (if interesting and relevant); significant experiences from church, mosque, or temple; and community organizing or political campaigns. Where else have you gained or demonstrated skills and abilities?

"GOING TO DO" VS. "ALREADY COMPLETED" EXPERIENCES

In making your listings, be aware that you need to include things you are *going to do* as well as those things you have *already done*. For example, if you are going to write a senior thesis, then you could explicate under a "research" heading that you are *going to* develop a topic in a specified area, gain approval for your research idea and methodology, conduct research, write up your findings, and defend your work at an oral examination. You may be *going to* prepare a paper for publication, or take a language intensive in Mexico City, or be a research assistant to Dr. Wilson. These items, also, need to find a spot in such categories as those listed above. Don't rob yourself of significant CV information that has not taken place yet, as long as it is something that you are definitely going to do.

THE EDUCATION LISTING: THE INCREDIBLY ELASTIC CATEGORY

Your education can be listed in a number of ways. Normally, you list all the universities and colleges you attended, but you don't have to; you can just list the ones granting you a degree. You omit high schools unless you are applying for a job on Wall Street and you went to an elite boarding or day school, or you are explicitly asked to include high school experiences on your resume or CV.

You can include honors and awards, political appointments, TA and RA assignments, Greek life, field studies, service and leadership experiences, presentations, theses, and special projects *under the education listing,* or you can make some of this information into full resume categories and feature the experiences at length. In some cases, you can do both. For example, being vice president of the pre-med club could be listed under "education" and/or under "leadership."

Being captain of the rowing team could be mentioned under "education," or it could be part of a section titled "sports and activities," or it could also find a home under "leadership."

You can also create tables of pertinent classes if you think this will help you establish for your reader that you have certain skills. This is an effective technique when your major or minor doesn't tell the whole story. Here's one example:

The University of Maryland, College Park
B.A., Musicology and Music Theory

Course work included:

Music and Recording Industry	Marketing
Arts Administration	Business Writing
History of Rock 'n' Roll	Introduction to Accounting

We have a much better understanding of this student's broader background as a result of reading the courses that the student took than if we only knew that the person received a degree in musicology and music theory. By using the term "course work included" instead of "classes included," you don't have to use the official title for each class. For example, "Music and Recording Industry" might have had an uninteresting or even misleading title, like "How to Earn a Living in Music," or "Senior Symposium: Open Topics."

Special Projects Category

A particularly useful category for college resumes is "special projects." Related headings are "thesis," "capstone," or "field study," but "special projects" can include a wider range of content. Special projects can fall under education or can become a whole section of their own. These headings are popular with artists and designers but can be used effectively by any student, from economics and business majors to architects and engineers. This is a particularly effective technique to highlight impressive experiences that took place in a classroom setting. Even if you only have one project, you can use this heading in the singular, that is, "special project." Here is one example:

EDUCATION
B.A., Interior Design, Academy of Art College, San Francisco, 2012

—Honors:
—Dean's List
—Merit Scholarship
—Senior Design Award (see first project below)

Activities:

—Membership Officer, College Chapter of ASID

—Usher, 2010 ASID National Meeting, San Francisco

Special Projects:

—Plans for 2,000 s.f. multilevel mixed-use design project, a 24-hour space supporting three businesses: a high-end retail by day, a wine bar and dance club in the evening, and a coffee shop in the early morning. Concept, drawings, surfaces, model.

—Remodel plans for 4,600 s.f. hospital ER waiting room, including business analysis of patient flow, triage, security, and daily cycle of use. Presented to hospital board of directors. Concept, as-built drawings, renderings, floor plan, utility trunks.

—Researched scents to brand a university admissions office. Mixed and tested scents, and created "Bookish," the smell of a library with a hint of coffee, which was adopted by Stanton University undergraduate admissions.

CHOOSING THE BEST CATEGORIES AND CONTENT FOR CVS AND RESUMES

As you can see, there are many choices you will have to make in designing your CV and resume. Back in the day when things were a bit simpler, a traditional resume had only two categories: "experience" and "education." In contemporary practice, resumes usually have an "objective" statement, but this is optional. They also now have a "profile" or "skills" section at the top that summarizes a candidate's skills and experience relative to a particular opportunity. Some resumes now may break experience into subcategories, like "sales experience" or "management experience" or similar topics.

CVs have *many* more category options. It's routine to have a section on areas of research, for example, "research interests"; to have dedicated sections for "publications" and "presentations"; and to have separate sections for typical academic endeavors such as "teaching experiences" and "research experiences." Also, for a variety of reasons, a person can combine or break out sections; for example, "honors and awards" can be combined or separated, "teaching and tutoring assignments" can be combined or separated, etc.

Organizational Structure

The classic organizational principle for resumes and CVs is to put the information *within each section* in reverse chronological order, that is, to put the latest experience at the top, then the prior experience below that, and so on going back in time. By carefully manipulating the order of the sections, an applicant can change the emphasis of a resume or CV without changing a single word in the document. For example, in applying for a job or fellowship emphasizing teaching, a candidate might start all experience listings with a section "teaching and tutoring experiences" even if the last job—first job listed—was in admissions. The order of the listings is just as important as the information within listings.

This Category? That Category? Or Both?

As noted above, the same item of information can be presented in many different places, depending on whether you want to emphasize it or not. For example, if you are a McNair, MARC, or SROP scholar, that fact could be presented under academic honors, research experiences, experience in general, presentations or academic conferences (if your program had you involved in these), or in more than one of these categories. For example, under "education," you might mention being a McNair scholar this way:

The University of California, Berkeley, California
B.S., Chemistry, expected May 2013

Honors and Awards:
> —McNair Scholar
> —Dean's List (every semester)
> —Watkins Distinguished Science Undergraduate (2011)
> —Faculty Scholar (Spring 2010)

Later in your CV, the same experience might be explicated more fully under "research experiences":

McNair Scholars Program, U.C. Berkeley, Fall 2010 to Present
Research Assistant
> Designed and conducted an original research project into a novel method to flip parts of sucrose molecule rendering them indigestible, but with the same taste effect as regular sugar, a National Science Foundation project carried out in the Watkins Laboratory at U.C. Berkeley under the supervision of Prof. L. Wilson, the Maudie J. Sternberg Distinguished Professor of Research Chemistry, and funded in part by the Ronald E. McNair Postbaccalaureate Achievement

Program. Findings will be presented at the McNair Scholars National Conference in Delevan, Wisconsin, October 28, 2012. Abstract selected for *Rising Up: A National Journal of Undergraduate Research,* in press.

Final Decisions

If your first step is to assemble all your pertinent information, your second step is just as important: to decide what to feature, what to omit, what to combine, and what to downplay. For example, you may have worked your way through college as a dishwasher at IHOP for the last four years, with more hours at IHOP than in any other experience on your resume. However, a reader of your resume or CV may be far more impressed that you were a student senator or a part-time research assistant or the winner of an academic award. Your restaurant experience can be relegated to a line near the bottom of your resume:

ADDITIONAL EMPLOYMENT WHILE STUDENT:
IHOP, Boston, Massachusetts, 2008–2012

You could even combine several less-than-relevant jobs into one line:

ADDITIONAL EMPLOYMENT WHILE STUDENT:
Boston-area Restaurants and Eateries, 2008–2012 (including supervisory
    roles)

Carefully consider your reader in deciding what to emphasize and what to deemphasize. Think more about your future than your past. What's going to be important in the future? Leadership and research experiences? Or washing dishes on the graveyard shift?

A resume or CV is a document designed to impress. By carefully choosing and organizing your categories, you can maximize the impact of your document.

COMMON VERSIONS OF CV CATEGORIES

The following list offers the most common categories found on CVs. You can experiment with the best formulation of the following headings for your particular CV. For example, you could have a heading, "Teaching Experience," or you could combine several related experiences under a single heading such as "Teaching, Tutoring, and Training Experiences."

Research Interests
Education
Other Schools Attended
Honors and Awards
Scholarships and Fellowships
Assistantships
Activities
Course Work
Study Abroad
Field Studies
Major Papers
Thesis
Dissertation
Capstone Project
Special Projects

Sample Research Projects
Research
Teaching
Tutoring
Training
Lectures and Presentations
Table Topics
Publications
Service
Leadership
Committee Appointments
Elected Positions
Academic Conferences
Symposia

Practica
Experience
Management Experience
Other Student Employment
Patents
Certifications
Laboratory Skills
Technical Skills
Computer Skills
Licensure
Languages
Affiliations
Sports
Travel

Additional

For more assistance with resumes and CVs, see Donald Asher's classic guide *The Overnight Resume*. It provides many more examples of how students can effectively package their student experiences into resume or CV formats.

Tobias W. Wilson

twwilson@stanton.edu / (413) 555-0195

255 Elm Street, South Arbor, Massachusetts 01074

OBJECTIVE: An internship in the trading department at Smith and Wollstein

Skills:

- Two Wall Street internships with strong recommendations
- Advanced analytical and research skills
- Proven work ethic

FINANCIAL EXPERIENCE:

Financial Analyst (Intern), The Opus, New York, NY, Summer 2010

- Co-developed a schema for analysis of sovereign debt risk, in collaboration with a senior partner
- Identified multiple sources to obtain sovereign debt data, researched and cross-referenced discrepancies
- Created a country-by-country risk profile for the Euro zone, with hedging strategies on multiple scenarios

Trading Assistant (Intern), Brubaker-Haan, New York, NY, Summer 2009

- Served as the "on-demand" research assistant to a trader specializing in REITs and construction- and real estate-related equities
- Responded to cascades of information requests in a real-time environment during a period of market crisis
- Simultaneously used Bloomberg terminals, live news feeds, and an array of research tools, including LexisNexis

A/R Accounting Clerk, Wilson Bros., South Arbor, MA, Summer 2007

- Prepared requests for progress payments for this high-end residential home builder with projects in Massachusetts and Connecticut

ADDITIONAL: **Campaign Worker,** Wilson for City Commissioner, Summer 2008
Construction Laborer, Wilson Bros., Summer 2006

EDUCATION: **B.A., Political Science,** Stanton University, expected May 2012

- Double minor in Mathematics and Business

Activities and Awards:

- Dean's List (every semester, will graduate with honors)
- Investment Club (president 2010, treasurer 2009)
- Habitat for Humanity (service spring break 2008)
- Language: Conversational Spanish
- Sports: Ultimate Frisbee Team, Intramural Flag Football

Special Project:

- Conducted a major research project for Macroeconomics 345: "International Influences on the U.S. Housing Bubble"

Dana Corwin Goodson   *Curriculum Vitae*

Applicant for the Harrison Fellowship
Application ID # 92148948
Sponsor: The University of New Stanton

AREAS OF INTELLECTUAL INTEREST

Contemporary International Law and Diplomacy
Modern History of the Middle East
Languages

EDUCATION

Degree:

The University of New Stanton, Stanton, Connecticut, USA
Bachelor of Arts, Comparative History of Ideas Program, expected May 2011
Self-Designed Concentration: Contemporary Middle Eastern Cultures and Civilizations
Honors Thesis: *From Hijab to Chador: The Idea of 'The Freedom of Concealment'*
Double Minor: Arabic and Political Science
GPA (as of January 2011): 3.94/4.0

Summer Programs:

University of Oxford, Oxford, UK
Special Summer Program–Readings and Lectures on the Role of the UK in the Creation of the Modern Middle East, 2010

The American University in Cairo, Cairo, Egypt
Arabic Language Institute–Arabic Language Intensive, 2009

Harvard University, Cambridge, Massachusetts
The Kennedy School–Summer Colloquium on Women in the Middle East, 2008

Monterey Institute of International Studies, Monterey, California
Summer Intensive in Pashto, 2007

Instituto Miguel de Cervantes, Guanajuato, Mexico
Spanish Language & Cultural Immersion, 2006

Conferences and Meetings:

Program in Peace and Conflict Studies (PACS), University of California, Berkeley
Policy, Peace, and Security: Foundations for a Post-War Era, May 2-3, 2010

United Nations, New York, New York

Dana Corwin Goodson   *Curriculum Vitae*
Page 2

Biannual Conference on Global Population and Migration, September 22–24, 2009

The Auerbach Institute, Boston, Massachusetts
Global Student Leaders Summit, April 22–25, 2008

Study Abroad:

University of Washington, Seattle, Washington

CHID Exploration Seminar, Tochni, Cyprus, Fall 2009
Intermediate Study in Arabic Language & Dialects and Middle Eastern and Pan-Arabic Nationalism, Regionalism, and Identification

LANGUAGES

English, native speaker
French, speak, read, write, translate, interpret
Arabic (modern), speak, read, write
Spanish, speak, read
Pashto, basic conversational ability only
Egyptian (hieroglyphics), basic reading ability only

Note: Farsi intensive language program planned for summer 2011, depending on travel schedule and visa restrictions.

ACADEMIC HONORS & AWARDS

University:

Honors College, 2007–present
President's Scholar, 2008–present
Dean's List, 2007–present

Mortar Board Honor Society, 2007–present
Most Outstanding Junior, Comparative History of Ideas, 2010
Faculty Scholar (most outstanding freshman), 2008
National Merit Scholar, 2007

Note: several major honors available at the university are not awarded until graduation.

High School:

Co-valedictorian, New Stanton Day School, 2007 (GPA: 3.7/4.0)

Dana Corwin Goodson *Curriculum Vitae*

Page 3

SCHOLARSHIPS

Hugh & Marta Steinberg Scholarship for Academic Excellence, 2010–2011

State Bar Association of Connecticut Scholarship for Future Leaders, 2010–2011

International Student Alumni Award for Students with a Global Outlook, 2010–2011

President's Scholarship, 2008–2011

Rotary Club Young Ambassadors Merit Scholarship for Central Connecticut, 2009

New Stanton Day School Alumni First-Year College Scholarship, 2007–2008

STUDENT ACTIVITIES

Student Senator, 2007–2008, Spring 2009, 2010–2011

President, Sophomore Class, 2008–2009

Member, Judiciary Committee (appointed by president of the university), 2010

The Cosmopolites Club

– Founder & First President, 2007–2008

– Membership Chair, 2008–2009

– Member, 2010–2011

    Member, Dean of Students Search Committee, 2008 (appointed by provost)

    Member, Stanton Investment Club, 2007–2011 (average return 18%)

RESEARCH PROJECTS

"U.S. Policy in the Middle East: A History of How We Got Here"

Comparative History of Ideas

Professor Charles Swenson, International Studies, University of New Stanton

– This paper was selected by the professor to be given to the department as a whole, October 1, 2010

"Education and Elite Women in Egypt, Lebanon, and Qatar: A Comparative Analysis"

Near Eastern Languages & Civilization

Professor Elias Goldfarb, Political Science, University of New Stanton

– Presented at the university's Annual Meeting for Undergraduate Research, Stanton, Connecticut, May 2, 2010

– Published in *Proceedings of the Annual Meeting for Undergraduate Research*

"Compound of Freedom and Constraint: The Home Life of Women in Afghanistan"

Comparative History of Ideas

Professor Marian Goedell, Anthropology, University of New Stanton

– Presented at the American Association of University Women annual meeting in Boston, Massachusetts, April 23, 2009

– Also presented (as the only student paper offered) at Summer Colloquium on Women in the Middle East, Harvard University, August 21, 2008

Dana Corwin Goodson   *Curriculum Vitae*

Page 4

TRAVEL

Albania, Bahrain, Bosnia, Croatia, Cyprus, Czech Republic, Egypt, France, Greece, Italy, Lebanon, Mexico, Morocco, Qatar, The Netherlands, Saudi Arabia, Turkey, The United Kingdom, UAE

VOLUNTEER & SERVICE

Africa and Middle East Refugee Assistance Program (AMERA), Cairo, Egypt

Intern, Summer 2009

–Assisted Egyptian lawyers with the preparation of legal documents to be submitted to the United Nations High Commission on Refugees

University of New Stanton, Stanton, Connecticut

Tutor, Research Methods, Writing, Study Skills, 2007–Present

SPORTS

Golf (fair), **Tennis** (good), **Field Hockey** (captain of league champions in high school)

CHAPTER 9
Obtaining Strong Letters of Recommendation

You have two tasks in getting great letters of recommendation: choosing the best recommenders and prepping them with the information they will need to do a great job on your behalf. Graduate schools want slightly different content in letters of recommendation than elite scholarship programs, so let's consider what graduate programs want first. Then we'll go on to elite scholarships and experiential opportunities. This way, you'll be better able to see the differences, which will help you choose the right recommenders and prep them with the right content to help you reach your goals.

RECOMMENDATIONS FOR GRADUATE SCHOOL

For High School Students

The rules for how to approach a recommender and how to prepare a portfolio are the same for high school students seeking that first scholarship as they are for the college senior seeking a major graduate fellowship or a grad student seeking a post-doc. So, high school students should read this chapter and apply the advice to their particular goals.

Graduate schools usually seek three letters of recommendation from faculty who have direct experience of an applicant's scholarly work in the classroom or laboratory setting. Your recommenders should be familiar with your work habits, mental acuity, maturity, demeanor in the classroom, and potential for success in a graduate program.

Making the Right Choices

If you're pursuing a graduate degree that is directly or closely related to your undergraduate program, readers in your prospective academic programs will want discipline-specific information. They will want to know about your knowledge of the discipline, in addition to your talents, abilities, and potential. Your recommender should be an insider—say, a biochemist, philosopher, or historian depending on your major—writing for another insider. (If your targeted program is in a different discipline from your undergraduate major or minor, you can choose from a wider range of faculty. See the next section.)

The usual rule for a graduate program in an academic discipline is to select faculty in your department or a closely related department. It is fine to have all three recommenders come from the same department. It is also appropriate to reach outside the department for the third recommender but wise to stay within the division. So, the rule for sourcing recommenders is: department, department, department, or department, department, division. The rule applies to both humanities and science disciplines. Here are examples: math, math, math—or math, math, physics; English, English, English—or English, English, history.

There are some obvious recommenders that graduate programs will expect to be writing a recommendation. If you conducted a major undergraduate research project, wrote an undergraduate thesis, or spent a summer as a research intern in a laboratory, reviewers will expect the supervising faculty member to be a recommender. They may wonder if there was a problem if that faculty mentor is not among your recommenders. There are plenty of good reasons for choosing other recommenders, but keep this caveat in mind.

About Unrelated and Nonfaculty Recommenders

In general, for academic programs, faculty believe faculty and are most likely to believe those faculty who are most familiar with the discipline. They are less interested in recommendations from nonfaculty, even nonfaculty with significant prestige. However, professional and practitioner programs, such as business, law, medicine, public health, public policy, nursing, international relations, and similar, are more liberal about accepting recommendations from nonfaculty. They may even request recommendations from supervisors in employment settings or from those who have supervised you in service or volunteer settings.

In general, unless a program specifically requests that letters come from specific authority figures, think twice before choosing to seek letters of recommendation from anyone who doesn't know you very well or doesn't know your academic work very well. Sports coaches, religious leaders, and politicians are often willing to write letters for graduate applications. With notable exceptions, these types of letters are not persuasive to graduate programs.

RECOMMENDATIONS FOR ELITE SCHOLARSHIPS AND EXPERIENTIAL PROGRAMS

When applying for elite scholarships and awards, you will also want to choose your recommenders carefully, but the rules are different. If at all possible, identify recommenders who have knowledge of the particular opportunity you are pursuing. In some cases, recommenders will be suggested or even provided by the scholarships committee at your school. In other cases, you'll have to ask around to find out which professors have knowledge of the programs that interest you. If you are working with a scholarships committee or adviser, always start this conversation with them. Their guidance about how to identify and prep recommenders for each specific opportunity will be extremely valuable.

You—and your recommender—should know that writing letters of recommendation for elite scholarships and experiential programs is not the same as writing letters for graduate school. Graduate school recommenders usually need to have direct knowledge of your performance in the academic setting. So, for graduate school, an assistant professor who knows your actual work in the lab or classroom is a better recommender than a dean who knows your character but not the details of your scholarship. For elite scholarships and opportunities like many in this book, the opposite is often true. A dean or vice president of academic affairs who has interviewed you carefully and knows the specific scholarship selection criteria may be a much better recommender than an assistant professor focused on a narrow discipline.

If you do work with a recommender who has never helped someone apply for these types of opportunities before, some learning curve may be involved. Students who try to "instruct" faculty face a dangerous task. Faculty, in general, do not want or seek instruction from students. So you need to be very careful in how you approach faculty about writing for you. We'll have more on this in a later section in this chapter.

READ THE INSTRUCTIONS!

Whether a recommender knows the ins and outs of writing letters for elite programs or not, your job is to know what the programs want, so read the instructions—carefully—several times, if necessary. You have to know exactly what is wanted before you can decide whom to approach to write your letters.

Whom does the program want writing the recommendations, and what criteria does it suggest to you in choosing recommenders? Are the reviewers looking primarily for faculty in certain disciplines as recommenders? Or are they open to recommendations from supervisors in internship, work, service, or volunteer settings?

What about content? Are they looking for people to comment on your knowledge of a particular area of biochemistry, the depth of your concern for social justice, your potential for leadership, or all of the above? Are they interested in you as a person or simply as a scholar? Are they going to consider whether you have overcome any barriers in your journey as a student? In some programs, your whole character, personality, and life history are of concern. For others, your performance and potential in a specific discipline are the entire focus of the selection process, and your personality and life experiences outside the academy are irrelevant. In particular, some science-intensive grants may not request nor have any interest in your personality or life history; they may care only about your promise and background in the particular discipline.

The information in this chapter may be a bit general for some readers. Be sure to make the instructions provided by each scholarship or program *your primary guide in* choosing recommenders and having letters of recommendation written. Let this chapter be your secondary guide to help you manage the process well and not miss anything obvious.

PREPARING YOUR LETTER OF RECOMMENDATION PORTFOLIO

After you have chosen your recommenders, based on guidance from a scholarships adviser and a careful review of the application process instructions, you need to prepare a portfolio to help your letter writers do a great job of recommending you. Develop your portfolio based on the following guidelines:

- Prepare a list of the programs that interest you with a summary of the selection criteria for each opportunity.
- Provide any handouts or instructions offered by each opportunity to guide recommenders.
- Provide the URL for the Web site for each scholarship or experiential opportunity.
- Summarize any contacts you have had with each opportunity. For example, have you met with any representatives of the program? Have you met with prior winners? Have you gone to any information sessions? Make sure your recommender knows about all your contact with and exposure to each opportunity.
- If you are applying for several opportunities, you will need to clearly differentiate what each requires in a recommendation so you don't get letters that are insufficiently customized in each case.
- You will almost always need to provide your recommender with a printout of your transcripts. An unofficial printout is usually fine. If there are any curious, odd, or troubling data in your transcripts, you may need to provide brief, written explanations for consideration by your recommender. For example, if your grade point average dropped in a particular semester because you were sick, there was a crisis in your family or home life, you unwisely took an onerous overload of credits, you had a financial crisis, etc., your recommender might benefit from knowing about that situation. Keep such information brief and unemotional. If recommenders want more information, they'll ask for it. Those students whose academic record has been consistently strong may not need to provide commentary on their transcripts.
- Some recommenders will want to know your SAT/ACT scores, as well as your scores on any graduate examinations you have taken, such as the GRE, LSAT, MCAT, GMAT, or similar. Provide these only if they are impressive or someone requests them.
- It is often useful for a student to provide some work or writing samples to show the quality of their academic work. If you have a thesis, a major research paper, a

particularly clever lab write-up, or published academic work, you should consider providing a copy to each recommender. If you don't have any particularly impressive or germane examples, skip this step.

- You will definitely want to provide a comprehensive resume or CV that includes all your experiences that might shed light on your interests, preparation, drive, talent, and accomplishments.
- If you have to write a statement of purpose or an application essay, your portfolio should include the latest draft or outline of that essay.
- You may want to provide some suggestions for content. These may be anything from stories (the explosion in your freshman chemistry lab) to data points (your IQ or your GPA in classes involving original research) to family and personal issues (family connections, early exposure to a discipline, personal challenges overcome). You might title this "some things you may not know about me" or "some ideas for your consideration." Do not title it "talking points." You are not in charge of anybody's talking points.

A Cautionary Note

On this whole topic of suggesting content, it is extremely important that you not try to influence your recommenders by being overly specific about what you want them to write about you. Your judgment may be off-key about the best content for such a letter, and your recommenders may resent you for not trusting them. They may be offended that you would think, for one moment, that you knew better how to construct a letter of recommendation. Remember, most recommenders write letters like this every year. They have their own theories about what works. Your portfolio should support the recommender's efforts, not direct them. The wrong tone from you, in person or via your portfolio, and your recommender may turn sour on the whole project.

The following page is based on a form that a fellow faculty member shared with one of the authors. He provides it to those who ask him to write a letter of recommendation for them. Consider adopting it for your own interactions with your recommenders; they'll thank you.

LETTERS OF RECOMMENDATION

This is a relationship, not a transaction. I prefer a month's notice; two weeks is the minimum. I have made exceptions in extraordinary cases (late decision or late discovery of a very attractive option), but these are exceptions.

I need a portfolio from you with the following contents:

1. A preliminary list of the graduate programs and/or scholarships you are considering, and how you differentiate them. Most faculty recommend you apply to two safe schools, two reach schools, and two schools from the middle of the spectrum, more for law and medicine. If you are going to go to the trouble to apply to graduate school, please have a strategy to succeed at the process. Be mindful of the level of competition for some of the elite scholarships, and be sure to have alternate plans.

2. A printout of your transcripts.

3. Copies of two or three graded work projects, theses/papers/ labs/write ups that represent the quality of your work.

4. A rough draft or outline of your personal statement or statement of purpose. If you want help with this, see Donald Asher's *Graduate Admissions Essays: Write Your Way into the Graduate School of Your Choice,* a best-selling guide to the graduate admissions process, which also includes essays for many of the elite scholarships.

5. A CV or resume, including student activities, volunteer, and service experiences, etc. If you have a different CV or resume crafted for submission to scholarship applications or graduate schools, I'd like to see that version also.

6. A brief list of what *you* think would be most important for a program to know about you.

7. Clear instructions for submitting the letter. Web links and codes that work, or if there is a paper process, all forms or envelopes filled out in advance, and stamps (correct postage) for anything that I have to mail. The less secretarial work I have to do, the more effort I can put into your letter itself.

8. *A very clear indication of when you need the letters submitted.* Otherwise, I will assume that anything ahead of the deadline is satisfactory.

After I submit your recommendations, I need two more things:

1. You need to share with me any communiqués from the programs about secondary inquiries, award or admission offers, wait-list notices, other funding/support/fellowship/assistantship offers, telephone contacts, meet-and-greet events, and so on. This helps me be a better advisor.

2. I need to know what awards you decide to accept or where you decide to go!

This form originally appeared in a slightly different version in *Graduate Admissions Essays: Write Your Way into the Graduate School of Your Choice,* by Donald Asher. Used with permission.

APPROACHING PROFESSORS ABOUT LETTERS OF RECOMMENDATION

Most students approach professors for a letter of recommendation as if they were involved in a small-scale transaction. "If you'll give me a letter of recommendation," they seem to be saying, "I'll give you appreciation." This is an old, and some consider obsolete, model for human interaction called, appropriately enough, the Transactional Model of Communication.

Your recommenders should be part of your corps of advisers for the entire process of applying for elite opportunities. So they should be involved early and often in considering which directions to pursue and in helping you prepare to be a strong candidate. Approach the process of getting letters of recommendation as part of a larger conversation you're having with advisers. So instead of asking a professor, "May I have a letter of recommendation?" our suggestion is to ask, "Professor Wilson, would you have some time to discuss my scholarship application process with me this week?" or "Dr. Johnson, would you have some time to discuss my graduate school application process with me after class on Wednesday?" The letters should come up naturally in this meeting.

Four Tips to Cultivating a Good Relationship with Recommenders

You can help recommenders write better letters for you by following these four tips for managing the process.

1. First and foremost, give recommenders plenty of time to write your letters. Most faculty will say they like four to six weeks to write a letter, so it doesn't interfere with their many other obligations. Two weeks would be a rush request. For a major award, such as a Rhodes or a Marshall, a committee might prefer to have months to craft perfect letters as part of an overall strategy of advancing a student for an award. So plan accordingly.

2. If you ask someone to recommend you, give the person room to say, "No." Say something like, "I know you're really busy, and I'll certainly understand if you don't have time to do this." If the person gives any hint of reservation, you should consider another recommender. In fact, you don't have to ask a possible recommender for a letter directly. Ask instead, "Do you have any suggestions for someone who could write a strong and persuasive letter to a committee for such and such?" If professors are willing, they will nominate themselves.

3. Bring your portfolio to this meeting! Everything in your portfolio should be a copy, not an original, so you can leave it behind. You need to be ready to talk about all its content right then and there, out of respect for your recommender's time. For some of the most prestigious programs, recommenders may want to meet with you several times and may contact others about you. They may prepare a draft of the letter and show

it to others. But for opportunities that are not so competitive and for recommenders who are either very confident or very busy, this meeting may be the only time you will have a chance to represent yourself, your interests, and the content of that portfolio.

4. Promptly provide anything a recommender may request that you did not bring to your meeting. Any delays you create in the process will be interpreted as a lack of interest in the process and its outcome. Don't create delays!

YOUR OBLIGATIONS TO YOUR RECOMMENDERS

As the handout reproduced above shows, you have several obligations to your recommenders. First and foremost, you need to be respectful of their time. Some recommenders may be part of your fan club and comfortable preparing you for interviews and helping you through all those hoops along the way to be selected for an elite opportunity. But some may want to trade that letter for a small expression of appreciation, so they can then get on with their other critical responsibilities. Be sensitive to the difference.

Giving Gentle Reminders

As part of being respectful of a recommender's time, it's your job to nudge the professor, supervisor, or dean a couple of times before the due date arrives. First of all, be sure to highlight when you want the letter to be submitted, *not the deadline* to submit the letter. You will want to have all your materials in well before the deadline, so you don't want to call attention to the deadline. You want to call your recommender's attention to your target submission date.

At least two weeks before the target date, gently remind your recommender of the project. "I just wanted to check in with you," you might say, "and make sure I gave you enough information and the right kind of support materials. Do let me know if you need anything else. As you know the target date for submitting the letter, October 1, is fast approaching. Do you need anything from me?" Then, again, one week out, gently check in and ask if everything is on schedule, and ask again if your recommenders need anything from you. On the target date, at around 6 p.m., ask for confirmation. "Dr. Wilson, I just wanted to check in with you and be sure you were able to submit the letters of recommendation today."

Two check-ins and a confirmation are not rude. But if you harass your recommender every couple of days, you're crossing that invisible line and abusing their time.

Saying "Thank You"

You absolutely will send a formal thank-you note to the recommender when the letter has been submitted. Writing a recommendation letter for you is a big deal; recommenders are putting their reputation on the line and putting out effort to support you in your goals. An actual, paper (not e-mail), thank-you note is appropriate. You should also consider giving recommenders a modest gift, something that shows your appreciation but not so grand that it makes them uncomfortable. The price limit on this is rather low, around $20 or $30 or so. Appropriate gifts are a bottle of wine, an office plant, or something related to a hobby, such as a kitchen gadget for someone who likes to cook. Avoid anything with a cash value, which is why gift certificates are not the best choice.

Also, you need to let your recommenders know what happens to you in the selection process. As you are advanced or rejected, you will need to update your recommenders. This is an implicit requirement. They will expect it, and they will note it if you fail to let them know your outcomes.

These courtesies, thank-you notes, a small gift, and updates on outcomes, are not just a matter of following etiquette and protocol. You may need these same people to help you prepare later for interviews or to help you apply for other opportunities (doctoral programs, post-docs, or fellowships) or even for jobs.

CHAPTER 10
Interviewing to Win

Not every scholarship, fellowship, or experiential learning opportunity will involve an interview—but many will. The most competitive opportunities, such as the Rhodes, the British Marshall, the Truman, and the Mitchell, will involve a fairly extensive interview process, usually over several days. This chapter describes in general terms the interview process and offers advice on how best to prepare should you have the very good fortune of being called in for an interview.

Bear in mind that all opportunities that involve an interview will have their own variations on the process. Your campus scholarship adviser or the representative of the program itself should be able to provide you with final interview details specific to your application.

WHAT IS THE PURPOSE OF A SCHOLARSHIP OR FELLOWSHIP INTERVIEW?

The scholarship or fellowship interview, like any interview, gives the review committee the opportunity to meet with the best candidates for the opportunity. By the time candidates for major scholarships, fellowships, or other experiential opportunities make it to an interview, committees will have spent a great deal of time whittling down applications to a small number of candidates. The interview is the last step in making a decision about who should receive the award(s), about who will be the best ambassador for the particular vision of the program. For example, the Truman Scholarship program has described potential candidates as those with an interest and the potential to become "agents of change." In an interview, the committee will be looking for someone who, both personally and academically, fits that description.

The review committee has come to know you on paper, and now the members want to meet you in person and have a real-time conversation with you. Interviews for scholarships, fellowships, and other experiential learning programs should be viewed as extensive conversations about what you have written in your personal statement, your CV, and your application. In this way, these interviews are different from an interview for traditional employment, which tends to focus solely on your resume.

POSSIBLE PRE-INTERVIEW SOCIAL EVENT

In some instances, such as the Rhodes, British Marshall, and Rotary Scholarships, there is also a social component to the interview process. This often involves a dinner-event the evening before the formal interviews take place. The social event is built into the structure of the process to allow the interview committee to see how you engage with fellow applicants as well as themselves in a social setting. What you say, don't say, do, and don't do is picked up by the committee. Depending on your personality type, this may in fact be more challenging than the actual interview. However, like the formal interview, you should prepare for any social gathering as well.

Don't look at the social event as a hostile experience, however. Rather, think of it is as chance to gather in a less-formal setting to get to know the review committee before your interview.

It is important for you to remember that you have been given an opportunity to spend time—in the interview or at dinner—with a group of people genuinely interested in what you care about, your studies, and your future ambitions. With the right preparation, interview experiences can prove enjoyable, aside from the obvious nerves one would expect. It is also good to remember that every interview committee and interview experience is unique, given the makeup of the committee and applicants each year. Interviews are meant to be rigorous and challenging, but they are not meant to be taken as profoundly personal. Being invited to an interview is an achievement in itself. Try to keep that in mind as you prepare.

WHAT SHOULD YOU EXPECT?

The variables that go into determining a scholarship or fellowship review committee are complex and, therefore, make it difficult to predict *exactly* what to expect. But, there are some aspects we might call "typical" based on our experiences and those of our students.

Broad Range of Topics

In most cases, your interview committee should be seen as friendly and well-educated and very serious about their professions and their roles on the committee. They have been charged with the responsibility of selecting the very best student(s) to receive an award, and they prepare to make such a decision with great care. Committees are made up of experts in a particular academic field, deans and other university leadership, prominent businesspeople and politicians, lawyers, and previous award-winners.

While you can expect a committee to be well-educated and capable of discussing your specific subject area, you should not assume that there will be a faculty member or dedicated committee member entirely versed in your area of academic pursuit. This intentional structure of a review committee is meant to reflect what you, as a potential scholarship or fellowship recipient, will encounter in the "real world."

The expectation is that while you will eventually be an expert in your own specific field, you will also be engaged with others from varying professions and positions in life for the duration of your career. Broad-ranging, well-educated conversation is an important factor to review committees, and an interview is an opportunity for them to determine your potential for such interactions while representing their program and beyond. That said, there is always a chance that you *will* have an expert in your specific discipline on a review committee. If so, you will need to be prepared for very pointed questions about your academic pursuits.

No Softball Questions

Be prepared to be pushed and, in most instances, hard! Review committees are determining who may go on to become world leaders, future faculty, diplomats, founders of nongovernmental organizations, scientists, and advocates for societal and cultural advancement. You aren't there quite yet, but a review committee has that vision for its awardees. Therefore, in an interview situation, you will be pressed to discuss in depth anything that may come to their attention through your personal statement, CV, and other application materials.

It is precisely for this reason that you need to be aware that anything in your personal statement may be a talking point in your interview. Or, to paraphrase a familiar line, "anything said (or written in a personal statement) can, and will be, used in a scholarship or fellowship interview."

Committee Size

Review committees vary in size, but you should expect a fairly significant group. You can certainly expect more than 2, but generally fewer than 10. The committee can be quite formal or more relaxed, depending on the committee members. The interview may take place at a variety of locations determined by the program leadership. For example, the final interviews for the British Marshall are usually held at the closest regional British consulate.

"I Have Nothing to Wear!"

Perhaps the most important factor for the fashion-minded of the world is: What to wear? These are formal interviews, not unlike an interview for employment. Men should expect to wear a suit and tie or slacks and a jacket and tie. Women should also plan to wear a suit or jacket and pants or skirt and a comfortable but professional top.

The locations of these interviews are unique to each program, and you shouldn't expect always to have a conference table in front of you. You may actually be sitting in a parlor chair and should keep that in mind when selecting your attire. This is also something worth noting when you're doing a mock interview.

In a nutshell, don't wear anything you will be remembered for. You want the committee to remember you for what you had to say; not for your fashion sense—or lack thereof.

Common Courtesies

Finally, do take a moment to walk around the room and shake the hand of each member of your interview committee at the beginning of the interview. You may have met them at dinner the night before, but it is a common courtesy. By the same token, be gracious and thank them for their time following the interview.

HOW TO PREPARE

If you are fortunate enough to be at an institution with a dedicated scholarship and fellowship office, you should be able to receive some guidance and assistance on interview preparation. That said, the following suggestions are useful to any applicant and are highly recommended.

Know Thyself

First, you need to review your application materials thoroughly and know your personal statement, CV, and academic records inside and out. This is the primary fodder for your interview. You should also try to anticipate any question that might develop as a related issue to something in your application. Of course, you can't be an expert on absolutely everything— no matter how peripheral—about your own subject. But, for example, if you are a student in development studies, you should be prepared to discuss competently broader questions about water management. Or, if you study Jane Austen, you might want to be prepared to tackle questions on contemporary views of marriage and the reception of her work in the twenty-first century.

Know About the World

A part of your preparation should also involve keeping up to date on current affairs. One of the more difficult aspects of these types of interviews is that committee members may in fact try to steer you away from what you are most comfortable with (your personal statement, etc.)

and into subjects they expect you to be aware of as a global citizen. You may be a philosophy major, but they may be interested in your view on Darfur or Indonesia.

Staying up with current events and differing points of view about those events is critical in navigating questions that aren't specifically related to your field. Regularly following the BBC, *The New York Times,* the *Washington Post,* and other similar news sources will help in preparing you for your interview. You will be expected to draw from a wide range of resources related to your specific interests and demonstrate the capacity to connect what you know with what you don't know. An interviewee may need to connect what he or she is comfortable with in terms of studies, interests, etc., with something generally unrelated. This is the "test" of an interview: how to adapt the question to the interviewee's own experiences. Finally, do expect questions that seem to come out of thin air like "what book is currently on your night-stand and why?"

Stage Mock Interviews

Like candidates for president of the United States who participate in mock debates before the real thing, you should, if possible, stage a mock interview for yourself. Whether at an institution with a scholarships office or not, it is important that you plan a series of mock interviews. If you can engage the faculty who wrote your letters, other academic staff, and fellow students in the process, you will be able, in part, to create the interview experience.

- Aim for at least 6 people who are generally familiar with your application materials and can press you on the ideas you've presented in your materials.
- If possible, include someone who is an expert in your discipline and another who has no idea what you're studying.
- Dress the part.
- Practice pausing when you need to think about the best possible answer to a question. Often, students back themselves into a corner because they think they must answer immediately. Ask for a moment to consider the question, gather your thoughts, and answer when you are ready.

If you can, videotape your mock interviews. This will give you a chance to go over what you've said and consider alternative responses to questions. It will identify "hot-spots," areas in your application that may prove problematic. It will also give you an indication of any nervous habits you may have that could prove distracting to the interview committee. Perhaps you fidget with a pen or pencil, or you don't make appropriate eye contact with your committee. A video will assist you in correcting such things.

All this preparation may seem a bit over-the-top, but participating in a mock interview will not only affect the success of your interview, but it should also help alleviate some of the nervousness you will naturally feel the day of the interview. The more prepared you are, the less nervous you will be.

SOME DO'S AND DON'TS

Interview committees are intent on learning more about your potential and the things you care about. But, as has already been said, they have a job to do. Here are two things you should do in an interview and one thing to avoid:

1. **Be honest.** If you don't know the answer to a particular question, acknowledge that fact and pause to gather your thoughts. Suppose as a philosophy major, you've been asked your thoughts on the violence in Iraq and the current administration's position on the situation in both Iraq and Afghanistan. It's appropriate to say that it's not your specific area of specialization, but then work out a way to connect it, if remotely, to what you're studying. Perhaps it is an opportunity to explore some type of ethical conversation on the subject. Regardless, be aware of digressions and potential holes in your own background.

2. **Be aware.** If you are a student of politics, religion, or any other subject for that matter, be very aware of potential pit-falls, the areas of extensive debate and of critique in your area. An interview committee will use that to determine your ability to engage multiple points of view.

3. **Don't appear to be better than your fellow applicants** at any social event sponsored by the scholarship or fellowship organization. Posturing is never attractive, and your interviewers are bound to recognize it. You are there to engage and learn from one another and from the committee.

WHAT HAPPENS NEXT?

Following your interview, you may be asked to remain on site for a time while the committee determines who the best candidates are. Bring a book and find ways to fill your time. If it's the Marshall, Rhodes, Mitchell, or Truman, you will likely know before the day is over if you have been successful in applying for the award. Opportunities like those provided by the Rotary Foundation may take a bit more time. Be prepared both to be called in for a second interview and to wait for the outcome. If you receive an award, be in touch with your financial aid adviser(s) and remain aware of tax consequences.

CHAPTER 11

Advice for Parents: Helping Your High School Student Plan for Success

Parenting is really about keeping the end result in mind: Raising kids to be less dependent on us and ready to be contributing members of our global society.

Just as your child did not arrive with a book of instructions, neither is there a written guide that provides a step-by-step formula for helping your child gain academic and professional success. When your son or daughter reaches the high school years and is preparing to launch from small nest to big world, you may find that you need some help yourself in navigating this phase of parenting. Before your child or children launch, let's think about your role as the coach who will help give them the direction they need to exit adolescence and prepare for future academic and professional roles. As a parent, you have enormous potential to shape and mold your child, and it is our hope that the strategies and resources we discuss in this chapter will help you mentor your child to achieve his or her academic and professional potential. We wish you our best.

FIVE WAYS TO HELP YOUR CHILD IDENTIFY HIS OR HER GIFTEDNESS, PERSONALITY TRAITS, AND PASSION

Every individual has his or her own unique set of skills, attributes, and interests. This variety is what makes the world work as well as it does. Have you ever thought about the vast depth and breadth of human knowledge and the application of that knowledge in such areas as technology, industry, commerce, science, medicine, and education? It's pretty impressive. The fact is, however, not every person is talented in all these areas; people have strengths in some areas and not in others. Our society enables individuals to specialize based on their unique characteristics and, as a result, our society flourishes. Some of the most remarkable individual and group accomplishments can be traced to the alignment of individual giftedness, personality traits, and passion. Many experts describe the alignment of these areas using sports metaphors such working in the "zone" or the "sweet spot."

Your child also has his or her own unique set of aptitudes, personality traits, and interests. The challenging part can be helping your child align these characteristics in a productive direction. Some find their "sweet spot" very naturally, whereas others struggle a bit. As you think about your role in coaching your child, consider the following five suggestions to help guide you:

1. **Be Intentional in Discussing with Your Child His or Her Giftedness, Personality Traits, and Interests.** This intentional discussion is not about empty praise that tells children they are good at everything. That kind of language never helped anyone. Instead, the discussion we are advocating is deliberate, constructive communication to your child about what makes that child unique and talented in *certain* areas. Astute parents can evaluate their son or daughter, focus in on specific talents, and capture and communicate that picture for the child to see. Over time that image becomes clear and identifiable by the child.

    This is not about encouraging your child with words like, "You're so smart." What we are talking about is a type of coaching that is clear and concise and is geared toward your observations of your child's giftedness and effort. "Wow! Claire, I am impressed with how hard you studied for that algebra test. You show the kind of perseverance needed to develop your math abilities. Not only are you excelling in algebra, but you are learning how your continual hard work pays off."

    This kind of coaching follows a simple formula:

    identification of specific giftedness + clear communication to child about observed giftedness = a child who develops clarity of her or his giftedness

2. **Provide a variety of opportunities and experiences for your child.** A wide array of life experiences will help your child discover more about his or her likes and dislikes. These experiences can range from tutoring younger children to teaching salsa dancing to seniors to organizing a collection drive for the local food pantry, or the experiences can be athletic and academic. (Leadership and service opportunities are discussed more fully later in this chapter.) You and your child may be surprised at what you both discover.

3. **Meet with your child's teachers and career/guidance counselor at school.** The career/guidance counselor may already be working with your child and be able to provide some insight into the process in relation to your child. Teachers are also a great source of information. Take time to attend parent-teacher conferences and ask your child's teachers where they see strengths and growth areas in your child. The more sources of information you have the better.

4. **Don't be afraid to call on a career development professional for help.** These professionals are well-trained to work with children and families and will likely administer some of the tests listed below. They have the expertise to explain results and map out a plan of action as your child prepares for the next level of education.

5. **Be flexible and patient.** Don't be frustrated if you don't see the alignment right away; just remind yourself that you are planting seeds for a future harvest. Not all adolescent

children can align giftedness, personality traits, and passion while they're still in high school. In fact, most will not. Most will find their way in college, the traditional time of great self-discovery. However, the foundation you build at home will help your children connect the pieces of their unique self in the future.

Part of the challenge related to giving your child assistance in this area is setting aside your own wants and desires for your child and allowing your child to discover what his or her own passion in life is. President Harry Truman once said, "I have found the best way to give advice to your children is to find out what they want and advise them to do it." This may seem a bit cavalier an attitude, but there is some truth to it. A parent can't make a child into someone he or she is not.

The following are a few tools and resources that may help you identify your son's or daughter's talents and gifts. Some instruments may require the assistance of a career counselor:

> ### For More on the College Years and Self-Identity
>
> If you're interested in learning about how students develop in college, consult *Education and Identity* by Arthur W. Chickering and L. Reiser.

- **StrengthsFinder**
  http://www.strengthsfinder.com/
- **Campbell Interest and Skill Survey**
  http://psychcorp.pearsonassessments.com/HAIWEB/Cultures/en-us/Productdetail.htm?Pid=PAg115&Mode=summary
- **Strong Interest Inventory**
  https://www.cpp.com/products/strong/index.aspx
- **Myers Briggs Type Inventory**
  http://www.myersbriggs.org/my-mbti-personality-type/mbti-basics/
- **TypeFocus**
  http://www.typefocus.com/s_complimentary.html
- **Keirsey Temperament Sorter**
  http://www.keirsey.com/sorter/instruments2.aspx?partid=0
- **Holland Codes**
  http://www.hollandcodes.com/holland_code_career.html

BE YOUR CHILD'S ADVOCATE WITHOUT BECOMING A "HELICOPTER PARENT"

Can good intentions bring bad results? In the case of being over-involved in your child's life, the answer may at times be "yes." A recent trend in parenting, characterized by parents being overly attentive to their child's well-being and success, is evident worldwide. Rooted in a desire to protect and give their children the best in life, these "helicopter parents," as they are nicknamed, may be doing harm to their children. A recent study suggests that these over- involved parents may be contributing to the development of neurotic personality traits in their children.

A recent *Time* magazine article describes helicopter parents who text teachers before class has even ended because their children texted them during class that they made a bad grade on an exam. In another instance, a mother called her daughter's college professor to explain why her daughter had not been doing well in class. There are parents who provide the "hotel wake-up call" to their college son or daughter, so they don't sleep through an 8 a.m. class. Some colleges are setting up "Hi Mom!" Webcams in common areas of campuses, so parents can see what their children are doing.

Given a culture of over-parenting, what is a parent to do? How can you make sure that you give your children the help they need without hovering over them? For starters, know that it is good to be a support in your child's life. Verbalize it and live it. The key, however, is to set limits in how involved you are in your son or daughter's life. For example, don't be the one to do all the research work in finding scholarships. Point your child in the right direction, help him or her get started if necessary, and then hand over the process. A helicopter parent, on the other hand, will constantly check to make sure the work is done and may even write or rewrite essays.

Remember that your children need to be invested in their future; it's their future. Of course, you care, and you want the best for your child, but success is earned, not given. What you can give is space—the space for children to surprise you with how well they can do on their own.

For More on Helicopter Parenting

- 'Helicopter' Parents Have Neurotic Kids, Study Suggests
  http://www.livescience.com/culture/helicopter-parenting-100603.html
- Gibbs, N. "The Growing Backlash Against Overparenting." Time, Nov. 20, 2009.
  http://www.time.com/time/nation/article/0,8599,1940395,00.html

DON'T BE AFRAID TO LET YOUR STUDENT EXPERIENCE FAILURE

This point is tied to helicopter parenting. Rooted in fear and anxiety; with an inherent belief that discomfort is a bad thing to experience, many modern parents seek to cushion their children from experiencing failure. The same *Time* magazine article mentioned above refers to this kind of parental fear as a "parental fungus" that robs parents of peace and, in turn, drives them to try to prevent their son or daughter from being knocked down in this big, scary world.

Let's state a plain, but profound, truth: Failure never hurt anyone. In fact, failure is often the main ingredient needed to drive people to push ahead and pursue their dreams. Sounds strange? Counter-intuitive? Perhaps yes, in this current parenting culture. But from a historical perspective, it's neither strange nor counter-intuitive. Consider the stories of Abraham Lincoln, Michael Jordan, Stephenie Meyer, Steve Jobs, Steve Wozniak, and Walt Disney.

Lincoln lost several elections and experienced other professional failures, before he became one of history's greatest and most respected presidents. Michael Jordan was cut from his high school junior varsity basketball team but went on to be the golden number "23," motivating boys to "Be like Mike." Stephenie Meyer, author of the *Twilight* series, had a degree in literature but the only job she could get was as a receptionist, until she pursued a writing career. Even then, she was hardly an overnight success. Her work was rejected by a number of publishers until one gave her an unprecedented advance of $750,000 for three *Twilight* novels. Her books have since sold more than 100 million copies. Steve Jobs and Steve Wozniak's idea of what would come to be known as the Apple Computer was turned down by both Atari and Hewlett-Packard. Can anyone say iPhone or iPad? Walt Disney was told he lacked imagination and went on to build the Disney franchise from Mickey Mouse to Disneyland—not bad for a man supposedly short on creativity.

So failure can breed success. Yet its counterpart, fear, leads some parents to believe that failure will result in ruin and is to be avoided at all costs. Failure can breed success. This is true in the lives of people like Steve Jobs and Stephenie Meyer, and it is true in the life of your child as well. So our advice is: don't spare your child the opportunity to grow through failure—or fear of failure—even when you may have the power to do so. When your child fails, be there to comfort. Then, help your son or daughter evaluate the effort and its outcome. When needed, give your child the encouragement to try again or to pursue the next goal. Discuss what your child learned and what steps he or she can take to be more successful in the future.

HELP YOUR CHILD LEARN TO BE COACHABLE

Many people who achieved greatness give credit to someone in their lives who saw potential in them and helped them to craft their talents into something remarkable. This is the moral of the ancient Chinese parable of the Red Horse. The Red Horse was considered useless by its owner and was abused and ignored by the villagers. "Who would want an odd horse like that?" one would say to another. "It's such a wild and undisciplined thing," others would say. "You can't ride it, and it can't be trusted to pull a cart," was another condemnation. "And look at it! It's so red!" But an Old Man took an interest in the horse. He saw talents that others did not see. He saw that it was big and powerful but untrained. The Old Man was gentle with the horse, and he tamed it to be ridden. The Red Horse became the fastest racehorse of its time; no other horse could pass it. The moral: The Red Horse and the Old Man needed each other. The talents of the Red Horse needed to find the teacher in the Old Man.

It is critically important for you as the parent to help your child develop a coachable spirit, that is, to be willing to be helped to reach his or her potential by people with the appropriate expertise. We believe a coachable spirit can be cultivated. As parents, the challenge is to help your child accept both encouragement and critique and balance giving both to your child. Sometimes parents err on the side of too much praise or too much criticism. Too much praise leads to a child's thinking he or she is impervious to failure and prevents the child from understanding that some change is needed. Too much criticism can squelch the spirit and lead to the child's feeling inferior and incapable of success.

Children need an honest, yet encouraging, voice in their lives. Be that voice for your child so he or she can be coachable Young people sometimes do not appreciate the value in an honest critique of their performance, so don't always expect a big "thank you." However, as you give constructive feedback that is marked with positive regard, your children will learn to see that you and others who coach them are seeking to bring out their best.

Enlisting Outside Coaches

Everybody has coaches. The best Olympic athletes, the highest paid football players, and the winningest tennis players have coaches and would not think of going forward without them. In addition to thinking about cultivating a teachable spirit in your child, think about other people who can help you. Is there a professional academic tutor in your area who specializes in SAT preparation? What about the well-respected and academically challenging English teacher at the high school? Would this teacher be interested in doing some private lessons to help in developing essay-writing skills? Be willing to explore options. This will involve some expense, but utilizing another's expertise can be worth it.

INSTILL THE "GROWTH MINDSET"

In the body of literature on achievement and success, the work of Dr. Carol Dweck is important to consider. Dweck is a world-renowned Stanford University psychologist who wrote *Mindset: The New Psychology of Success.* In her book, Dweck differentiates between a "growth mindset" and a "fixed mindset," explaining that a "growth mindset" is optimal for ultimate success. Here is an excerpt that helps to explain the concept:

> The *growth mindset* is based on the belief that your basic qualities are things you cultivate through your efforts. Although people may differ in every which way—in their initial talents and aptitudes, interests, or temperaments—everyone can change and grow through application and experience.

Do people with this mindset believe that anyone can be anything, that anyone with proper motivation or education can become Einstein or Beethoven? No, but they believe that a person's true potential is unknown (and unknowable); that it's impossible to foresee what can be accomplished with years of passion, toil, and training.

More About the Growth Mindset

We highly recommend Dr. Dweck's book *Mindset: The New Psychology of Success* and, in particular, Chapter 7, which is geared toward parents, teachers, and coaches.

According to Dweck, instilling a "growth mindset" in your child cultivates a way of thinking and behaving. It involves teaching your children to love challenges, to show resiliency through mistakes and failure, to enjoy and respect the effort behind accomplishment, and to continue learning through experience. The "growth mindset" insists that effort matters. This is exactly the message that future applicants for major scholarships and fellowships need to hear.

LOOK FOR OPPORTUNITIES TO ENHANCE YOUR STUDENT OUTSIDE OF SCHOOL

The U.S. educational system is constantly scrutinized and critiqued. Many of the critiques center on student performance in this country compared to students in other countries. One recent article that appeared in *The Economist* stated, "American children have it easier than most other children in the world, including the supposedly lazy Europeans. They have one of the shortest school years anywhere, a mere 180 days compared with an average of 195 for OECD countries and more than 200 for East Asian countries." The article goes on to point out that most U.S. children get three months off in the summer and this long break has an impact on learning. Children begin to forget large chunks of what they learned during the school year, especially in mathematics.

As a parent, your challenge is to combat this phenomenon. Regardless of how you feel about where your child attends high school and the quality of the education, it is our contention that schooling alone cannot help children reach their full academic potential. Enriching activities in the evenings, in the summers, and during holiday breaks are necessary. These experiences have several benefits:

- Exploration of subjects outside of traditional school curricula
- Connection to a new network of friends and professional adults
- Exposure to new perspectives and ideas
- A sense of accomplishment
- Memories that students will cherish for a lifetime

Be careful, though, that your child is not over-programmed.

The following are some opportunities that we think have a great impact on young people:

- summer enrichment camps
- precollege academic camps
- sports camps
- mission trips
- outdoor camps
- professional shadowing experiences
- volunteer work
- internships
- international travel/educational opportunities

Many of the opportunities listed above will be available within a stone's throw of your residence. A good place to start your search is at a college or university near you. Other opportunities are available across the United States. The following are five top-notch academic-based opportunities available nationally. Many more great opportunities can be found at http://www.teenink.com/Summer/.

- **A+ Summer Program Held at Stanford University**

  The A+ Summer Program is an academic-based program held annually at Stanford University. The A+ Web site reports that the experience is "a one-of-a-kind opportunity to be immersed in an environment that encourages advanced thinking, creative problem solving, and a lifelong love of learning."

  http://www.educationunlimited.com/camp/category/3/a+-summer.html

- **4 Star Summer Camps**

  This organization offers summer camps in the areas of academics, golf, tennis, and sports (general). Sessions take place at the University of Virginia in Charlottesville, Virginia, and Stony Brook University in Stony Brook, New York.

  http://www.4starcamps.com/

- **Duke Youth Programs**

  Duke University offers a variety of academic experiences for precollege students. Programs range from creative writing to science and computing. Students live in residence halls at Duke. The program Web site states, "All programs seek to engage learners in innovative, interactive, transformative learning experiences. Co-curricular social and recreational activities are carefully planned and delivered to complement the instructional day. The camp 'learning community' approaches learning as a shared responsibility among students, instructors, and counselors."

  http://www.learnmore.duke.edu/youth/

- **Harvard Secondary School Program**
  The Harvard Secondary School Program allows high school–age students to experience college life at Harvard University during a summer session. Students take Harvard courses for credit and live in the residence halls at Harvard.
  http://www.summer.harvard.edu/2010/programs/ssp/default.jsp

- **Summer Focus at UC Berkley**
  According to the Summer Focus Web site, "Summer Focus precollege camp for high school students at UC Berkeley is designed to provide a small-group learning environment for talented and motivated high school students who want to experience college life. Students attend an actual UC Berkeley Summer Sessions class, receive support from our Education Unlimited program staff, tutoring as necessary, and have fun learning with other high schools students from around the United States and from other countries." http://www.educationunlimited.com/camp/category/8/summer-focus-at-uc-berkeley.html

HELP YOUR CHILD EXPERIENCE A VARIED SET OF LEADERSHIP AND SERVICE OPPORTUNITIES

In preparation for future award applications, guiding your child toward experiences that allow for leadership and service is important. One impressive example is the story of Austin Getwein, an eighth-grader who founded Hoops of Hope. Getwein was moved by the poverty and suffering he saw in Africa and decided to do something about it. He started a "shoot-a-thon" to help raise money for orphaned children in Zambia. The first year, he raised $3,000. Eventually his idea caught on around the country and Hoops of Hope has raised over $1 million to build a school and two medical facilities in Zambia.

Not all leadership/service activities will be this newsworthy, but they can be as satisfying to young people. The key is to help your children tap into some leadership/service activity that interests them and stirs some passion in them. Remember, however, that this passion is not what you give them, but what they find within. A well-intentioned mom once shared that, after moving to a new town, she wanted to get her daughter involved in some activities to help her meet people. The mother had a friend who worked at a local nonprofit for disadvantaged youth, so she arranged for her daughter to go with the friend to check it out. Surprisingly, the daughter discovered an untapped passion in helping disadvantaged youth and in tutoring. She started volunteering regularly, and her mother thinks these early experiences led her to pursue a career in English and nonprofit work.

It doesn't take long to discover there are significant unmet needs in our world. Many outstanding organizations are continually looking for willing, committed volunteers to help further humanitarian work locally, nationally, and internationally.

It's our contention that service brings out leadership. To be a true leader, you need to know how to serve others. By giving time and energy in serving others, your son or daughter is learning how to relate to and work with people, identify needs, carry out a plan to fulfill those needs, and show compassion through action, all ingredients of great leaders.

The Self-Interest Aspect

Many colleges and universities are looking for students who have participated in service work prior to entering college. Your son or daughter does not want to leave that part of the application blank because he or she was never involved. Trust us; this does not look good to prospective colleges and universities.

In addition, some organizations offer scholarships to youth who have been involved in leadership/service activities and are planning to pursue this work in college. While this should not be the motivating reason to serve others, it can be a helpful by-product of leadership/service opportunities. While in high school, one young woman decided on her own to take small plants to nursing home residents in her town during the Christmas break. She walked up to the counter at the nursing home and asked if there were some residents who didn't have any family coming to see them over the holidays. The staff pointed out the residents with no family, and the young woman went to these strangers' rooms and delivered the plants to them. Most were bedridden and some were unresponsive, but this young woman's compassion did not go unnoticed. During her senior year of high school, she received a college scholarship from JCPenny for her volunteer work.

The following are some excellent organizations that your child can check out to find a place to make a difference:

- United Way (most mid-size communities have local chapters that help to raise money to support local nonprofit organizations)
- Boys and Girls Clubs
- March of Dimes
- Habitat for Humanity
- Red Cross
- Meals on Wheels
- Feeding America and local food banks

FINAL SUGGESTIONS

If you believe your child is hyperintelligent or just precocious in terms of intellectual maturity, consider early entry into college or enrolling him or her in a high school or college program designed for gifted students like the ones listed below.

- **Bard College at Simon's Rock**

  Simon's Rock is also known as the Early College. It accepts bright, mature students who are ready for college-level intellectual work at an early age. It was founded by Elizabeth Blodgett Hall, who believed that young people were capable of so much more than we asked of them in traditional high school. The program is affiliated with Bard College but is a separate school entirely. This college and other unusual options are covered in Donald Asher's Cool Colleges for the Hyper-Intelligent, Self-Directed, Late Blooming and Just Plain Different. Check out Simon's Rock at http://www.simons-rock.edu.

- **The Davidson Academy**

  The Davidson Academy is a high school for students way at the top end of the Bell curve, the top 1/10 of 1 percent. The school is affiliated with the University of Nevada, Reno. The school was started by software entrepreneurs Bob and Jan Davidson, the husband-and-wife team who dreamed up Math Blaster™, among other releases. They are also authors of Genius Denied: How to Stop Wasting Our Brightest Young Minds: What You and Your School Can Do for Your Gifted Child. The Academy's Web site leads to the book's Web site, and you can sign up for a newsfeed for families with gifted children. Check it out at http://www.davidsonacademy.unr.edu.

An important resource is:

- **Hoagies Gifted Education Page**

  Hoagies is a clearinghouse portal with something for everyone interested in education for gifted students. It calls itself "The 'All Things Gifted' resource for parents, educators, administrators, counselors, psychologists, and even gifted kids and teens themselves!" It's a great place to explore the gifted community in the United States, which includes an eclectic mix of home-schoolers, educators, and psychologists. Hoagies lists conferences and meetings of interest to students, families, and academics. You can find it at www.hoagiesgifted.org.

CHAPTER 12
Advice from Student Winners: What's the Secret?

This chapter lets you hear the voices of students who have had great success in applying for the types of awards described in this book. As we interviewed students, we wanted to hear primarily about how they approached the process of applying for these awards as well as advice they would like to pass on. In reading their comments, you will see several important themes emerge that will help you in crafting a strong application. These include the following five actions: (1) start your application process early; (2) ask for help to craft the strongest application; (3) be creative, unique, and genuine as you present yourself in your application; (4) research your particular award so that you know what the committee is looking for; and (5) be ready to have a life-changing experience.

HOW LONG BEFORE YOU TURNED IN YOUR APPLICATION DID YOU BEGIN WORKING ON IT? WHAT WAS THE PROCESS LIKE FOR YOU?

"I worked on the application for the Truman Scholarship for about three months. The workload was the equivalent of about one 3-credit-hour course, so I wanted to give ample time for reviewing, editing, and preparing for the interviews (should I be called back). There's nothing worse than cramming for such a high-stakes, high-pressure situation (interviews for scholarships feel like both!). I always buy-in to the phrase "Failing to prepare is preparing to fail."

In terms of what the application looked like, the Truman Scholarship application (at least when I did it) required a series of long- and short-answer questions, as well as a 500-word personal statement and a 1- to 2-page policy memo on an issue of your choosing. The policy memo required quite a bit of research and analysis, specifically what are the barriers/constraints for such a policy? What is the evidence that such a policy is necessary (what is the "problem," per se)? The memo needed to be succinct and very compelling. And, since I had no previous experience writing policy memos in such a fashion, I'm glad I gave myself enough time to rework several versions of it. The process felt grueling at times because I worked on the application while managing my regular course load. Some of the questions were difficult to know how to answer (e.g., you wonder what *exactly* they're looking for), and I struggled with what angle to take for my personal statement. In the end, I had to trust my instincts to determine which anecdotes, responses, etc., would best capture my personality and why I was a good fit for the fellowship. While it was a lot of work, it was also a very good exercise for me to start thinking about my personal statement (how to sell myself for graduate programs or other programs) as well as the extent to which I enjoyed thinking and writing about policy."

* * *

"I found out about the Boren Scholarship in September and began working on it immediately, approximately five months before the February application deadline. Starting early on this kind of award was essential, for I needed to first research exactly what the admissions committee was searching for in applicants, as well as learn about the program so that I could tailor my application to the Boren program itself. One of the points that the Boren Scholarship looks for in applicants, for instance, is a strong desire to work for and serve the U.S. government. I spent weeks researching various career paths associated with the government and all of its various branches until I found a career that really excited me, Foreign Service Officer. This process allowed me not only to write a genuinely enthusiastic personal statement that had a clearly defined and tangible goal, but further allowed me to express my desires and path with precision and clear understanding about what I desired, as well as how this goal coincided with the purposes of the Boren Scholarship admissions committee. The earlier you start, the less stressful the process is, the more tailored your essays can be, and the better chance you have of finding willing and enthusiastic professors or employers to write letters of recommendation on your behalf."

* * *

"During the academic year, I need about six weeks prior to the deadline to assemble a competitive application.

Week 1: Research the mission statement of the organization and merit criteria of the award. Find examples of winning applications from online postings, from past winners at your institution, and from your institution's scholarship coordinator. Ask for letters of recommendation due in five weeks and ask qualified people if they would review your application in the next two weeks. Good people to ask for application reviews include your recommendation writers, past award winners, and your scholarship coordinator.

Week 2–3: Complete all the forms, submit transcripts and test scores, and write as much as you can for the essays and response sections as a first draft. Revise the drafts and augment with citations.

Week 3: Give draft application to reviewers for comments and allow one week for reviews. Remind recommendation writers that the application is due in three weeks.

Week 4: Receive back application reviews, discuss proposed changes with reviewers, and revise accordingly. Confirm that transcripts and test scores were received.

Week 5: Finalize your application and submit.

Week 6: Hooray! You finished with a few days to spare!"

* * *

"The application was due at the end of January, and I began at the end of summer vacation, i.e., August. The process was, therefore, not as stressful as would be expected; I was able to give a higher level of concentration on the initial drafts."

* * *

"I started working on the application about three months before it was due. I began the process by meeting with the university scholarship coordinator. During the initial meeting, we compiled information on all of the academic and extracurricular work I had done, as well as talked about aspects of my personal life that were relevant to the scholarship. I then wrote rough drafts for the short essays and reviewed them with my adviser. After about three reviews of the short essays, we moved on to the large essay. I started out with a detailed outline for the essay and then wrote the rough draft. In the end, I went through about six or seven revisions on the essays before both my adviser and I were happy with the application."

* * *

"Teach For America has a multi-step admission process. There are several phases, or waves, of being admitted and you have to stay on top of everything if you really want to stand out. If you don't have all your ducks lined up in a row, I'd imagine that's a clear indicator that you're not someone who is completely committed to TFA, so you'll probably be phased out early on. It may sound crass, but to be fair to TFA, when you have 46,000 people applying for 5,500 spots (roughly 12 percent), there isn't time to get to know everyone.

For part 1 of my application, I started about a month in advance. Fortunately, at the time, I had already put together some rough drafts of the required documentation so I was able to edit, revise, and rewrite those things I already had. My deadline was September 12, and I began at the beginning of August. Because school hadn't started yet, I was able to focus the majority of my time on the application. I had a few friends who helped edit and gave me feedback on my application. However, even with all of this support (already-built resume, consultation with profs and friends, etc.), I literally worked until the application deadline. So I worked for about a month straight and that was just for part 1.

If you get through part 1, you're invited to a phone interview. You have a certain deadline by which you have to schedule the interview, and then you have to make sure you're available for that interview. In some ways, it's a mini-test to see how organized you can be. At least, I felt that way. Being organized, meeting deadlines, etc., I have learned that these are all huge essentials to succeeding with your children when you become a TFA teacher. The phone interview lasts 30 minutes. I actually got dressed for mine.

If you get past the phone interview, you're invited to a FINAL Interview, which takes place in specific cities around the country. Because I was on a McNair Scholars trip in Chicago during the time of the interviews, I signed up for one at Loyola University in Chicago. At the FINAL Interview, you present a 5-minute mini-lesson and do a group interview and then a one-on-one interview, followed up with a Q-and-A session. Before the FINAL Interview, however, you have to submit your regional/grade level assignment preferences as well as your transcripts. You also have to make sure that your recommenders fill out their online recommendation questionnaires."

* * *

"The strategy of making a daily routine out of scholarship applications is useful for the small awards that didn't require extensive preparation. Applications for scholarships awarding less than $2,000 can generally be completed in two to three days, but the big scholarships ($5,000, $10,000, full tuition) need much greater forethought. To direct my search for these scholarships, I first defined my strengths and passions. I knew I was very interested in psychology and neuroscience, so I looked for science-based scholarships that offered large awards. In January of my freshman year, I came across two scholarships that seemed like perfect fits for me: the Science, Mathematics, and Research for Transformation (SMART) scholarship awarded by the Department of Defense, and the Department of Homeland Security Scholarship. Both awards sought students with extensive course work in the sciences and who were defining themselves as undergraduate leaders in their respective fields. The deadline for the SMART scholarship wasn't until the fall and the DHS scholarship was approaching in the next month. After looking over the requirements of the DHS scholarship, I decided I was currently underqualified for the award (I didn't have contacts to write letters of recommendation on my behalf, didn't have research experience, and did not know how my career goals fit in with the interests of the DHS), so I decided to apply for both scholarships the following academic year.

I spent the next year continuing to apply for small scholarships while also working to gain experiences that I could use in my applications for the two big awards. I became a member of the psychology majors honors society, which allowed me to make new contacts with professors and make a name for myself in the psychology department; I frequently spoke outside of class with my favorite professor who ended up writing a letter of recommendation on my behalf; I was accepted into a pharmacology research program at the University of Texas as the only freshman attendee; and I found a job on campus in the lab of a leading cognitive psychologist where I continued to work for my remaining three years of college. In short, I identified my interests, utilized the resources of my university, and continually reviewed the application requirements in order to set myself up in the best position for success.

When I finally wrote the essays for those two scholarships, I had a year of preparation to draw from as I typed. I explained that my measure of devotion set me apart from other candidates; I cared deeply about science and wanted to utilize my experience in the service of the federal government. By the time I heard a response from either of the scholarships, the well had just about run dry. I had won only a couple smaller scholarships, had amassed large loans my first two years, and knew my parents could not afford to pay out of pocket for my education much longer. I was sent a letter of denial from the SMART scholarship in February of my sophomore year, and I was convinced I would have to transfer to another school or take time off before I could finish my education. Then the fateful call came in early April: I was informed that I was one of a handful of undergraduates accepted into the DHS Scholarship Program! This program was accompanied with a full-tuition scholarship, a monthly living stipend, and opportunities for summer internships. My financial burden had been lifted."

* * *

"I began working on my application five months prior to the due date. This semi-early start allowed for ample review by friends and faculty. The process for me consisted of an initial application, screening interview, resubmission of my application, and three essays. The initial application was least stressful because I knew the process involved a lot more than just that application. After selection for an interview, I became nervous. The interview was essential in ensuring that my proposal was doable and my conception of a full year of immersion was realistic and grounded."

* * *

"I started working on my application seven months before it was due. I was not chosen the first time, so I made it a priority the second time around and began reworking my application after I was told the results. The process as a whole was not very difficult once I broke up the application into several distinct parts. It essentially all hangs on the personal statement, assuming your academics are up to par."

HOW MANY PEOPLE HELPED YOU? WHAT ROLE DID THEY PLAY IN HELPING YOU?

"I did not have a great deal of outside assistance when I applied for the Boren Scholarship. My two recommendation writers, of course, played an integral part in helping me earn the scholarship, and my adviser at the study-abroad office had alerted me to the existence of the Boren Scholarship. My mom also proofread my essays before I gave them a final edit. Other than this, though, this scholarship application did not really require outside assistance."

* * *

"The NSF Fellowship was more work than the Goldwater, and seven people helped me perfect the application. My four recommendation writers critiqued my application and provided comments. Two past scholarship winners and a scholarship coordinator also advised me on my application."

* * *

"My professor (for whom I was also a research assistant) provided a tremendous amount of guidance and insight. He was also an informal scholarship coordinator for the college and had previously helped students apply for (and win) the Rhodes and other fellowships. He was the one that suggested I apply and gave me enough encouragement to do so. He also helped proofread and provided advice regarding the application, the interview questions, and other interview prep. I definitely couldn't have done it without him. I had a few other friends and professors help with the mock interview and some one-on-one questioning for practice."

* * *

"Nine people were intricately involved in my application process. Two of them were coordinators for the scholarship and study-abroad program. They played a huge role in providing me with information about what I needed to complete and when it needed to be completed. The other seven people were split between helping me prepare my application and mentally and physically prepare for the experience."

* * *

"The director of our Office of Special Scholarship Programs was my primary editor. I went only to her with drafts. She provided suggestions and guidance, both stylistic and contextual. She also organized the final application, which required a plethora of recommendations, transcripts, and essays. Other people, such as family and friends, played supportive roles, but on a much less significant scale."

* * *

"I had professors I knew; professors I didn't know but consulted because I knew of their experience; staff and administrators at my university; friends and family; people who were already in the corps that I knew; people in the corps whom I didn't know; my recruiting director from Teach For America—the list goes on and on. I even went so far as to take a trip to New Orleans and spend some time visiting with teachers and principals in the Recovery School District and even the Superintendent of the Recovery School District. Never was there a moment during my admission process that I wasn't consulting someone, some book, some article, or the TFA Web site. There are two main ways that these people helped me: as consultants and as encouragers or cheerleaders. People were behind me, supporting me in any way they could, because they wanted good things for me."

* * *

"My department chair in Comparative Literature, my foreign language professor in Portuguese, the dean of the College of Arts and Science, the poets in Brazil, and two professors at my sponsor university in Brazil all assisted me at various levels. My chair read my application several times. The dean, a specialist in Lusophone Literature, connected me to Brazilian scholars and emerging literature in the United States and Brazil. My foreign language professor stretched my Portuguese-language skills. The sponsoring university in Brazil was excited about my ideas although my area was not one of its principal areas of interests. My real work was with a small group of poets who published a journal, but the university had a comparative literature program that could sponsor my scholarly work."

* * *

"The most obvious help in my application was my research professor. He helped not only with my research project but also with editing the proposal section of my application and guided me to some relevant scientific literature. In addition, he wrote the most influential letter of recommendation. I was also lucky to have a scholarship coordinator at my university who sent out deadline notifications and who, with her years of experience in competitive scholarships, was a great sounding board for ideas and questions."

* * *

"My friend and my professor helped me edit my short questions/essays. I chose editors who specialize in fields different from mine to ensure that my answers could be easily understood."

* * *

"My roommate had just received a Fulbright ETA grant to Chile, which is what inspired me to apply for Hungary. My undergraduate institution has an Office of Fellowships and Pre-Professional Advising. Even though I applied the fall AFTER I graduated, Vassar let me apply through it, which means that I received application support and the college managed all the mailing of my application materials. A member of the faculty committee discussed suggestions for my application essays once, and I was able to ask the staff member procedural application questions. One of the faculty members, who received a Fulbright grant from Hungary to the United States many years before, did my language exam for me. Finally, a grantee from two years ago also answered some of my questions."

HOW DO YOU PREPARE FOR INTERVIEWS?

"First and foremost, I had the cliché "good night's sleep" and a meal before the interview. Second, and perhaps even more important, I made sure to research the scholarship itself so that I knew the statement of purpose, the goals, and the kind of individual the committee was searching for. It is always good to be able to demonstrate knowledge about the program that you are applying to, as it shows a genuine interest in the program. The Boren Scholarship is a government award to fund students to study abroad with the intention of producing informed and cultured individuals who will serve the U.S. government in some form in the future. Thus, I assumed that the interview would hit on key points such as (1) which career path I wanted to take and why; (2) why I was a good fit for the Boren; and (3) why I chose the country I did, that is, how it relates to U.S. foreign policy and security and how aware I am of the current events regarding this nation.

Thus, I made sure to research in great depth the career path that I had stated in my personal statement that I wanted to pursue, so that I could truly demonstrate an understanding of the path I needed to take and the obstacles I would encounter. I wanted be able to express enthusiasm and knowledge about the topics I was sure I would be questioned about. Furthermore, as I was applying for the scholarship in order to study abroad in Moscow for the year, I made sure to catch up on current events in Russia and research the State Department's reports on safety and foreign relations with Russia. The preparation definitely paid off, and I was able to get through the interview calmly, knowledgeably, and with very few stumbles or pauses."

* * *

"My experience interviewing before scholarship committees has led me to believe that panels view prospective scholars as investments. I have found it helpful to prepare for interviews by practicing describing a future of concrete and positive action as the inevitable consequence of my period of study and research, thus presenting my proposal as a solid investment."

* * *

"Everyone prepares differently for things, but I went a little bit overboard. I used a 3-inch binder to collect necessary documentation for my interviews (you were required to fill out certain legal documentation, collect transcripts, etc., and present it at your interview); I collected the "Region Profiles" that the TFA had on its Web site and put those in separate folders so I could study the regions one-by-one; I collected news articles (from *The New York Times,* the *Washington Post,* etc.) about particular cities I was interested in so I could get a richer understanding of what I was getting myself into; I read books related to the educational crisis; and lastly, I went to experience it as best I could. I flew to New Orleans and sat down to observe what I was about to get myself into, and I also called corps members. That was the prep part. I also created a personal portfolio that I carried into the interview with me as a supplement. Even if committee members weren't going to look at it, I wanted them to know I meant business. I wanted to look and act as professional as possible."

* * *

"First, I reviewed my application, essay questions, and personal statement and made sure I could clearly and succinctly summarize what I had described in the application package. If it's in your application package, expect that you *will* be questioned about it. Second, with the help of a professor, we came up with a list of likely or possible questions I might get. The list was quite random and encompassed questions about current affairs, what books I was reading, what books or thinkers had a great impact on me, where I saw myself in five years, etc. These are the types of questions aimed at gauging how you think and how you view the world.

I also developed particular themes in my responses, so that if I *did* get a total curveball question, I wouldn't get flummoxed but could respond with a general sentiment or story that I wanted to use to articulate what I believed, cared about, and why. Finally, my professor set up some mock interviews with other professors, and they conducted a fake interview session and provided feedback. Getting feedback at this level is really painful but worth it. If you're not looking someone in the eye, or you are shifting nervously, or saying "um," or are using the same anecdotes over and over, it's good to know that ahead of time! Get as much feedback as possible, so you can improve well ahead of the actual interview."

* * *

"Ask for help from your recommendation writers, from the scholarship coordinator, and from your institution's career center. If you're lucky enough to know an actual application reviewer at your institution, ask him/her for advice and a trial run."

* * *

"I studied the Fulbright Web site and other Fulbright alumni projects. I practiced my Portuguese. I knew the history and geography of Brazil and Brazil's relationship with the United States as well as its bordering countries. I was prepared to answer some general knowledge questions about Brazil that were not particularly related to my field. I knew how to make an argument about why my project was unique and how it would contribute to my field. I could give a one-sentence summary of my project in nontechnical terms. I also did not assume that everyone would have the necessary background to understand my project. I smiled and made sure to make body language show that I was excited about my project and Brazil!"

* * *

"Become comfortable talking about yourself. I tend to talk about myself as little as possible, but it's important to be able to present yourself coherently. I prepared answers to questions that I expected I'd get and also had friends ask me wide-ranging questions to be able to practice answering random questions on my feet."

* * *

"I solidly formulated my reasons and logic for wanting to study abroad and how my credentials would benefit the funding agency. It was crucial that the committee see the advantages and strengths that I brought to my proposal. Without a clear vision of what I wanted to accomplish and how that fit in with the sponsoring organization, I would not have received the scholarship."

* * *

"I make a list of potential questions that I would ask myself if I were an interviewer and collect questions from university career services Web site. Then I ask my friend to act as an interviewer and try to answer all of the questions impromptu. This process boosts my confidence and reduces my nervousness."

* * *

"I prepare for interviews by reading my personal statement sentence by sentence with a friend and asking myself "why is that important to you." Then my friend critiques my answers. Also, I try to assume that the interviewers are on the same side as I am and want to see me through, which helps my nerves."

WHAT DO PEOPLE MISUNDERSTAND ABOUT WINNING THESE AWARDS?

"I think some people do not understand the time that must be put into preparing for the awards in order to produce a winning application. A good application often takes time, determination, and attention to detail. People also forget that because one doesn't receive the award, it doesn't necessarily mean that the applicant was not 'good enough.' It could instead mean that the qualifications and goals of the applicant did not match up with the goals of the award provider."

* * *

"People underestimate the amount of commitment it takes to make a competitive application. You must convey enthusiasm for your proposal! Don't expect your ideas to sell themselves, so market yourself and target the specific objectives of the organization to which you are applying. It is crucial to appeal directly to the mission statement in the award description. Expect the review committee to spend no more than 10 minutes judging the merit of your application."

* * *

"I've met some people who think that Teach For America is a great way to get into an Ivy League B school. It's rated in *Business Week* as the #7 "Best Place To Launch Your Career", ahead of Microsoft, J.P. Morgan, and the CIA. And all of it is true. Most of the alums I meet in D.C. are interning for the White House, finishing up at Harvard or some other Ivy League Program, or helping to run the District of Columbia public schools reform efforts. They're in big places, but none of this is about you. TFA is about kids, kids in this country who are receiving much less than just a lackluster education, and live lives day to day that do not expand their horizons. Once you step into the classroom, you realize that you are their only chance and you can't depend on anyone else to do your job for you. This past year in my classroom, I learned that missing a day was crucial for my kids because there's really no one to replace me. Budget cuts have sent staffing shortages across the district, and what that means is that if I'm not there, my kids suffer. Even more, if you think that somehow you'll just cruise by over the course of two years so that you can get into some nice program, you're incredibly mistaken. If you want to Teach For America, you've got to understand that there are millions of students across the country who desperately need great (not just good) teachers."

* * *

"Since many awards (Rhodes, Truman, Marshall, Fulbright, etc.) have such a prestigious aura and open up many prestigious opportunities, sometimes I think people can get wrapped up in just that—the prestige. Now, I don't want to speak on behalf of the other scholarships or fellowships, but with the Truman Scholarship, the underlying thing reviewers were looking for was a genuine commitment to public service. Of course, my writing had to be of high quality and my grades good, and I had to be polished in the interview, etc. But I also think the reason I won was because I walked into that interview room and I was *myself*. I didn't try to be overly impressive or intellectual; I just told them who I was and why I wanted to advocate for kids and why that mattered to me.

Another possible misconception is that you've really got to maintain a professional image and be incredibly serious. Have fun with the process and the interview! Don't be afraid of emotion. I think I nearly cried when I told them why I cared so much about fighting on behalf of kids. I didn't plan it or mean to; it just happened. But because it was authentic, I think that was okay. Be yourself.

I also think people might underestimate themselves when considering applying. It's overwhelming to look at your peers and see an impressive array of titles, jobs, resume-bolstering experiences, an Ivy League college, etc. But those are all just words. When scholarship committees look for leadership experience or examples of persistence and tenacity, they're not looking for a line on your resume that says you headed such-and-such committee for four years. They want to know—and see—your passion and your leadership skills. They want to pick people who are compelling, who can write and speak with conviction, and whose passion isn't just a flat sentence on an application, but really takes life and is evident during interviews.

Finally, while winning a scholarship like the Truman really opens your opportunities ten- and twenty-fold, don't think that being announced as a winner will make obvious your career path. Choosing where you want to go, what you want to be, what your "theory of change" is, what sector you belong in, etc., is still very difficult. You might still doubt yourself even though you've won a really prestigious scholarship and think you *should* know what you're doing. That's just life; it's part of venturing out and figuring out the best place for you and where you can find the niche where your interests/passions and ability to have an impact intersect nicely. I'm 27 and have a master's degree and various other experiences and sometimes I still doubt myself—that's just life! Don't take yourself too seriously. Don't judge your own success by looking at people around you; trust your instincts, your passions, and give yourself some credit now and again because you deserve it."

* * *

"Some fellow applicants seemed to only want the award for financial reasons. While that is a significant reason for any applicant, understanding the purpose of the award is vital to a successful application. Selection committees want to see that an applicant will support the mission of the award."

* * *

"Before receiving the Udall Scholarship I, like many people, thought that these awards are so difficult to receive that the chance of winning one is very slim. However, I learned that with passion for environmental/tribal issues, a strong academic background, and involvement in extracurricular activities, anyone can receive the Udall scholarship."

* * *

"One misconception I had about finding funding for college was: *I'm smart. Finding funding will be easy for me because I have a strong GPA and a lot of leadership positions in high school.* The fact is, even though I graduated in the top of my class and was one of two African Americans in the top 50 in a senior class of over 600 people, financial aid was a nightmare. I had so much faith that I would be able to earn merit scholarships with ease that I did not put in the legwork of finding more obscure, less-competitive scholarships until I was already enrolled in college and had to juggle the scholarship search along with the college curriculum and the social adjustment from high school to college life. I wised up once I got to college and carefully planned my freshman year to accomplish my goals for finding funding. I made scholarship applications a part-time job: every day, I devoted a few hours of my time to searching for scholarships and preparing to apply for them. The support of my family was pivotal to my success: they would e-mail me any scholarships they happened to find online and would proofread the essays I wrote. Meanwhile, I also made it a point to become involved on campus and build solid relationships with my professors. I credit the professor of my favorite psychology class, my mentor from a summer internship, and my boss in the psychology lab for providing phenomenal letters of recommendation that strongly influenced my scholarship success."

* * *

"[My Fulbright experience] was not just a year of personal enrichment abroad, but service to U.S. foreign relations and cultural exchange. Fulbright supports real research that is continued for years. Books are published, lives are changed, and life-time relationships are formed. After nine years, I am still in touch with my Fulbright cohort, Fulbright sponsors, and some State Department program coordinators (not only in Brazil). If you are willing to invest the time and energy, Fulbright is not only a lifetime achievement but a lifetime network."

WHAT ADVICE WOULD YOU GIVE FUTURE APPLICANTS?

"First, start early. Second, seek guidance and support. Do not presume that what you say or think is clear to anyone else. Try out your arguments on friends, mentors, instructors, and counselors; they will have questions and comments that will improve your application. Third, finish your application completely with care and intention. In the process of putting together a quality application you will learn a lot about yourself, which will help your future endeavors."

* * *

"Be arrogant enough to believe that you can do it but humble enough to actually achieve it. Applicants must be confident in themselves and their ability; however, they must also be honest in their actions, diligent in the work, and nice to everyone they meet. At the end of the day, evaluators are humans. They want to reward people with the highest potential and the best character."

* * *

"The advice I would give future applicants is to find out where the funds come from for the scholarship or award, and to focus their essays to that organization or branch of the government.

These scholarships often have evaluating criteria that give points to certain applications if they mention certain things in their statement."

* * *

"First, give yourself plenty of time to complete the application. I'm not just talking about time to write and do the requisite research, but also time to reflect, ponder, change your mind, and really think about the application as a whole and whether it really represents *you*.

Second, make sure your writing is excellent—beyond excellent, actually. Reviewers have no idea who you are and the only way they'll get to know you (before inviting you to an interview) is through the written word on the page. Be compelling. Write succinctly. Don't use terrible jargon and clutter up the application. Have five or ten people you trust review your writing, if necessary. Write something memorable. After all, this is your story; it's your only chance to get the message across about why you deserve to win. After I applied to graduate school and was accepted, and several months into my first year of the program, someone came up to me and said that one of the original reviewers of my application was so moved by it that he wanted to meet me. Months later, he remembered my essay. This wasn't because my policy memo was the most brilliant or had the most facts. It was because I really poured my heart and the essence of *who I am* into that application and, luckily, I left a mark on the folks who read it. I'll never forget that. Write an application that'll make people remember you.

Finally, when it comes time to interview, prepare as thoroughly as possible. Set up mock interviews with professors or friends. Anticipate questions and practice responding. Get feedback and try to improve, even on the little things. At this stage in the process, *all* the applicants are strong and while your hesitation to respond, not making eye contact, seeming nervous, or tripping up on a question might not seem like a huge deal, sometimes it's the only thing distinguishing you from another candidate. Practice, practice, practice. If you've gotten this far, it's worth the extra work to put you over the edge!"

* * *

"When answering questions or writing essays, it is important to tell a unique story. Find an experience in your life that no one else has had and tell that story. Immerse the readers in the experience and allow them to empathize with the main character, you!"

* * *

"Know that Teach For America is a huge commitment. Without a doubt, this is the hardest program I've ever been in. I go to graduate school full-time, I work well over 40 hours a week, and in between all of that, I try to have a normal life by spending time with my fiancé, cooking, hanging out with friends. It is a huge sacrifice. Your children (in your class) have to come first or else you will ultimately fail. Before you commit, know that you will commit to serving children and attending to their well-being and their future every day that you are a corps member and even beyond your commitment."

* * *

"Be interesting! All scholarship selection committees need something to keep them interested. Present a piece of *yourself*, drawing upon your own experiences in order to demonstrate your abilities and qualifications for the scholarship. Those who have studied or traveled abroad before, for instance, might mention how this experience demonstrates a passion for culture and international travel, interests which are essential for effectively fulfilling a position relating to national security. Everyone who applies for major scholarships has made good grades, so it is the expression of unique experiences that will catch the eye of the reader and set the applicant apart from the crowd."

* * *

"The best advice I can give is to start the search for awards as early as possible, and to start working on applications as soon as you know which awards will work best for you. I have run into countless peers who would have been perfect candidates for the Boren Scholarship, for instance, but they did not start the search process early enough and thus missed out on their chance for receiving $20,000 in funding. By starting early, you can begin to prepare for the award, make time to write a very finely tuned essay, and find individuals to write your letters of recommendations.

With regard to the personal statement and essay, do your research to prepare the best work possible, and EDIT, EDIT, EDIT! Express your voice clearly and decisively, with as little fluff as possible. Active sentences and succinct, confident expression of ideas are a great indicator of one's true knowledge. Furthermore, highlight something unique about yourself in your essay. Make yourself stand out from the masses of applicants, and state why this uniqueness makes you the best candidate for the award. Admissions committees do not want to read wordy, trite, cookie-cutter papers. After you edit your essay, have at least a second pair of eyes look at it as well. Also, start making personal connections with professors or employers who you think could be potential recommendation-letter writers. By establishing a personal relationship, the writers will be more enthusiastic about helping you, and their enthusiasm will undoubtedly be evident in the letters they write on your behalf."

* * *

"Garner enough experience before you apply for a really big award like a Truman or a Rhodes: internships, publications, grants, scholarships. Otherwise, you are wasting your time."

* * *

"My advice is to look at the scholarship's Web site, former winners' bios, etc., very carefully. It is smart to write your personal statement truthfully but to address characteristics, accomplishments, etc., that the foundation is clearly looking for in its applicants. If you look carefully, most foundations describe ideal candidates. Also, my advice is to do one or two activities well in high school, college, or medical school. Two big interests/activities/organizations in which you have a leadership role and are passionate about are better than a few smaller, one-time activities. I don't see this as padding your resume; everyone can find one or two things they feel passionately about or are interested in and the time to do them."

* * *

"Even if you do not normally keep a planner or some calendar system to remember dates and deadlines, you will probably want to for the Boren Scholarship. The application process can take several months, and it is important to be able to remember all the dates and deadlines for material submissions."

* * *

"I knew that the people reading my essay would be reading hundreds, if not thousands, of others as well, so I wanted to write something that would not just be the same thing they had already read over and over again. I chose to start with a short personal story, not only because I hoped that would be an interesting lead-in to my essay, but also because I wanted to show my personal connection to what I was writing about."

* * *

"Do your research! For example, the Boren Scholarship tends to be awarded to those individuals who express a desire to use their experience abroad to pursue a career related to foreign policy. Having a clear idea about the kinds of available government jobs and being able to express clearly why such a career field is attractive are important aspects of a successful application for a Boren Scholarship. Furthermore, it is crucial that applicants be able to express how their particular program will advance national security interests. Furthermore, knowledge of the proposed country itself and its relation to U.S. national security is essential for a persuasive application. An individual applying for study abroad in Russia, for instance, might mention the importance of correcting negative stereotypes concerning Russia in order to build healthy relations between it and the United States because Russia can be an extremely valuable ally in terms of U.S. national security."

* * *

"For scholarships like the Udall that involve a number of short essays, it's important to not only create a narrative arc that ties all of your essays together but also to use each of them to describe a slightly different part of who you are. More generally, my advice is to enjoy

the application process. All of these scholarships are incredibly competitive, so the odds are against you for winning the money. But you can still learn a lot about yourself and how you tick in the process of putting together an application."

* * *

"First and foremost, know your individual institution's protocol for the application process for each scholarship. At my institution, for example, the internal "deadline for submission" was two months before the deadline of the competition itself because the university must select its best 3 candidates for nomination to the scholarship. I know this was a much different process than for other institutions. Secondly, because the Goldwater is a science research scholarship, do research in an area you are passionate about. While it may seem obvious, many students gravitate toward research in "world-saving" issues like cancer or AIDS simply because they feel it will give them a better chance at this award. The research must be novel and unique and no matter the scope (whether the research is on honey bees or a molecule in the atmosphere), being passionate about the project will come through in the application and give you the best chances."

* * *

"The greatest advice I could give to younger students starting the scholarship search would be to start early and often. Make the most of your time in high school to begin identifying scholarships that apply to you: read books on scholarships; think about your unique experiences (debate team, theater, math club, sports, etc.) and background (ethnicity, disability, religion, etc.). Then try to find specific scholarships that focus on them. Ask for the help of family, friends, and school counselors to guide and support you as you apply for your scholarships. If you find yourself without enough funding in college (as I did), don't give up! Make the scholarship search a priority, one you're willing to sacrifice a few parties and movie nights for.

Take the application process very seriously, and put yourself in a position to make yourself a top candidate. Think about how different aspects of your life tie in to one another, and speak to this in your essays. In my case, my mentors, course curriculum, internship experiences, and organization memberships were all part of a network that encouraged my success as a young scientist. Find out where your own passions lie, and work toward making the interactions with those around you extensions of those passions."

* * *

"Your institution has likely offered seminars on how to write winning applications and proposals in the past. Find out about these seminars, the speakers, and the materials disseminated. Regardless of your field within the humanities, social sciences, or natural sciences, all applications share common traits, and advice from actual review committee members is invaluable. Do not underestimate the importance of your GPA and GRE scores for academic

applications. Grades and test scores are the easiest way to filter candidates. If you need to give any caveats (e.g., explain a low grade) or highlight any experiences, ask a recommendation writer to include this in his/her letter."

* * *

"Have as many people as possible review and edit your essays. This includes any scholarship centers in universities. Part of the reason why I think I received a Boren Scholarship was because of the help I received at my school's Scholarship and Research Center. Also, edit yourself as much as you can. The Boren Program is looking for refined, clear, well-organized, and interesting essays. A good rule to remember is: If it may be superfluous, it probably is and should not be in the essay."

* * *

"View writing these essays as a way to gain more insight into who you are and what you want to do with your life. Putting the application together is a valuable reflective experience regardless of whether or not you win the scholarship. View the other applicants as potential friends and colleagues rather than competitors; some of my closest friends now are people I met through these scholarships. Only apply for the award if you really want to do what you'd get the award for; don't apply if you're just looking for the prestige. That way, you'll (1) have a better chance of actually getting the award and (2) enjoy the experience that comes along with the reward."

* * *

"The most important aspect of the application process is to find a good faculty adviser or scholarship coordinator to support you. Make sure this person is someone who will set deadlines and is not afraid to enforce them, as well as someone who has a strong background in editing. Start the application process at least three months prior to the deadline. Writing and revising the essays can take months to do, so applicants will want to make sure to leave plenty of time. Finally, keep in mind that academics and extracurricular activities are extremely important components of a scholarship application like the Udall. Applicants need to be involved in their communities and college campuses and have a strong passion for environmental/tribal issues."

HOW HAS THIS AWARD AFFECTED YOU PERSONALLY AND PROFESSIONALLY?

"This award gave me an opportunity to expand my vision of the world. Personally, I have become more curious and critical of habits and standards that were previously second nature. Professionally, I have gained a valuable language skill, foreign experience, and great network."

* * *

"I would say the biggest effect the Goldwater had on me professionally was to put me on the same footing as top-notch scholars across the country. To clarify, I attend a state university, which does not have the same reputation as does a Harvard, Stanford, or Princeton. With the Goldwater, when I apply professionally, my resume says I have competed nationwide with the upper echelon of scholars and been successful. Had I not had the Goldwater, it is difficult to put my application (even with good grades) on a comparable level. Along those same lines, the personal effect of the Goldwater was to validate me to myself as a scholar. I would not have applied for this scholarship if it were not for the insistence of a professor—because I undervalued my potential. I told myself there was no chance I could compete on a nationwide scope. Winning the Goldwater has given me the confidence to keep striving toward the top academic level."

* * *

"The Truman Scholarship is awarded to college juniors on the basis of their commitment to public service and the likelihood of their becoming a "change-agent." Winning the scholarship helped reaffirm my commitment to public service and gave me an immediate community of peers around the country who were committed to similar work. Moreover, it was incredibly validating, coming from a small place like Messiah College and competing against students from Ivy League universities. Knowing that I could keep up with them, in a sense, really opened my eyes as to what was possible for me professionally. The Truman Foundation also has a relationship with various graduate programs, so this opened doors for me to have access to some of the best public policy programs around the country. I will be forever grateful for those opportunities.

On a more fundamental level, the process of applying and going through the rigorous interviews and really being drilled about what I believed, why I cared about public service, why it mattered, etc., forced me into a process of reflection that I was fortunate to undergo at such a young age. I came away from the entire process and *really* knew, and was able to articulate very clearly, why I cared so much about public service. I emerged with a deep understanding of how my personal life experiences had impacted me and had driven me to advocate on behalf of kids, and this gave me confidence to take a somewhat nontraditional path by joining Teach For America and teaching elementary students in Camden, New Jersey. Joining this

program had an irreversible impact on me and changed my perspective entirely. I knew I wanted to work in education policy after teaching in one of America's poorest communities for two years. But it's all connected. Had I not applied to and won the Truman Scholarship, I might not have considered the public service path and detoured into public education."

* * *

"Winning the Boren Scholarship has greatly affected my life. It allowed me to achieve my dream of studying abroad in Russia for a year and gave me an experience that helped shape me as a person. By enabling me to live in Moscow, the scholarship allowed me to gain an incredible level of language proficiency in a relatively short period of time. The experience furthered my knowledge of Russian culture, politics, history, and mindset, which are crucial for my intended career. As a result of this experience, I have been granted additional fellowships. The committees saw the receipt of the Boren as an indication of excellence and viewed my study-abroad experience as unique and a demonstration of determination and drive. I have also been admitted to the top graduate schools in international relations, despite the tendency of these schools to reject applicants lacking professional experience. As a result of the Boren and my study-abroad experience, I will be attending Johns Hopkins SAIS [School of Advanced International Studies] master's program.

Another great, and unexpected, impact of the award has been its effect on my professional career. Indeed, it was the very process of applying for the Boren that made me look into serving as a Foreign Service Officer for the State Department. The research I did to prepare for the Boren actually helped me discover and decide upon the career path that best suits my drive and desires and sparked an incredible excitement in me to begin working for the State Department. Furthermore, the acceptance of the award requires me to serve the government for one year. The award program has a network that specifically helps award recipients fulfill this service requirement. I really am not exaggerating when I say this award significantly changed my life."

* * *

"The experience of being a Teach For America corps member has helped me to learn things about myself. For instance, I've learned that I need a lot more alone time than I thought and what I learned after that was that I need to create alone time in my schedule. On that note, time management is something else I learned. As a corps member, you have all of these things you have to be responsible for: School Documentation, School Meetings, All Corps Meetings, School District Professional Development, Teach For America Professional Developments, Teach For America Professional Development Saturdays (separate from TFA PDs), TFA Program Director Observations, TFA Observation Debriefings, School District Observations, Principal Observations, Weekly Graduate Courses, Graduate Assignments,

Weekend Courses During the Semester, Grading Your Student Papers, Lesson Planning, Unit Planning, Designing Student Assessments, Planning Interventions, and the list goes on and on. It's a ridiculous number of things to be responsible for, but that's what you sign up to do. Learning to manage your time is the most crucial lesson I have learned this year. You cannot be a flake or hold back in any part of your commitment to changing kids' lives. These are obviously basic things, but probably the biggest thing I've learned is that there are kids in this country who need people; there a ton of people who don't know that; and for kids, you have to do something, and you absolutely can't quit. If you don't do something, then who will?"

* * *

"The award has affected me personally because I made some close friends at the Udall Scholarship orientation that I keep in contact with. Also, it has given me the confidence to pursue the high goals I have set for myself. It has affected me professionally by giving me an edge in the hiring process because employers in my field usually recognize the Udall name. When I apply to graduate programs, I believe that the Udall scholarship will help me be accepted into the programs of my choice."

* * *

"It sounds trite to say, but this award changed my life. I got the Fulbright for a gap year between my M.A. and Ph.D. studies in history. I applied for the English Teaching Assistantship position so I could teach university classes on American history and culture and learn more of the Hungarian language and some Hungarian history on the side. The teaching confirmed my desire to become a professor of American history. But I also realized that the history of East Central Europe is fascinating and understudied. I am too invested in my background in American history to make the full switch, but I realized that the best path for me is to study Central European immigration to the United States. This allows me to do new research, use my Hungarian-language skills, and even have a legitimate reason to go back to Budapest. Personally, my Fulbright roommate has become one of my most influential friends. We have been able to navigate living in Budapest, travel to Slovakia and the Balkans, tackle historical questions, and practice Hungarian together. I have no doubt that, because of the personal and professional elements of our friendship, it will be a lifelong connection."

* * *

"My scholarships changed the way I look at my life and my profession. I realized that I have a responsibility to be the best in my profession to help my society. Many movies and books have shown that a single technology or event can dramatically change the fate of humankind, and it is up to me and my generation to prevent disasters and help civilization progress.

The application process, more than the award itself, allowed me to reflect and gain a deeper understanding of what motivates me and what I want to pursue in the future. The networks of other people who have won the same scholarship are quite possibly worth more than the actual scholarship money for the links to professional and personal development opportunities, resources, and support systems."

* * *

"Personally, this award validated much of the work I had done and inspired me to continue. Professionally, it opened the door to other awards and scholarships. The Goldwater is quite prestigious, and corporations recognize what it entails, which lends subsequent applications another facet of legitimacy."

* * *

"I have been extremely successful in teaching, publishing, and securing other grants. I have had students secure positions in the U.S. State Department as well as teaching abroad. I have successfully managed a Study Abroad Program, as well as traveled and conducted research abroad. Three of the poets from my Fulbright research have visited the United States. One of them was sponsored by Vanderbilt University, where I completed my Ph.D. Another poet was sponsored by Lipscomb University, my first tenure-track position upon completing my Ph.D. at Vanderbilt. These invitations are the ultimate acts of cultural exchange. I look forward to more exchanges of this nature.

In addition, I was invited to be on the U.S. State Department Speakers List and have traveled and spoken to audiences in Africa about my Fulbright research and publications. Personally, I have maintained my passion for Latin American Studies and continue to research, teach, and publish in the area of my Fulbright studies. Professionally, I am considered a leading expert in the area of Afro-Brazilian women's literature."

Appendix

This appendix contains additional resources that we feel might be helpful to you in your educational journey.

RECOMMENDED WEB SITES

https://www.essayedge.com

https://www.e-education.psu.edu/writingpersonalstatementsonline/

http://apps.collegeboard.com/cbsearch_ss/welcome.jsp

http://www.cblbank.com

http://www.finaid.org

http://www.fastweb.com

http://www.fastaid.com

http://www.college-scholarships.com

http://www.collegenet.com

http://www.cos.com

http://www.collegefunds.net

http://www.absolutelyscholarships.com

http://www.internships.com/welcome/MichiganStateUniversity

http://www.nafadvisors.org/scholarships.php

http://www.studentscholarshipsearch.com/

http://www.scholarships.com

https://www.e-education.psu.edu/styleforstudents/

https://www.collegeanswer.com/index.jsp

http://www.petersonspublishing.com/

http://www.free-4u.com

RECOMMENDED BOOKS

Graduate Admissions Essays: Write Your Way into the Graduate School of Your Choice by Donald Asher

College Student's Guide to Merit and Other No-Need Funding 2010–2012 by Gail Ann Schlachter and R. David Weber

Financial Aid for Study and Training Abroad, 2010–2012 by Gail Ann Schlachter and R. David Weber

The New Global Student: Skip the SAT, Save Thousands on Tuition, and Get a Truly International Education by Maya Frost

Funding for United States Study 2009 by Institute of International Education

Funding for United States Study: A Guide for International Students and Professionals (Funding for US Study) by Marie O'Sullivan and Sara Steen

Scholarships, Grants & Prizes from Peterson's

Foundation Grants to Individuals by Phyllis Edelson

Annual Register of Grant Support: A Directory of Funding Sources by Beverley McDonough

Scholarship Handbook from The College Board

The Ultimate Scholarship Book: Billions of Dollars in Scholarships, Grants and Prizes by Gen Tanabe and Kelly Tenabe

The Vault Guide to Top Internships by Carolyn C. Wise

NOTES

NOTES

NOTES

NOTES

NOTES

NOTES

NOTES

NOTES